Guilty Pleasures

LAW AND CURRENT EVENTS MASTERS

David Kairys, Series Editor

Also in this series:

Icarus in the Boardroom
David Skeel

In Search of Jefferson's Moose
David G. Post

In Brown's Wake
Martha Minow

Advancing the Ball
N. Jeremi Duru and Tony Dungy

Unequal
Sandra F. Sperino and Suja A. Thomas

Guilty Pleasures

Comedy and Law in America

Laura Little

Foreword by Bob Mankoff

OXFORD
UNIVERSITY PRESS

Oxford University Press is a department of the University of Oxford. It furthers
the University's objective of excellence in research, scholarship, and education
by publishing worldwide. Oxford is a registered trade mark of Oxford University
Press in the UK and certain other countries.

Published in the United States of America by Oxford University Press
198 Madison Avenue, New York, NY 10016, United States of America.

Library of Congress Cataloging-in-Publication Data
Names: Little, Laura E., 1957– author.
Title: Guilty Pleasures : Comedy and Law in America / Laura Little ; foreword
by Bob Mankoff.
Other titles: Comedy and Law in America.
Description: New York, NY : Oxford University Press, 2019. | Series: Law &
current affairs series
Identifiers: LCCN 2018018997 | ISBN 9780190625764 (hardback)
Subjects: LCSH: Law—United States—Humor. | Forensic oratory. | Law—United
States—Language. | American wit and humor. | BISAC: LAW / General. | LAW
/ Media & the Law.
Classification: LCC K184.L58 2018 | DDC 349.7302/07—dc23 LC record available at
https://lccn.loc.gov/2018018997

1 3 5 7 9 8 6 4 2

Printed by Sheridan Books, Inc., United States of America

To my parents, Meg and Deacon, who taught me how to laugh.

CONTENTS

Foreword by Bob Mankoff   ix
Acknowledgments   xi

Introduction   *1*

    A. On, About, In . . . Law's Intersection with Humor   *1*

    B. The Power of *New Yorker* Cartoons   *3*

    C. Humor Scholarship   *5*

        1. Humor Inventories   *5*

        2. Major Theories of Humor   *9*

1. "On": Law's Effect on Humor   *21*

    A. An Unwitting Passage into the Comedy Business: How Courts Become Humor Critics When Indirectly Regulating Humor   *23*

        1. Intellectual Property Law: Parody as a Favored Child in Trademark Law   *24*

        2. Tort   *28*

        3. Contract   *36*

        4. Workplace Humor and Harassment Claims   *40*

        5. Endnote on Indirect Regulation   *46*

    B. The Frontal Attack: Punishing the Joker, Muzzling the Comedian, and Regulating the Punster   *48*

        1. Punishing the Joker   *48*

        2. Muzzling the Stand-Up Comedian   *51*

        3. Regulating the Punster and the Rebellious Wordsmith   *57*

    C. The Unusual Case of Hate Speech   *61*

    D. Humor's Pushback on Law: Censorship Humor   *64*

2. "About": Humor About Law   *71*

    A. Lawyers   *76*

1. Crafty and Cunning: Disloyal Lawyers as Allies of the Devil   *79*

2. Money-Grubbing Vultures   *85*

3. Proliferating Lawyers   *88*

4. The Future of Lawyer Jokes   *93*

B. Judges   *94*
C. Juries   *100*

1. Stupid Jurors   *101*

2. Lazy Jurors   *103*

3. Misbehaving Jurors   *105*

4. Common-Sense Jurors   *108*

D. Gender, Race, and Sexual Orientation Meet Humor and the Law   *112*

1. Gender   *113*

2. Race   *123*

E. The Legal System and Legal Texts   *125*

1. The Legal System   *126*

2. Legal Texts   *134*

F. Can Satire Inspire Change?   *140*
3. "In": Humor in Law   *143*
A. Funny Lawyers   *144*

1. Advice Giving, Media Spinning, and Social Justice Advocacy   *145*

2. Negotiation and Mediation   *146*

3. Adversary Litigation   *148*

B. Funny Judges   *156*

1. In-Court and Extrajudicial Humor   *156*

2. Humor in Opinions   *165*

C. Funny Legal Instruments   *171*

1. Contracts   *171*

2. Wills   *174*

D. Funny Laws   *178*
Conclusion   *182*

Notes   *185*
Selected Bibliography   *209*
Index   *211*

FOREWORD

This is a seriously funny book.

It's a primer on humor theory and a primer on law—including just enough to teach the reader to be interesting about the intersection of both at a cocktail party. And once you leave the cocktail party it actually offers a lot more than charming chit-chat. The book's two undertakings—revealing how both humor and law operate—weave throughout the text. With lawyerly agility, professorial rigor, and . . . duh . . . humor . . . Professor Little, James G. Schmidt Professor of Law at Temple University's Beasley School of Law, or as I call her, Laura, because I'm her friend and can't remember that entire title, sweeps us through the complete law and humor story. But she goes further, using the lure of humor to have us wrestle with important ideas that the meeting of humor and the law highlight: free speech principles, democratic theory, and, yes, legal doctrine. Look, she's not the James G. Schmidt Professor of whatever for nothing.

Most books in this area simply compile funny bits about law. Some target a specific topic: lawyer jokes, funny laws, things like that. This book, however, covers all ways that law and humor collide: how law affects humor and how humor affects law (to very good effect, I might add, just to show I know the difference between "affect" and "effect").

What follows is a tsunami of original thought enlivened by Laura's dry humor as well as the slightly damper humor of *New Yorker* cartoons. Among Little's enlightenments is her theory of what's funny and what's not *to the law*, which, unbeknownst to its own magisterial legal parsing, largely mirrors the analysis of humorologists. (Yes, there are such things and please don't you make fun of them.) She shows you what works well before the court and what gets you thrown in the clink, giving specific and instructive examples. So, heed her advice and your humor will be protected by the law's shield. Ignore it and the law's gavel, guillotine, and halberd are waiting for you. Actually, the law doesn't have a halberd, but reportedly the attorney general of the United States is looking into it.

All that is good as far as it goes but Little goes further. She connects humor to big issues: individual expression, democratic debate, and social relationships. Little shows how satire and other comedy allow jokesters, comedians, and cartoonists to poke the underbelly of politics, government, and the law itself. She also explains how humor that is inappropriate and unquestionably offensive should not always amount to actual legal offense.

Tricking us into consuming her considerable wisdom and legal knowledge, Little also shares insights through her curation of cartoons in this volume. (Did someone say cartoons? That's where I come in.) Little's choice of *New Yorker* cartoons displays a mash-up of tropes and domains bearing directly or indirectly on law. The cartoons are funny simply "for the fun" of being funny. But they also provide a striking picture of two controlling dynamics in the law and humor world:

(1) **Law uses humor as a scapegoat** (occurring when courts and legislatures target humor as a subject of regulation); and

(2) **Humor uses law as a scapegoat** (occurring when humor finds a rich trove of raw material in legal actors, proceedings, and texts).

This is where I exit. Law and humor are scapegoats, but I'm not volunteering to be one too. I'm delighted to have contributed to Little's efforts—but when it comes to the law's strong arm, I'm outta the picture. That said, I am most happy to have this insightful and important book at my side. My guess is that you too will enjoy this book's fun ride. I also guess that you'll appreciate its guidance. By the power vested in me, I warrant that you'll be amused and educated. Read on.

Bob Mankoff, Former Cartoon Editor of
The *New Yorker* Magazine and Current Cartoon
and Humor Editor of *Esquire* Magazine

ACKNOWLEDGMENTS

I am particularly grateful to former *New Yorker* Cartoon Editor Bob Mankoff for his encouragement and support for this book. Both Bob and the *New Yorker* magazine were both helpful and generous throughout the process of developing this book.

My colleagues and friends also provided much support for the project. Professor Finbarr McCarthy provided laser-sharp editing. Professor Jules Epstein patiently answered my questions about evidence and trial practice. Professor Susan DeJarnatt provided a never ending stream of funny legal anecdotes. A mother lode of talented Temple Law students provided research assistance and editing support: Tom Bosworth, Elizabeth Bukis, Adam Johnson, Daniel Kaufman, Merideth Ketterer, Richard Lynn, Rachel Reznick, Zakary Rosenberg, Dylan Taylor, Riana Yancy, and Laura Zipin. Erica Maier provided all manner of technical help—large and small. And, as always, I am grateful to my wonderful husband, Rich Barrett, and children Cate and Graham Barrett, who continue to buoy me and keep me in line.

This volume features the following cartoons, which are reproduced under a license granted by the *New Yorker* magazine and Conde Nast Publications, Inc.: Warren Miller/The New Yorker Collection/The Cartoon Bank/ TCB-30539; Frank Cotham/The New Yorker Collection/The Cartoon Bank/ TCB122480; Mick Stevens/The New Yorker Collection/The Cartoon Bank/ TCB 28015; Liam Walsh/The New Yorker Collection/The Cartoon Bank/ TCB-142264; Drew Dernavich/The New Yorker Collection/The Cartoon Bank/ TCB-140192; Mick Stevens/The New Yorker Collection/ The Cartoon Bank/ TCB-40526; Jack Ziegler/The New Yorker Collection/ The Cartoon Bank/ TCB-44255; Mick Stevens/The New Yorker Collection/ The Cartoon Bank/ TCB-40526/017390-313; Charles Barsotti/The New Yorker Collection/The Cartoon Bank/ TCB-25446; Leo Cullum/The New Yorker Collection/The Cartoon Bank/ TCB-10562; Michael Maslin/ The New Yorker Collection/The Cartoon Bank/ TCB-38842; Lee Lorenz/ The New Yorker Collection/The Cartoon Bank/ TCB-43841; Leo Cullum/ The New Yorker Collection/The Cartoon Bank/ TCB-40418; Roz Chast/

The New Yorker Collection/The Cartoon Bank/ TCB-125361; Robert Mankoff/The New Yorker Collection/The Cartoon Bank/ TCB-31076; Lee Lorenz/The New Yorker Collection/The Cartoon Bank/ TCB-39380; Christopher Wyant/The New Yorker Collection/The Cartoon Bank/ TCB-141351; Robert Mankoff/The New Yorker Collection/The Cartoon Bank/ 8A TCB-31031; Zachary Kanin/The New Yorker Collection/The Cartoon Bank/ TCB-133318; Charles Barsotti/The New Yorker Collection/ The Cartoon Bank/ TCB-124968; Danny Shanahan/The New Yorker Collection/The Cartoon Bank/ TCB 51550; Danny Shanahan/The New Yorker Collection/The Cartoon Bank/ TCB 40288; Richard Cline/ The New Yorker Collection/The Cartoon Bank/ TCB 41623; Michael Maslin/The New Yorker Collection/The Cartoon Bank/ TCB 122120; Leo Cullum/The New Yorker Collection/The Cartoon Bank/ TCB 29804; Leo Cullum/The New Yorker Collection/The Cartoon Bank/ TCB 122644; Lee Lorenz/The New Yorker Collection/The Cartoon Bank/ TCB 47739; J.B. Handlesman/The New Yorker Collection/The Cartoon Bank/ TCB 40228; Leo Cullum/The New Yorker Collection/The Cartoon Bank/ TCB 34205; Lee Lorenz/The New Yorker Collection/The Cartoon Bank/ TCB 45345; Mick Stevens/The New Yorker Collection/The Cartoon Bank/ TCB-33123; Matthew Diffee/The New Yorker Collection/The Cartoon Bank/124660; C. Covert Darbyshire/The New Yorker Collection/The Cartoon Bank/ TCB 121801; Leo Collum/The New Yorker Collection/ The Cartoon Bank/ TCB 30465; Michael Maslin/The New Yorker Collection/The Cartoon Bank/ TCB 34221; Mick Stevens/The New Yorker Collection/The Cartoon Bank/ TCB 29630; Michael Maslin/ The New Yorker Collection/The Cartoon Bank/ TCB 89571; James Stevenson/The New Yorker Collection/The Cartoon Bank/ TCB-30220; Michael Crawford/The New Yorker Collection/The Cartoon Bank/ TCB 43024; Al Ross/The New Yorker Collection/The Cartoon Bank/ TCB 40329; Al Ross/The New Yorker Collection/The Cartoon Bank/ TCB 79852; Robert Weber/The New Yorker Collection/The Cartoon Bank/ TCB 80616; Joseph Mirachi/The New Yorker Collection/The Cartoon Bank/ TCB 35520; Henry Martin/The New Yorker Collection/The Cartoon Bank/ TCB 75912; Peter Steiner/The New Yorker Collection/ The Cartoon Bank/ TCB 44049; Al Ross/The New Yorker Collection/The Cartoon Bank/ TCB 79666; Charles Saxon/The New Yorker Collection/ The Cartoon Bank/ TCB 81917; Edward Franscino/The New Yorker Collection/The Cartoon Bank/ TCB 33803; Leo Cullum/The New Yorker Collection/The Cartoon Bank/ TCB 22412; Danny Shanahan/The New Yorker Collection/The Cartoon Bank/ TCB 38582; Danny Shanahan/The New Yorker Collection/The Cartoon Bank/ TCB 119472;

Paul Noth/The New Yorker Collection/The Cartoon Bank/ TCB 122488; Leo Cullum/The New Yorker Collection/The Cartoon Bank/ TCB 43341; Danny Shanahan/The New Yorker Collection/The Cartoon Bank/ TCB 33227; Robert J. Day/The New Yorker Collection/The Cartoon Bank/ TCB 95051; Perry Barlow/The New Yorker Collection/The Cartoon Bank/ TCB 46294; Mike Twohy/The New Yorker Collection/The Cartoon Bank/ TCB 36774; Edward Steed/The New Yorker Collection/The Cartoon Bank/ TCB 142327; Liam Frances Walsh/The New Yorker Collection/The Cartoon Bank/ TCB 136942; Emily Flake/The New Yorker Collection/ The Cartoon Bank/ TCB 140413; Paul Noth/The New Yorker Collection/ The Cartoon Bank/ TCB 142325; Robert Mankoff/The New Yorker Collection/The Cartoon Bank/ TCB 41390; Drew Dernavich/The New Yorker Collection/The Cartoon Bank/ TCB 132410; Ed Fisher/The New Yorker Collection/The Cartoon Bank/ TCB 36761; Robert J. Day/ The New Yorker Collection/The Cartoon Bank/ TCB 38948; Drew Dernavich/The New Yorker Collection/The Cartoon Bank/ TCB 132928; J.C. Duffy/The New Yorker Collection/The Cartoon Bank/ TCB 67654; Peter C. Vey/The New Yorker Collection/The Cartoon Bank/ TCB 37009; Roz Chast/The New Yorker Collection/The Cartoon Bank/ TCB-67854; Peter Arno/The New Yorker Collection/The Cartoon Bank/ TCB 39953; Whitney Darrow, Jr./The New Yorker Collection/The Cartoon Bank/ TCB 67280; Dana Frandon/The New Yorker Collection/The Cartoon Bank/ TCB-42588; Mike Twohy/The New Yorker Collection/The Cartoon Bank/ TCB 25296; Michael Shaw/The New Yorker Collection/ The Cartoon Bank/ TCB 121932.

Guilty Pleasures

Introduction

L aw is everywhere. First are the obvious places—our government, our courtrooms, and our lawyers' offices. But it is also in our homes, our jobs, our relationships, and our casual interactions. Humor is everywhere too, so we should not be surprised then to discover that law crosses paths with it in every realm.

A. ON, ABOUT, IN . . . LAW'S INTERSECTION WITH HUMOR

Despite law's pervasive intersections with humor, an easy approach to understanding this relationship rises to the surface: an approach organized by on, about, and in. "On" centers on how legal rules wrestle with humor and sometimes silence its fun. "About" focuses on the national sport of jesting about lawyers and the legal process. Lawyer jokes, operation-of-government jokes, judge jokes, jury jokes, and this-law-is-preposterous jokes abound. Moving to "in," one can see that law itself overflows with funny parts. Judges and lawyers sometimes think they are (and indeed sometimes are) just *so* funny. Statutes and regulations can be funny. Judicial opinions too. Court proceedings have an occasional side-splitter: funny facts, funny testimony, funny mistakes by participants. These are part of humor "in" the law.

Starting with law's great effect on humor, we observe how powerfully law can constrain humor, such as when the government directly punishes or censors a communication. Joke about bombing an airport to kingdom come? Expect to get yourself in the slammer. Quip about killing the president? If you don't duck a conviction on account of mental illness, serious prison time may await you. And don't forget more indirect forms of legal regulation, which channel (or force) humor to take certain paths and to avoid others. The threat of a lawsuit can send a potent signal—silencing categories of jokes that could lead to liability while allowing others to flourish.

Let's take for instance our inclination to tell others in print or on the Internet about a seriously awful meal we've experienced. Should we report that the fish we ate "taste like old ski boots"?[1] Did the digestive reaction we had to the spicy meal truly make us into "a human flame thrower"?[2] Both of these descriptions indeed appeared on peer review websites. Did legal liability await those who posted and those who published? (See Chapter 1.) How about the fabled *London Sunday Telegraph Magazine* review crowning a dining establishment "one of the very worst restaurants in Christendom," describing its "meals of crescending monstrosity," and comparing one dish to a weapon of mass destruction that could be "found in a canister buried in the Iraqui desert"![3]

Restaurants reviews do not have a lock on colorful language like this.[4] Lawsuits asking for law to put its controlling hand on flamboyant (and often funny) statements appear in nearly every legal corner: laws regulating contract, intellectual property, employment discrimination, and defamation provide particularly vivid examples.

When law influences humor, we first see how legal principles and court decisions can control humor—encouraging some humor and muzzling or punishing other types. Since people (even brave and funny people) respond to the law's grip through fear, inaction, or by diluting their messages, legal regulation stifles creativity. The human spirit being what it is, however, legal regulation also inspires comedy—often with jokes ridiculing censors. Thus is an especially important wrinkle on how law influences humor. In all these contexts, law "regulates funny."

The words *humor and the law* also evoke stories, cartoons, and jokes about the foibles of lawyers, judges, and the legal process. For humor about the law, lawyer jokes are by far the most prominent. Bad lawyer jokes saturate the humor world yet nonetheless hold interest on many levels, containing anthropological, moral, and professional lessons. Most seem to agree that lawyer jokes are not really funny—amounting to an overworked trope at best. But they still grip our culture. One does not need to look far for pointed examples:

Q: What do you call a smiling, courteous person at a bar association convention?

A: The caterer.[5]

Q: What's the difference between a vacuum cleaner and a lawyer on a motorcycle?

A: The vacuum cleaner has the dirt bag on the inside.[6]

Are you laughing?

Often these jokes convey entertaining social critique. Real legal practices and events also reveal those messages: that is, humor *in* the law provides a rich medium for understanding of law and humor's role in government and society. Indeed, an equally important part of the law and humor story comes from what lawyers and judges show when they aspire to *be* funny as they dispatch the drudgery of their duties. Sometimes these characters succeed in their comedic aspirations, but often not. The jokes and cartoons showing lawyers or judges trying to be funny that are presented throughout this book capture this vanity. A rich trove of examples from books, formal Internet sites, and blogs compile transcripts (or at least allegedly real transcripts) of testimony showcasing witnesses who deviate from the formal seriousness of the proceedings:

ATTORNEY: How was your first marriage terminated?

WITNESS: By death.

ATTORNEY: And by whose death was it terminated?

WITNESS: Take a guess.[7]

ATTORNEY: The youngest son, the 20-year-old, how old is he?

WITNESS: He's 20, much like your IQ.[8]

These transcripts each present a comic classic: the "stupid question." Did you also notice that the lawyer was the object of the gag? Further analysis follows in Chapters 2 and 3.

B. THE POWER OF *NEW YORKER* CARTOONS

Narrating and analyzing the crossroads of humor, published and unpublished cartoons from the *New Yorker* magazine play a key role in telling the law and humor story. Most cartoons reproduced in this book provide the raw material for analysis: critiquing how lawyers act, judges act, the litigation process betrays justice, and legal rules tie themselves in knots. A handful of the cartoons simply illustrate how the law regulates funny bits of life.

Why use *New Yorker* cartoons as primary source material? The *New Yorker* magazine is a cultural icon in the United States—sharing salient analysis of current issues, impeccable manners, artistry, and consistently excellent writing. Reinforcing this *New Yorker* mission, the cartoons bridge generations, ensnaring an emerging group of power brokers as readers. Pitched at those with social status and education, the *New Yorker* even captures the attention of young children, who struggle to decipher cartoons. Writing for the *New York Times* in 1975, cultural critic John Leonard described the *New Yorker* as "the weekly magazine most educated Americans grew up on." Tipping his hat to the cartoons, Leonard added that "[f]or better or worse, it probably created our sense of humor."[9]

To be sure, most Americans never experienced this privilege of having the *New Yorker* cultivate and shape their sense of humor. And many have become very well educated without the magazine serving any part in their passage into adulthood. That restricted scope for *New Yorker*–style wit turns out to be an important part of the humor and law story. One can certainly find instances when other, non–*New Yorker* media illustrate how law and humor intersect. Some of this alternative media deviated from the higher-class humor of the *New Yorker*, laying for itself the foundation for legal liability. This book features examples of this as well.

But the influence of *New Yorker* cartoons among American culture brokers is strong. For avid fans, the magazine represents quality.[10] Even those who do not have the time and inclination to consume the magazine's more complex news stories and literary offerings identify with the magazine. Business people, lawyers, and other professionals may post cartoons outside their office doors and send particularly apt ones to a friend. Casual readers confess that when they encounter a *New Yorker* magazine (whether by subscription, happenstance in a doctor's waiting room, or as a hand-me-down from a friend), they always enjoy the cartoons first. This usually means starting with the back page caption contest. No one understands exactly why, but the caption contest draws in the fans, who marvel at what inspires such clever captions.

Lawyers feature prominently among the magazine's fans, relying on the magazine for information and opinion leadership. And lawyers, like other readers, enjoy *New Yorker* cartoons because they provide insight—funny insight—into the current political scene, legal institutions, and shortcomings of U.S. culture and government. Not surprisingly, then, the cartoons play to their audience. The compilation of *New Yorker* cartoons, available online at "The Cartoon Bank," is chock-a-block with cartoons about lawyers, judges, litigation, judicial proceedings, and legal themes. This trove provided the pool for this book's cartoons.

Yet the magazine's cartoons decidedly do not mirror the full array of American humor. As one observer has noted, the magazine's readership is largely "affluent professionals or business people with higher education, socially well established, living in one of the great metropolitan areas."[11] Their careful adherence to high standards of propriety ensures that many staples of American comedy—the bawdy, the scatological, the mean, and the crass—go unrepresented. The cartoons fastidiously avoid any whiff of bad taste. For more edgy American humor and its relationship with law, we must look elsewhere: television, the Internet, and the like. That said, the *New Yorker* cartoons provide key contemporary lessons on law and humor, even despite the magazine's steadfastly prim style. And despite its old-fashioned self-control, the *New Yorker* has impressively kept up with rapid change in media platforms and cultural expression, preserving important parts of its original format, while also opening "its windows, and . . . listening to the sirens of the streets."[12]

C. HUMOR SCHOLARSHIP

Although law touches all parts of what being human means, understanding law is a decidedly cerebral enterprise. Perhaps surprisingly, studying how humor works can enlist that same headiness. For centuries, a diverse collection of scholars from philosophy, literary theory, sociology, linguistics, psychology, medicine, and other disciplines have studied and dissected humor, declaring it an essential part of human cognition. Humor scholarship has depth and breadth, ranging from empirical and computational to literary and whimsical.

Surprisingly well represented are technical disciplines. Examples include engineers developing designs for a laugh-measuring machine, data scientists teaching computers to make jokes, linguists parsing and graphing joke taxonomies, and medical professionals conducting longitudinal studies of laughter's health benefits.

Legal scholarship on humor is sparse and narrow, largely confined to analyzing jokes about lawyers and juries,[13] compiling antics of participants in actual judicial proceedings,[14] or analyzing how one legal subject intersects with humor.[15] This book takes on a broader task, seeking to identify and to use common themes across the wide spectrum of legal contexts and humor types.[16] To guide this more global approach to law and humor, two parts of humor scholarship from non-law disciplines offer useful expertise: inventories of humor types and theories of how humor operates.

1. Humor Inventories

Scholars have identified at least twenty-one varieties of humor,[17] and given the nature of academia, it will surely generate more. With little effort, however, one can scour the existing taxonomies to narrow the varieties to six that are useful for understanding how law and humor interact: formal jokes, practical jokes, "satire, sarcasm, parody, [and] puns."[18] While these categories overlap, distinct examples of each exist within the world of law.

Formal jokes are rehearsed or "prepackaged humorous anecdotes" that people share with each other.[19] Formal jokes about law proliferate in the United States and are important mirrors of cultural attitudes about lawyers and the justice system. Humor scholars have noted that formal jokes tend to be a gendered enterprise: men more than women have traditionally indulged in joke-telling. The consensus reflected in popular and academic literature is that joke-telling provides a safe, non-emotional way for men to make a personal connection with others. Women, on the other hand, tend to favor situational humor—arising from the back-and-forth of personal repartee with others. Although formal joke-telling in intimate social situations may be on the wane, lawyer jokes continue to hold sway, particularly on the Internet. While some are long narratives with a punchline crescendo, others are short, snappy, and ... well ... you decide if they are funny:

Q: Why don't lawyers go to the beach?

A: Cats keep trying to bury them.[20]

Lawyer jokes are not the only legal genre well-represented in formal jokes. Also represented are lawsuits asking for courts to control wayward humor (think: sexual harassment and defamation). Sometimes formal jokes also pop up in court proceedings, particularly opening statements and closing arguments. Chapter 2 surveys common themes in these jokes.

Practical jokes usually take the form of "tricks" played on a person.[21] This trickster humor most commonly intersects with law either when a practical joke goes awry and creates legal liability—a matter covered in Chapter 1— or when frisky participants in the legal process perform a practical joke— illustrated in Chapter 3's discussion of humor within the legal process.

As for sarcasm, Chapter 3 discusses quips made during legal proceedings, which often include acerbic statements.

In contrast to pre-planned jokes, sarcastic remarks usually depend on context for their humor and convey unflattering personal commentary about another. Take, for example, this juror statement made during jury selection:

ATTORNEY: Do you remember the context in which your husband brought the issue up?

PROSPECTIVE JUROR: Not really. I try not to listen when he talks.[22]

Sarcastic commentary also generates defamation suits as reviewed in the discussion of the law's regulatory effect on humor in Chapter 1.

Sarcasm is related to parody and satire, two of the most pervasive genres at the intersection of humor and the law. Parody and satire appear often in critiques about laws, the legal process, and legal agents, discussed in Chapter 2. An important debate—also explored in Chapter 2—concerns whether satire promotes action or whether it assuages and diverts people from action. Parody and satire also feature in cheeky judicial opinions, discussed in Chapter 3.

Importantly, parody and satire regularly inflict pain and consequently provoke a variety of civil damage suits—that is, suits between private parties seeking money—which are covered in Chapter 1. What is the source of this central role for parody and satire in lawsuits? Both parody and satire usually include ridicule and operate without subtlety.[23] This ridicule can hurt people. Law's response is to provide a theory for fighting back: the primary business of civil law is to provide a remedy for hurt and damage. In addition, because their humor is generally obvious (not subtle), parody and satire inspire notice, can withstand rigorous standards of legal proof, and thus can be analyzed successfully using legal theories of harm.

Because satire attacks "some irritating aspect of the world," it has a sharper edge than parody: parody manipulates "pre-existing works, usually for comic effect," while satire is "an attack on some irritating aspect of the world."[24] As these two definitions suggest, parody includes lightheartedness more often than satire, which has a sharper edge than parody. Satire lacks one of parody's important qualities: something academics call "intertextuality,"[25] which involves interweaving references or qualities from parody's object. This overlap, which allows the audience to recognize the original text (or object) within the parody,[26] can arise through a number of techniques: the parody might contain the original's visual characteristics (such as an image resembling the Coca-Cola logo), the original's genre markers (such as the form generally associated with popular song lyrics or the narrative structure of a romantic story), or the original's actual words, characters, or plot lines (such as the words "I'll huff and I'll puff" in a *Three Little Pigs* parody, a character who resembles Little Red Riding Hood, or the plot of *Hansel and Gretel*).[27] How does this work in the law? The parody label can save the parodist from a damages judgment for an otherwise highly offensive presentation. Take, for example, the famous case covered in Chapter 2 when the parody characterization saved *Hustler* magazine from liability for its graphic description of a world religious leader having sex with his mother in an outhouse.[28]

Particularly acknowledging the overlap between the original and the parody, law treats parody as a favored child. Although law does not clearly explain this favoritism, I hypothesize that it originates in the tradition of debate and hearty criticism that U.S. society celebrates. By highlighting its roots in an original object, parody communicates that it exists primarily to comment on the original. Sometimes, however, parody can also commandeer the original object to comment on something else. So, for example, Cartoon i-1 that follows, which plays off the familiar trope of *Wizard of Oz* characters, primarily pokes fun at professions—entrepreneur, accountant, and attorney—and not the actual *Oz* characters.

But this explanation for why law favors parody can go only so far, since parody can be hard to distinguish from other forms of humor, particularly satire. Indeed, many works tracking parody's form are also satiric. Take, for example, the TV show *The Simpsons*, which satirizes suburban America but also parodies its own genre: situation comedies.[29]

Finally are puns. Definitions of puns span from rudimentary ("a play on words") to complex. Humor scholars have identified at least six categories of puns. Some of their distinctions are quite filigreed, although not necessarily significant to the blunt force of legal regulation of puns discussed in Chapter 1. The following straightforward definition serves well: A pun arises when "[t]wo or more meanings are packed into a verbal space which they do not ordinarily occupy."[30] Here's an example:

Q: How does an attorney sleep?

A: First he lies on one side, then he lies on the other.[31]

THE STRAW ENTREPRENEUR, THE TIN ACCOUNTANT, AND THE COWARDLY ATTORNEY

Cartoon i-1 (cartoon 75—TCB-30539) Warren Miller/The New Yorker Collection/The Cartoon Bank

For law's work in regulating discord in society, the controversial nature of puns proves important. As the above illustrates, puns can have a punch. (Hmm, *puns* have *punch?*) Puns also are especially effective for executing meta-humor—that is, humor about humor. Here's a meta-humor example of a (bad) lawyer joke alluding to the nature of puns as homonyms:

> Q: What's the difference between a lawyer and a liar?
> A: The pronunciation.[32]

As a matter of linguistic taste, different people have drastically different reactions to puns. Some believe that puns are the lowest form of wit while others are irresistibly attached to playing the role of the punster. Oppressed peoples can be drawn to them as an under-the-radar mechanism for communication. Totalitarian regimes prohibit them. And American courts have a tendency to favor them as a cerebral and cultured form of comedy. Puns hold an interesting status in the intersection of law and humor.

2. Major Theories of Humor

In much of life, a three-part structure guides our human understanding. The "rule of threes" holds that arguments or thoughts are more persuasive and effective when they travel in a pack of three. Humor is no exception—as comic technique often counsels that jokes should have a three-part structure, two parts carrying the setup and the third delivering the punchline. The comedy coming from the rule of threes arises in many contexts, but some say it is funniest if the last in the list is opposite from the first two:

> "She's hateful, she's despicable, I'm in love."[33]

And so it is with analytical humor theory. Over hundreds of years, scholars developed three theories to describe the source and structure of different types of humor: superiority, release, and incongruity theories. Although contemporary scholars have contributed new approaches to explaining why something is funny, the three classic theories still dominate. Though each has a unique heritage, they are not mutually exclusive and they are easily combined to explain why something inspires a laugh. Most quips or jokes do not sort naturally into distinct analytical humor categories.

Moreover, the different theories are not universal in that they fall far short in explaining the creation of humor.[34] Content, time, place, and presentation are crucial to prompting an authentic laugh and none of the theories adequately accounts for why humor depends on these factors. Nonetheless, the three theories of humor—superiority theory, release theory, and incongruity theory—provide a useful starting point for understanding the law and humor relationship.

a. Superiority Theory

Superiority theory derives from ancient thinkers, such as Aristotle, Plato, Socrates, and Cicero, who associated humor with aggressively disparaging others in order to enhance oneself.[35] Jibs and jabs have been going on for a very long time. Gazing backward, one discovers that Thomas Hobbes had a similar view. Hobbes used his life-is-brutish theme to analyze humor. He is often named superiority theory's progenitor.

Focusing on how humor connects with egocentricity and power, Hobbes suggested that a joke delivers amusement only if the jokester feels personally superior as a result. In a now-classic passage, Hobbes states: "*Sudden Glory*, is the passion which maketh those *Grimaces* cause LAUGHTER; and is caused either by some sudden act of their own, that pleaseth them; or by the apprehension of some deformed thing in another, by comparison whereof they suddenly applaud themselves."[36] We laugh because we feel a sense of triumph over the butt of a joke or the hapless protagonist in a story.

With this type of humor, ridicule, teasing, and taunts probably first come to mind. Certainly those uncharitable jokes fall within the scope of superiority humor, as do sexist, racist, and ethnic jokes. But the net spans even wider to include less obvious types that simply refer to the occasional stupid question or unthinking reaction by a protagonist. Consider the following cartoon—Cartoon i-2—as an example of the "stupid question" joke.

Superiority theory plays a key role in understanding law's effect on humor, humor about the law, and humor in the law. Because superiority humor may hurt people (and the law seeks to remedy hurt), this humor features large in lawsuits. The suits are sometimes successful, thus allowing law substantial latitude to stifle this type of humor. For humor about the law, lawyer jokes are the most prominent example, as they nearly always ridicule lawyers. Consider this little trio:

> Three surgeons were discussing their work. The first said: "I think accountants are the easiest to operate on. You open them up and everything inside is numbered!"

The second one said: "I think electricians are the easiest. You open them and everything inside is color coded!"

The third one said: "I think lawyers are the easiest. They are heartless, spineless, and their heads and asses are interchangeable."[37]

And here's an example of superiority humor coming from witness testimony memorialized in a (assertedly) real-life transcript—with a lawyer as its object:

ATTORNEY: Now doctor, isn't it true that when a person dies in his sleep, he doesn't know about it?
WITNESS: Did you actually pass the bar exam?[38]

Superiority humor makes powerful cameo appearances in humor in the law. Sometimes laws, legal analysis, and legal proceedings are really, really stupid and provide great raw material for jokes. That said, superiority theory has its limits.[39] Debasing people is usually not funny—even for the person who is delivering the blow. Satisfying, maybe. Funny, no. Understanding humor requires much more than appreciating the power and motivation of a taunt.

"Can you please identify which hand was mistakenly amputated?"

Cartoon i-2 (cartoon 4—TCB122480) Frank Cotham/The New Yorker Collection/The Cartoon Bank

b. Release Theory

What do sex, excretion, death, disability, and incest have in common? According to humor scholars, people generally hold repressed pleasure or anxiety about these matters, and jokes about them allow us to release tension.[40] Scholars credit Sigmund Freud and two philosophers—Alexander Bain and Herbert Spencer—with identifying this release theory of humor.[41] Because laughter allows relief from pent-up nervous energy, the theory is also called "relief theory."

Alexander Bain explained that we experience a sense of release when humor embraces "degradation" or reflects "personal pleasure in naughtiness."[42] Freud built on this observation in showing how jokes express taboo desires. Drawing on his work with dreams, Freud hypothesized that both joking and dreaming work by analogy, sidestepping both formal logic and literal meaning in order to elude our minds' internal censors.[43] By allowing forbidden thoughts to express themselves—the argument goes—the joke frees repressed energy through laughter, thereby inspiring mirth's pleasure. As support, Freud pointed to how jokes often focus on "sexual facts and relations."[44] Contemporary scholars have expanded the list to include other taboo or sensitive topics targeted by release humor.[45] Because jokes allow us to treat these forbidden subjects lightly—the theory goes—the jokes allow us to express ourselves in otherwise unavailable ways.

One sees strong evidence of release humor in lawyer jokes. Consider the following fine example—which contains the added sizzle of yoking a Baptist minister with the image of sex:

> A Baptist minister had the misfortune of being seated next to an attorney on a flight. When the flight attendant asked for drink orders, the attorney requested whiskey and soda. After giving the attorney the drink, the attendant asked the minister for his order. The minister said, "I'd rather savagely ravish a brazen whore than let liquor touch my lips." The attorney handed the drink back to the attendant, saying, "I didn't know that was a choice!"[46]

Perhaps because the questioning of witnesses involves huge amounts of interpersonal tension, one sees release humor in many funny, allegedly real, transcripts that make the rounds on the Internet and elsewhere. Consider the proliferation of transcript snippets dealing with coroners. Playing on our discomfort with death and other bodily matters, the common theme among the transcripts is striking. Here are just two examples:

> ATTORNEY: Do you recall the time that you examined the body?
> WITNESS: The autopsy started around 8:30 P.M.

ATTORNEY: And Mr. Denton was dead at the time?

WITNESS: If not, he was by the time I finished.[47]

ATTORNEY: Doctor, before you performed the autopsy, did you check for a pulse?

WITNESS: No.

ATTORNEY: Did you check for blood pressure?

WITNESS: No.

ATTORNEY: So, then it is possible that the patient was alive when you began the autopsy?

WITNESS: No.

ATTORNEY: How can you be so sure, Doctor?

WITNESS: Because his brain was sitting on my desk in a jar . . .

ATTORNEY: I see, but could the patient have still been alive, nevertheless?

WITNESS: Yes, it is possible that he could have been alive and practicing law.[48]

Because jokes in this category are about sensitive subjects, they—like superiority jokes—can easily inflict harm when they focus on real people. Release humor is often the target of the government's strong arm, working to prevent or to remedy injury. As such, release humor often plays a starring role in lawsuits based on jokes. In addition, when a judge or a lawyer occasionally forays into the off-color topics associated with release theory, then disciplinary sanction, mistrial, or malpractice liability can result. Take for example the judge who encountered negative career sanctions for telling a court employee that his wife's obstetrician offered to add "an extra stitch to his wife after childbirth in order to ensure the judge's later pleasure."[49] Equally egregious examples appear in Chapter 3.

But it is not just the law that censors these jokes. Informal disapproval of these jokes is an important part of the humor regulation story. Motivated by discretion—not law—editorial judgment also stifles release humor. Not surprisingly, bathroom jokes, incest quips, and raunchy sex cartoons are rarely found in polite conversation and are completely absent from the pages of the New Yorker. Yet taste, decorum, and editorial judgment do not prevent all sensitive topics from making their way into respectable, button-down comedy. One delicate legal theme—consistently present in New Yorker cartoons over the years—is the writing and reading of wills. These cartoons, discussed in Chapter 3, seem always to depict will-reading rituals in a lawyer's office.

What do these cartoons have to do with release theory? They presumably provide a vehicle for rehearsing and processing fears of a loved one's death, fears of losing a relative's affection, fears of one's rightful inheritance going to an interloper, and the like.

Though modern thinkers disparage much in Freud's thinking, most recognize as valid the key point of his joke theory. For jokes on restricted topics, we confront a conflict: we want to laugh, but we are not sure that we should. Ironically, this conflict ensures that the jokes are satisfying.[50] This is not a form of humor to ignore or marginalize.

c. Incongruity Theory

Of course, not all jokes relieve anxiety about taboos or express superiority. Most humor theorists believe that another quality characterizes all jokes: incongruity. Indeed, nearly all theorists agree that incongruity is necessary for a communication to inspire laughter. The general agreement that a joke may need some incongruity to be funny suggests that incongruity theory is by far the most important of the three fundamental theories. Also key to analyzing humor's intersection with law, incongruity theory gives courts a way to evaluate legal arguments about whether to protect or to punish humorous expression.

Philosophers and other thinkers have long connected humor and incongruity, tracing the connection to Aristotle's view that comedy springs from surprise and deception. Building on this view, Immanuel Kant and Arthur Schopenhauer further enhanced the intellectual pedigree of incongruity theory.[51] Today, most incongruity definitions in humor scholarship share the idea that incongruity arises when a joke joins two or more otherwise diverse or contrary phenomena. One modern theorist describes incongruity as "something unexpected, out of context, inappropriate, unreasonable, illogical, exaggerated,"[52] while other thinkers emphasize joinder of opposites, concluding that incongruity suggests "a conflict between what we perceive and our expectations."[53]

Humorous incongruity can appear in at least four ways. First, a joke demonstrates incongruity when it places something familiar in a foreign, unfamiliar context.[54] Incongruity can also result from the rhythm of a joke, which suddenly alters a viewpoint, such as changing something profound into something mundane (or vice versa).[55] An example might be a joke that begins with a child asking "where did I come from," the parents answer with a detailed description of human reproduction, and the child responds, "I was just trying to figure out if I came from New Jersey."[56] Character role reversal provides yet another example of an unexpected turn, such as when an apparently worn-out old woman shows great stamina in her sexual prowess.[57] Likewise, verbal incongruity can emerge from confusion about the context in which a term is used, with the process of resolving the confusion requiring an often fun or satisfying mental exercise. Abbott and Costello's "Who's on First" provides an example of this. Theorists suggest that the comedy in all these techniques is rooted in surprise (unforeseen insight) or, paradoxically, being satisfied by hearing what one actually thinks will follow from a joke's setup.[58] Sometimes one might delight in the fulfillment of expectations formed as the joke develops, sometimes one enjoys an unanticipated surprise in a joke's twist, and sometimes a joke contains elements that play to both of these emotional reactions.

This understanding that humor can result from both the thrill of surprise and the satisfaction of fulfilled expectations can shed light on a form of incongruity humor based on priming.[59] According to this view, humor occurs when a listener is primed with a script and required to apply the script in an unusual context. In this instance, the listener gets satisfaction from correctly guessing at the joke's next steps or from resolving an interpretation problem by replacing the original conception introduced in the joke with a less obvious or salient one.

Consider the following joke:

Q: How many scientists does it take to change a light bulb?
A: Ten—one to hold the bulb and nine to spin the room around.

Life experience provides the joke's primed script (twisting a light bulb), but resolving the joke requires reconceptualizing the script (twisting the room).[60] Room twisting appears incongruous, of course, because twisting pairs naturally with a light bulb, not with a stationary living space. But one expects that the joke's setup calls for a quirky punchline, and that expectation is fulfilled.

Consider also the primed script in Cartoon i-3 on the next page. We see someone asked to put a hand on a book. Common knowledge tells us (1) that action occurs when someone takes an oath of truthfulness and (2) that the book traditionally used in this scenario is a Bible. The caption then provides an unlikely surprise by substituting a holy book with a decidedly unholy one.

Thus emerges an important—arguably ironic—insight about humor: incongruity becomes funny by reference to congruity.[61] It makes sense that someone in a courtroom would be putting his hand on a book; it makes no sense that the book is a *TV Guide.*

Computer scientist and humor theorist Tony Veale explains how incongruity works within a world of congruity: "[Consider] four of the most primitive and fundamental drives guiding the instinctive behavior of mammals ... commonly known as the *four F's,* namely *Fight, Flight, Feeding* and *Mating.*"[62] The vaguely jarring incongruity is, of course, that mating is not an "F-word." Yet as an impolite F-word would fit very well on this list, the word choice "mating" is unexpected, albeit semantically appropriate. Veale explains, "We thus see past the foregrounded *Mating* to grasp the

"Wait a minute! This is a copy of 'TV Guide.'"

Cartoon i-3 (cartoon 2—TCB-28015) Mick Stevens/The New Yorker Collection/The Cartoon Bank

backgrounded F-word that lies underneath, and in doing so, preserve the validity of the phrase *four F's*."[63] Veale further reasons that the joke "relies on the complicity of the audience, both in their understanding of the speaker's desire to avoid any mention of a vulgar word and their desire to enjoy the frisson generated by this four-letter Anglo-Saxon expletive."[64]

One sees this process at play in the following two examples of legal humor. In both Cartoon i-4 and the following joke, one party makes an admission that would be incongruous because it works against the party's apparent self-interest.

Here's an example using a trial joke:

O'Riley was on trial for armed robbery. The jury came out and announced, "Not guilty."

"Wonderful," said O'Riley, "does that mean I can keep the money?"[65]

In both the joke and the cartoon, we can easily grasp the gag because it fits within the parameters of reality: one does not need to take notes when one is taping a conversation and a man might well blurt out a delighted comment upon learning of his acquittal. But an admission against interest is a surprising twist on this expectation.

"I don't need to write it down, boss, I'm wearing a wire."

Cartoon i-4 (cartoon 1—TCB-142264) Liam Walsh/The New Yorker Collection/The Cartoon Bank

Understanding the role of incongruity in humor is puzzling. Freud called the process of resolving the incongruity in a joke as making "sense of non-sense."[66] Other thinkers have referred to it as "limited logic"[67] or "local logic."[68] Some argue that humor will fail if the audience cannot at least partially resolve incongruities that a joke creates. According to this argument, audience discomfort with unresolved incongruity undermines comedy.[69]

More contemporary scholars challenge this position that resolving incongruity is essential for an audience to appreciate humor. They argue instead that some listeners have a high tolerance for absurdity and can easily find a joke funny and satisfying even when it leaves an incongruity hanging— with no resolution.[70] For some, a bizarre situation that is neither resolved nor explained is alone enough for hearty laughter. Take the (real-life) judge who filed a complaint, which he styled as a "public interest lawsuit." What was the harm to be remedied? Answer: the dry cleaners lost his pants. What were the damages sought? Answer: 54 million dollars! How on earth could the judge have thought this would succeed? Answer: We never found out. The spectacle of a judge claiming that the public interest required him to get 54 million dollars is an unresolved incongruity. The only resolution we know is that he "fell short of that goal, by exactly 54 million dollars."[71] Yet one might conclude the situation is sufficiently outlandish to fall within the range of "funny."

Cartoon i-5 might also depict unresolved incongruity. Experience offers no peg on which to hang any explanation of Ping-Pong among justices in an appellate courtroom. The reference to the framers' original intent as a reference point for resolving controversy hardly offers enough to resolve the unconventional image.

Despite scholarly disagreement about incongruity resolution, the overwhelmingly dominant view holds that a communication needs incongruity to have humorous potential.[72] Only a handful of thinkers believe humor can thrive without incongruity.[73] Incongruity, however, is a curious phenomenon: some incongruity is hilarious while other incongruity is not the least bit funny. In scholarly lingo, incongruity may be a necessary condition for humor, but it is not always a sufficient condition. Thus, some incongruities, such as randomly connected concepts, "poetic metaphors, [and] magic tricks,"[74] may be insightful, quirky, illogical, or "irredeemably absurd,"[75] but not really funny. So, for example, humor does not arise when we hear about or observe a person meeting death when he or she falls into a deep fissure while casually walking on a public beach.[76] Consider also arbitrary word pairings such as "carrot/radiator." Incongruous? Yes. Comedy? Uh . . . no.

"The Founding Fathers were clear. You must win by two."

Cartoon i-5 (cartoon 3—TCB-140192) Drew Dernavich/The New Yorker Collection/The Cartoon Bank

Precisely what makes some incongruities funny and others not so funny has eluded comics, scholars, and consumers of comedy alike. The phenomenon has a strong "I know it when I see it, but I can't explain why" quality. Yet identifying incongruity is so key to identifying something funny that pinpointing what makes certain incongruities funny is essential to understanding how humor operates. This is especially true for courts trying to decide whether the funny quality of a communication saves a speaker from legal liability.

The first chapter explores how courts perform this role of evaluating whether a communication is "just a joke" and thus not a basis for liability. To assist in evaluating whether courts decide this question consistently with incongruity theory, the following guidelines for funny incongruities are instructive. First, humor scholars argue that incongruities are consistently funny only if they are "motivated by, and understandable within, the context of their use."[77] Non sequiturs are reliably odd, but not reliably funny. Second, the context should be playful and relaxed (lacking anxiety) when the incongruity emerges.[78] Next, surprise substantially contributes to the comedic quality of a joke. (Indeed, some theorists even maintain that surprise is an essential component of humor.)[79] Nonetheless, a vibe, a cue, or some kind of social connection must alert the audience that the joke teller is looking for a laugh. The cue may be just a verbal tip-off, a smirk, or an expression in the eyes. But through this mental connection with the joke teller, the audience can anticipate that a punchline is coming, wonder what it will be, and experience satisfaction when it gets there.[80] This human connection can ensure that even the most mundane (congruent?) incongruity may provide pleasurable comedic appreciation.

Incongruity is also an important concept for understanding humor about the law and humor in the law. For example, the contrast between the normally solemn tone of a judicial opinion and ridiculous case facts can create funny results, particularly for those who appreciate how seriously judges can take themselves. Consider this official legal holding in a personal injury case that hinged on whether a court could use its admiralty power to resolve a dispute about injuries from a plastic cup hurled onto a ship while the ship was sitting in knee-deep water:

> In sum, throwing an object like a coffee cup from land at an individual standing on an anchored vessel does not threaten a disruptive effect on maritime commerce.... Accordingly [the] claims do not satisfy the ... two-prong connection test, rendering the invocation of federal admiralty jurisdiction inappropriate.[81]

How about the court's formal approach here! Is the court secretly smirking at the absurdity of the case or is it just systematically doing its job applying law to fact? Either way, the incongruity between a ridiculous lawsuit and serious analysis of a standard two-prong legal test creates a somewhat silly spectacle. Adding to the possible comic effect is the court's observation that the so-called anchored vessel bore the name *One Love* and was owned by a limited liability corporation doing business as "Ferocious and Impetuous."[82]

A similar comedic anomaly arises when the controlled, rigid nature of an actual in-court proceeding is peppered with a participant's profanity or references to topics such as sex. These situations can inspire laughter even when the same communications might not be the least bit funny outside of the august courtroom setting. Here's an example in which the comedy arising from a mismatch between topic and context is enhanced by the incongruity of a judge's apparent ignorance:

> ATTORNEY: Now, do you recall telling Officer F. that after David went into the living room that Gary assumed the missionary position on top of you?
>
> WITNESS: Yes.
>
> JUDGE: Excuse me, Counsel. What kind of position?
>
> ATTORNEY: A missionary position, on top of—
>
> JUDGE: Like in a prayer?[83]

What follows in this book shares many more such examples. Chapter 3 features similar situations when unlikely statements or topics seep into litigation formalities. Chapter 2 presents examples when comedians use their imaginations to produce fictional, yet incongruous, law-related scenarios. As you read, consider which group of examples strike you as the funniest.

Final Note "Ridicule!" "Degradation!" "Tension Relief!" "Incongruity Resolution!" These concepts have significant limits. The comic imagination has secrets we don't understand and don't really want to understand. But law is serious business and when it enters the realm of humor, we need guideposts to help ensure that the intersection of the two does not lead toward mutual destruction. Theorized approaches to understanding at least part of what fuels the fire of comedy, I submit, are better than personal idiosyncrasy and unchecked emotion. Humor theories at hand, the remainder of this volume proceeds through the three-part tale providing examples of the effect of law on humor, humor about the law, and humor in the law.[84]

Starting first with humor's effect on law, Chapter 1 surveys funny (or allegedly funny) legal challenges in the areas of intellectual property, defamation, contract, and sexual harassment. Discussion of criminal penalties and authoritarian censorship appear in Chapter 1 as well. Chapter 2 presents sometimes-funny and usually not-so-funny lawyer jokes, judge jokes, jury jokes, and legal process jokes. Perhaps unsurprisingly, the best comic material appears in Chapter 3: humor in the law. As is often the case, unforced gags emerging from real-life contexts tend to be the funniest of all.

CHAPTER 1

༄

"On"

Law's Effect on Humor

Did you ever encounter George Carlin's "Seven Dirty Words" stand-up routine? (If yes, no need to disclose how old you were when you first heard it.) Have any trademark parodies ever caught your eye? How about funny, but smutty, cartoons? Did your parent ever shake a finger at you to keep your mouth shut as you were going through airport security: "No joking about bombing airplanes!"? All of these touch on law's effect on humor.

In the city of Philadelphia some years ago, prosecutors brought charges against a white hospital employee who hung a noose near the locker of a black co-worker. The white employee said it was "just a joke." Let's just say that the Federal Criminal Code suggested that was not an excuse, and federal criminal charges followed. The all-white jury acquitted the white employee of ethnic intimidation charges, apparently accepting his testimony that the noose was only a "practical joke," but one might guess the white employee will think twice before doing that again.[1]

In its most obvious form, law regulates "funny" by imposing direct constraints and criminal punishments for certain types of jokes. As is the case for jokes about bombing airplanes, federal criminal law takes a dim view of quips about killing the U.S. president. Likewise, as the noose case illustrates, the law criminalizes racist jokes that terrorize or violate civil rights. These crime definitions are just one way government pressures wannabe jokers into silence. A judicial or regulatory order prohibiting someone from telling a particular joke will subject the violator to a contempt-of-court sanction. Because contempt often includes criminal punishment, these orders act as "prior restraints" on joke telling: they effectively prevent the joke from being uttered. Imposing these restraints, governments have picked on stand-up comedians—and, somewhat more bizarrely, amateur punsters. This chapter surveys law's direct and indirect impact on humor, touching on restrictions and protections that discourage humor, inspire humor, or in some unusual circumstances have both effects.

In theory, all government constraints on speech in the United States beckon the oversight of the First Amendment to the U.S. Constitution, which admonishes, "Congress shall make no law . . . abridging the freedom of speech." First Amendment doctrine is concerned largely with ensuring that information flows freely into the marketplace of ideas. Indeed, courts interpreting the amendment find deep offense in any attempt by government to stop a thought from leaving a speaker's lips. The thinking is that prior restraints on speech suppress debate and creativity while also reducing the quality and quantity of ideas exchanged among people. Accordingly, courts tread carefully when a restraint touches something even as potentially trivial as a joke.

The message from the rule against prior restraints is straightforward: except in extraordinary circumstances, speech should be uttered and free to be heard. Once a thought is communicated, however, other speech regulation can occur. Take for example when someone sues for damages after a joker speaks. The joker may ultimately incur damages, which may discourage the joker (and others) from making a similar gag in the future. The law's decision to allow damages therefore acts as a future disincentive, regulating the joke indirectly.

The effect of targeted judicial or administrative orders and criminal statutes that provide for jokers to lose their liberty is more direct. These laws harness the strong arm of government, providing high-stakes penalties—prison time and the like—designed to dissuade potential jokers from ever even uttering banned jokes.

This chapter first discusses law's indirect regulation of humor. Why start there? Indirect regulation promises to reveal more about courts' attitudes on humor. When deciding lawsuits between private persons (rather than deciding whether to lower the hammer of government control through direct regulation), judges often show no awareness that they are sending messages about what types of jokes should flourish and what types should be condemned. Focused on the specifics of legal theories outlining liability principles and blind to the possibility that they might restrict communication, judges often exert power over jokes unselfconsciously. With direct regulation—covered later in this chapter—that innocence disappears. When asked to impose criminal liability for speech or to issue a prior restraint on speech, judges turn reflexively to the First Amendment. As usually applied by courts, our beloved First Amendment tends to hijack legal analysis, pushing to the side other laws and concerns that might inform whether a speech restriction is appropriate. For this reason, law professors sometimes celebrate what they call "First Amendment exceptionalism": the notion that First Amendment principles are not only special but superior to other laws. Consider this analogy: when an English language literary scholar analyzes a modern text, a reference to Shakespeare—even when indisputably relevant—easily transports the discussion into revered, more doctrinaire, and self-conscious terrain.[2] So it can be with the First Amendment.

That's not to say that law's frontal attack on humor is uninteresting or unimportant. For that reason, this chapter presents a cross section of direct regulations, implemented through criminal law or prior restraints targeted at stand-up comedians and punsters (and other wordsmiths). One context in which many U.S. citizens have called for direct regulation is hate speech. In some countries, law severely restricts hate speech—even when it occurs in joke form. This is not the case in the United States. Importantly, though, law is not the only force suppressing jokes that disparage a particular group: custom, shaming, and violence can silence speakers in any society, including the United States. Consideration of these social mechanisms highlights the power of censorship, both formal and informal.

Finally, when one considers censorship through humor's lens, one discovers a fascinating twist in contemporary popular culture. The term "censorship" beckons an image of government power preventing citizens from expressing themselves. In a book (such as this) by a freedom-loving academic, one might expect predictable scolding about the evils of suppression. But that's not the full message of this chapter. Rather, the chapter concludes with a frolic through the world of censorship *humor*, which is flourishing on TV, in print books, on the Internet, and beyond. Out of fear, defiance, or just plain chutzpah, humor practitioners (comedians, cartoonists, writers, lay joke tellers) have created this unique genre of humor in the United States—which both mocks and capitalizes on the process of censorship. It is in this context—censorship—that law both restrains and inspires humor.

A. AN UNWITTING PASSAGE INTO THE COMEDY BUSINESS: HOW COURTS BECOME HUMOR CRITICS WHEN INDIRECTLY REGULATING HUMOR

U.S. legal regulation can be organized in diverse ways. One approach is to sort laws according to which branch of government creates and enforces them. Another approach—more useful here—is to organize laws according to what part of life they control. As contemporary life complicates the different types of subject matters that touch on humor, regulations have proliferated. One way to understand how humor relates to this hodgepodge of subjects is to evaluate the subjects in light of the three traditional pillars of law: property law, the law of wrongs, and contract law. (Yet again in the humor world, things come in threes.) Collectively, the subject matter categories discussed immediately below reflect a cross section of these three pillars: intellectual property (a form of property law), defamation and other torts (part of the law of wrongs), contracts (regulated by . . . you guessed it . . . contract law), and sexual harassment (governed by a combination of principles from contracts and the law of wrongs). These various subjects also represent state law, federal law, court-made law, administrative law, and statutory law. As such, they provide a representative snapshot of precisely how law responds to jokes.

These legal theories also protect diverse human concerns: promoting certainty, encouraging innovation, protecting against reputational harm, ensuring gender equality, and the like. Regardless of context, though, courts show remarkable consistency in the types of jokes they discourage as well as the types they protect. Collectively, the cases show courts favoring incongruity humor, which arises when two unlikely phenomena appear together in a surprising fashion. The cases also illustrate courts imposing liability on (and thereby discouraging) two other categories of humor: superiority humor, which is characterized by ridicule of another, and release humor, which provides a mechanism for relieving tension about taboo subjects such as death, sex, violence, and excrement.

One wonders whether this pattern of regulation is curious. Is it mere coincidence that leads courts toward protecting incongruity humor? Or is it dumb luck? A shared judicial funny bone? Consider the following and see what you think.

1. Intellectual Property Law: Parody as a Favored Child in Trademark Law

When a person toils to create an original work or invention, intellectual property law steps in to protect the creator. If someone else tries to rip off or profit from the creative work, intellectual property principles regard these actions as theft. As with many legal frameworks, however, courts have not carefully charted the line between fair use of someone else's original work and unfair use. As Cartoon 1-1 illustrates, sometimes a spin-off or knock-off might be viewed as a law violation (such as plagiarism) and sometimes it might be viewed as a respectful tip of the hat (such as an homage) to an earlier creation.

"Go ahead. Don't think of it as plagiarism, think of it as an homage."

Cartoon 1-1 (cartoon 16—TCB-40526) Mick Stevens/The New Yorker Collection/The Cartoon Bank

This fuzziness between celebration and violation extends to intellectual property laws governing humor. Before exploring that uncertain territory, however, we first need to understand how intellectual property laws intersect with humor.

Perhaps a consequence of the relationship between creativity and intellectual property law, intellectual property cases often have funny facts and circumstances. Take the "Monkey Selfie" case, which arose out of allegations that a macaque monkey, Naruto, took multiple snaps of himself using a nature photographer's camera. When the photographer, David Slater, asserted ownership of the pictures, People for the Ethical Treatment of Animals (PETA) argued that the monkey, Naruto, held the copyright in the photographs. Whether or not one scoffs at PETA's decision to make a federal case about this issue, few would deny that the pictures—which feature close-ups of Naruto's toothy grin—are charmingly funny. (To get a look, just Google "Naruto selfie.")[3] How did the case turn out? The federal district court ruled that although Congress might be able to grant endearing non-humans like Naruto the power to hold a copyright, Congress had not yet done so. Naruto, the court ruled, is not an "author" within the meaning of the existing U.S. Copyright Act.[4]

Although other intellectual property cases share amusing facts, a more common context in which humor crosses paths with intellectual property law occurs when a comedian, comic writer, or comedic musician seeks intellectual property protection (usually copyright) for a literary, artistic, or musical creation. The question of whether the copyright shield protects these artists does not usually rest on whether their material is funny, but rather on whether the material is sufficiently original. Originality, unfortunately, can sometimes elude precise definition. Can a humorous takeoff on another's creation be *original*? Can jokes be too *factually accurate* to merit copyright protection? The questions proliferate.

Precise legal rules become even more elusive when courts actually try to measure whether a violation falls into the realm of funny. The following regularly occurs in trademark infringement cases: when ruling on federal trademark infringement claims, courts must often decide whether an apparent infringement is a protected parody. In concluding that parody protection insulates an alleged infringement, courts tolerate (perhaps even appreciate) a good measure of mocking, superiority humor. But even more significantly (and perhaps even more unknowingly), courts dissect the alleged infringement, searching for another humorous quality: incongruity. The parody doctrine instructs courts to protect gags that reflect significant incongruity and to impose liability for gags lacking incongruity.

How is incongruity relevant to these lawsuits? The answer lies in the crucial role of consumer confusion. Trademark infringement law seeks to protect two entities: consumers, who may be misled into buying something different from what they thought they were buying, and trademark owners, who are deprived of sales, and therefore of profit, derived from their investment in creating the trademark. Key to an infringement claim is possible consumer uncertainty about who created the allegedly infringing product. If a court finds a "likelihood of confusion" between the product protected by a trademark and the challenged creation, the court can impose infringement liability.[5] This "likelihood of confusion" test invites the search for incongruity: if the alleged infringement lines up with the qualities or purposes of the protected product, then a consumer may mistake the infringing product for the original. If, by contrast, the connection between the alleged infringement and the protected product is too preposterous, remote, or unexpected, then a consumer would not reasonably confuse them. With a true parody, courts reason, a consumer understands that a producer will not likely poke fun of itself or give others license to do so. To do so would be inconsistent with self-preservation instincts and profit-maximization motives.

In raising a parody defense, trademark infringement defendants tap into this reasoning about incongruity, but they must walk a fine line. To avoid trademark liability, the parody must depict something sufficiently like the original mark so that one appreciates that the parody actually concerns the original mark. But the parody must also be sufficiently unlike the original mark that a consumer could not reasonably confuse the two. In literary language, the parody must be more than a pastiche—more than a simple imitation. More colloquially, the parody must be "a takeoff, not a ripoff"[6] in order to enjoy protection.

For a handful of courts, the parody defense also ushers in the First Amendment—inviting courts to fret over whether prohibiting the parody would threaten a core value of free expression, such as encouraging political debate. That most courts do not even mention the First Amendment in parody cases is odd because the First Amendment's purpose of promoting debate dovetails well with incongruity analysis: we do not expect a trademark's creator to use the mark as a tool for critical or satirical commentary. Thus, we could reasonably assume that the commentary comes from someone else who may be critiquing the mark. Critique, according to First Amendment principles, should be encouraged, since it can lead to robust debate and understanding.

So, for example, the following two cartoons would easily enjoy both First Amendment protection and parody protection under the trademark infringement laws. After investing time and money in developing and marketing their character mascots, the maker of Planters Peanuts (Cartoon 1-2) and the Walt Disney Company (Cartoon 1-3)[7] would not likely create satirical caricatures.

The cases—funny cases—in this area are legion. Parodists often market products using something close or identical to a classic logo but with a new name. Pet fragrance marketed under the name "Timmy Holedigger" (rather than Tommy Hilfiger),[8] posters of a pregnant Girl Scout with the caption "be prepared" (as contrasted with a scout who actually honored that slogan),[9] and Lard Ass jeans (rather than Jordache jeans)[10] all join the many litigated parodies. In elegant fashion, many cases reflect disciplined incongruity analysis, quoting literary definitions of parody and celebrating parody's political and literary pedigree in U.S. society and culture.

Elegance and discipline notwithstanding, the fuzziness of the consumer confusion test emerges in cases that include the necessary unlikely juxtapositions (incongruities) but nevertheless fail to win the courts' protection as parody.[11] Consider the court's finding that a sex toy manufacturer created a likelihood of confusion over the General Electric trademark. In holding the manufacturer liable to General Electric, the court suggested that a consumer might reasonably conclude that General Electric—a manufacturer of household appliances—would affix the same logo to a *dildo* that would appear on a clothes washer.[12] Did the court seriously believe this reasoning? Perhaps the court's real concern was that General Electric was due damages because the unsavory nature of the parody sullied its revered trademark.

"*Counsellor will instruct his client to remove his hat
and put on some pants before sentencing.*"

Cartoon 1-2 (cartoon 17—TCB-44255) Jack Ziegler/The New Yorker Collection/The Cartoon Bank

Could the *General Electric* court have acted out of distaste for release humor on a taboo topic? Such an impulse is certainly consistent with other trademark law, which prohibits such activities as diluting a trademark by degrading the mark's associations with positive qualities and prevents the Trademark Office from registering "immoral, deceptive, or scandalous marks."[13] This impulse is reflected outside intellectual property law as well: indeed, when courts confront off-color humor in any context, they are much more likely to impose liability.[14]

2. Tort

A tort is a civil wrong—whether intentional or unintentional—for which one private person can sue another, usually for damages. When it comes to humor, the assault on dignity in the form of defamation (defined to include both libel and slander) is the most common theory that an injured person brings to court. Yet bad jokes trigger other theories too, including additional

Cartoon 1-3 (cartoon 18—TCB-40526/017390-313) Mick Stevens/The New Yorker Collection/The Cartoon Bank

torts that remedy intangible damage to dignity as well as tangible—indeed palpable—harm.

a. Defamation

As defined under state court-made law in the United States, a defamatory statement "tends so to harm the reputation of another as to lower him in the estimation of the community or to deter third persons from associating or dealing with him." Importantly, a successful defamation claim requires not only that the plaintiff show that a statement is defamatory but also that the statement is false.[15] In the realm of defamatory humor, a common defense asserts that a statement is neither defamatory nor false because it was "just a joke." Courts have a devil of a time figuring out what to do with this defense. Here is the root of their difficulty: humor, even lame humor, doesn't fit easily into the law's paradigm of truth and falsity. Humor is by definition not "serious," thus suggesting that it operates outside the realm of anything one could verify. Yet—we know that jokes can hurt, we can usually pinpoint why they hurt, and we know that "many a truth is said in jest."

U.S. courts and commentators take a variety of approaches to the challenge of fitting the round peg of humor into the square hole of defamation
law. One route uses the treasured label of parody: some courts even say that
parody is not capable of being defamatory.[16] Others provide a wider protective net, declaring that "unambiguously jocular" statements "set forth in
jest" can inflict no reputational injury.[17]

The more common approach, however, tries to distinguish between jokes
meriting defamation liability from those jokes that do not. The legal shield,
known as the privilege of fair comment, has long performed this sorting
process, insulating comical criticism relating to "matters of public concern"
and allowing liability for criticism on private matters. Applying this privilege, courts distinguished between humorous assertions that were factual
(which were legally actionable) and those based on opinion (which were
not). Courts further refined the concept, now formalized in the *Restatement
(Second) of Torts*: " '[a] defamatory communication may consist of a statement in the form of an opinion, but a statement of this nature is actionable
only if it implies the allegation of undisclosed defamatory facts as the basis
of the opinion.' "[18] Applying this idea to comedy, the *Restatement* explains
that "[h]umorous writings, verses, cartoons or caricatures that carry a sting
and cause adverse rather than sympathetic or neutral merriment may be
defamatory."[19]

The U.S. Supreme Court folded into First Amendment doctrine this
state law distinction between fact and opinion. Although one would think
that using an existing legal principle would give clarity to constitutional law,
lower courts have remained baffled and inconsistent. In deciding whether a
joke suggests actual facts, courts often omit discussion of "opinion," looking
instead to protect exaggeration, "rhetorical hyperbole," and "vigorous epithet." In other cases, courts simply perform a sorting exercise. If the joke
includes material that a reasonable reader might interpret as suggesting real
facts, the court chutes the case down the liability channel, concluding that
the joke is capable of defamatory meaning and of undermining a good reputation. A contrary conclusion (the humor suggests no real facts) funnels
the case into the opinion chute, resulting in insulation from liability.[20]

However straightforward this sorting exercise appears on the surface,
courts indulge an impulse to develop complex definitions of fact and
opinion, including multifactor tests and crystalline distinctions between
"pure, *evaluative* opinion" (which can't be proven true) and "pure, *deductive*
opinion" (which can be).[21] These developments are not surprising: the enterprise of defining truth is often fraught with contingency and analytical
complexity.

Despite its faults, the fact/opinion test does protect important interests.
Humans like to share and hear opinions. Opinions inform, entertain, and

sometimes promote quality of life. Don't we want the option of consulting candid opinions about restaurants posted by other consumers on Internet sites? Don't we want our professional reviewers to tell us what they really think when they write for popular media? And don't we want to insulate all of these folks from the chill of looming liability that threatens to shut them up?

Restaurant reviews present a context in which the fact/opinion dichotomy protects a reviewer's ability to convey distaste in highly extravagant, hyperbolic, yet deeply informative descriptions. While a restaurant had a chance of winning a defamation case several decades ago, enhanced constitutional protection for opinion has now virtually freed reviewers from fear. Consequently, the eating public gets the benefit of unrestrained reviews, such as the following by the *New York Times* reviewer Pete Wells:

> Hey, did you try that blue drink, the one that glows like nuclear waste? The watermelon margarita? Any idea why it tastes like some combination of radiator fluid and formaldehyde?

and

> Is the shapeless, structureless baked Alaska that droops and slumps and collapses while you eat it, or don't eat it, supposed to be a representation in sugar and eggs of the experience of going insane?[22]

By virtue of a federal statute that immunizes Internet platforms such as Yelp and TripAdvisor, these companies do not need to worry about exposing their deep pockets to liability for posting reviews such as the following (special note for everyone's personal inclination to skim or skip quotes. . . . This is a funny one):

> The Duck Biryani, a special not on the menu, I would say, is not worth it. It's two cups of rice and a duck thigh, and we were surprised to discover later that it cost $28. My wife thought it was going to be around $8. My sense of remorse doubled this morning as it ripped its way out of me in a raging fiery whirlwind of poopy terror.
>
> This meal was delectable, exotic, and incinerated everything in my intestines. My morning was an unforgettable thrill ride. . . . 4 stars for the truly delicious food and unimpeachable service, minus one star for expensive biryani, and for turning me into a human flamethrower.[23]

Although the federal statutory immunity would protect Yelp from liability for this review, that statute would not protect the customer reviewer.

For any resulting lawsuit, the reviewer would likely rely on the constitutional protection for opinion, asserting that the review is not factual. One questions whether the fact/opinion concept is well suited to handle this dispute. With its tenacious images, the review likely invoked for readers a primordial instinct to avoid poisonous food. Surely this could result in a precipitous drop in business for the restaurant. But how on earth could the restaurant prove that the description of a morning's "unforgettable thrill ride" contained a false fact alleging digestive distress resulting from the restaurant's food?

When evaluating comical, extravagant language, one encounters difficulty segregating fact and opinion. Humor operates in the realm of laughter, not truth. That said, some funny comments are indeed clearly opinion:

> In my humble opinion, that haircut makes your head look like a turnip.[24]

Yet most other quips are much harder to sort between the fact and opinion. Consider the following excerpt from a federal district judge's decision on the constitutionality of a police officer's conduct:

> Law-enforcement work is not easy, and no one doubts the correlation between preserving public safety and preserving a free society. Nor does anyone doubt the imperative of allowing officers to use ruses and lies in the course of this essential work, particularly if the tools of indirection ensure public safety.[25]

While some statements in this passage might qualify as factually verifiable (e.g., "the correlation between preserving public safety and preserving a free society"), other assertions are more difficult to characterize. The humorous, tongue-in-cheek tone shrouds the whole message, enabling it to penetrate before being fully evaluated. The humor also tends to address the topic of an officer's alleged unconstitutional conduct ambiguously, in a manner that is difficult to fully understand (e.g., "tools of indirection"?). Part of the humor in this passage arises from incongruity (e.g., the notion that guardians of the rule of law—police officers—have an imperative to use ruses). By definition, incongruity does not reflect the constellation of facts and emotions we readily experience but instead presents a surprising reality, unsettling our expectations.[26] That quality makes jokes entertaining but also enhances the challenge of definitively concluding whether they contain fact or opinion. While potentially thrilling and hysterical, an unanticipated reality does not beckon a clean vision of "truth."

And of course humor's message is filled with playful uncertainties, which do not sort into neat fact/opinion categories either. As one judge observed: "Laughter can soften the blows dealt by a cruel world, or can sharpen the cutting edge of truth."[27]

Consider the following example of metahumor (humor about humor). When (as in Cartoon 1-4) the comedian says, "Yo bitch"—is he disparaging women or is he disparaging people who disparage women? Also, is Cartoon 1-4 poking fun at white comedians, black comedians, or both? Can we say with any certainty whether it depicts something related to truth?

So, the opinion/fact dichotomy is ill suited for determining whether a humorous, although hurtful, statement can form the basis for a defamation claim. That said, we do have a concept to guide whether defamation law provides a remedy for harms caused by vicious and lacerating comedy: the concept of incongruity saves the day yet again.

Consider first the following classic case—*Polygram Records v. Superior Court*[28]—arising from Robin Williams's riff about wine snobbery and race. Williams developed his monologue around "the fantasy of a black wine 'tough enough' to be advertised by 'Mean Joe Green.'" Rejecting the defamation suit brought by wine industry representatives, the *Polygram*

Cartoon 1-4 (cartoon 22—TCB-25446) Charles Barsotti/The New Yorker Collection/The Cartoon Bank

court concluded that Williams's "suggestion that the hypothetical wine is a 'motherf*ck*er,' black in color, tastes like urine, goes with anything 'it' damn well pleases, is 'tough' and endorsed by ruffians are not assertions any sensible person [would] take seriously."[29] Rather, the court concluded, the riff distorted reality and gave us illogical references in its physically impossible depictions of wine. Williams's verbal images were too far afield (indeed too incongruent) from anything one would be expected to say about wine; the images failed to disparage a winemaker's reputation and the case stumbled and fell.

For a wildly different case also rejecting a defamation claim, consider *New Times v. Isaacks*.[30] In *Isaacks*, the newspaper *New Times* ran an apparently satirical story—headlined "Stop the Madness"—depicting Texas's attempt to ban the children's book *Where the Wild Things Are*. The satirical story described a "diminutive 6-year-old" jailed for celebrating the "cannibalism, fanaticism, and disorderly conduct" in the book. Texas officials thought this article defamed them, so they brought suit. Rejecting the officials' suit, the court identified a long list of incongruities establishing the story's status as non-defamatory satire. The incongruities included (i) an "unorthodox headline," (ii) a far-fetched description of a 6-year-old in shackles, (iii) reference to a "freedom-opposing religious group that bears a ridiculous acronym: God Fearing Opponents of Freedom (GOOF)," and (iv) an unlikely George W. Bush quote calling the book "deviant," "violent," and "sexual."[31] Clearly a joke, the court concluded, the article merited no liability.

Incongruity theory does not provide a sure-fire test for accurately evaluating when the law should favor or reject defamation liability. The theory does, however, provide a relatively emotion-free guide for identifying when a communication is something that is so wacky or disengaged from the ordinary course of events that it is easily characterized as "just a joke," that is incapable of inflicting reputational harm. That said, incongruity analysis does not account for when something really funny and incongruous also deeply wounds another. Surely, an authentic wound is relevant to whether the law should give a remedy for a communication. Also, another crucial, yet really hard to measure, ingredient belongs in the analysis: fun. Part of the trick for pinpointing whether or not a court should hammer a defamation defendant with damages is for courts to decide if a joke passed the line from good-natured fun into just plain mean. Said differently, jokes aren't funny without fun. If the communication conveys fun spirit, we may want the law to back off.[32]

Evaluating these components of defamation liability requires intuition and good judgment. While no rigid analytical test for intuition and good judgment exists, judges and juries might find assistance in the concepts of superiority and release humor. If jokes contain an air of ridicule (superiority humor) or if they embrace an unsavory topic (release humor), then the humor more likely might cause the type of harm that tort law is designed to remedy.

b. Other Torts

Defamation is only one of the so-called dignitary harms. Other torts that provide damages for personal harm to dignity include intentional infliction of emotional distress, invasion of privacy, appropriation of publicity rights, and others. Humor collides with these theories in varied ways, and courts generally handle the lawsuits as they do defamation suits: distinguishing between fact and opinion, celebrating parody, and occasionally (although unwittingly) deploying incongruity theory—all in service of identifying jokes that should flourish and those that should be regulated. Two examples are instructive.

The most famous example of a comic dignitary harm suit is *Hustler Magazine v. Falwell*.[33] The case arose out of a *Hustler* magazine ad parody that depicted Reverend Falwell having his first sexual experience *with his mother in an outhouse*. Falwell sued *Hustler* for intentional infliction of emotional distress. Denying liability for Falwell, the U.S. Supreme Court's decision contains a love letter to parodies, exalting their role in U.S. cultural tradition and declaring that our national "political discourse would have been considerably poorer without them."[34] The Court acknowledged that the *Hustler* parody "was at best a distant cousin of [America's beloved] political cartoons . . . and a rather poor relation at that."[35] Nonetheless, the Court reasoned, the First Amendment protected the *Hustler* parody, particularly since no one could reasonably interpret it as asserting "actual facts about [Falwell] or actual events in which he participated."[36]

A more obscure, but equally revealing, case is *Martin v. Living Essentials*,[37] decided by a federal district court in Chicago. Martin sued the manufacturer of an energy drink under a number of theories, including appropriation of Martin's identity and his right to publicity. The dispute started when the drink manufacturer ran a television advertisement boasting about the astounding things its product could empower a consumer to do: "disprove[] the theory of relativity, [swim] the English Channel and back, [find] Bigfoot, and master[] origami while beating the record for hacky sack."[38] The commercial included small print at the screen's bottom saying, "for comedic purposes only. Not actual results."[39] What was Martin's gripe about this ad? Martin, it turns out, proudly held the world record for "the most consecutive kicks (no knees) in the footbag (i.e., hacky sack) singles category."[40] Taking umbrage at the suggestion that someone else might possess an equal degree of athleticism and persistence in mastering the hacky sack, Martin argued that the manufacturer used one of Martin's key attributes (his hacky-sack record) to promote its product.

After seriously engaging with the specifics of Martin's achievements, the court turned to the crux of its reasoning: the commercial was meant as a farce and Martin should have interpreted it as a farce. It was extraordinarily improbable, the court reasoned, that anyone would believe that "in addition to unrivaled skill at keeping a footbag aloft, he possesses genius surpassing that of Einstein, twice the endurance of Diana Nyad, and hunting skills so refined that he is able to locate even mythical creatures."[41] The judicial voice here is jauntier than the usual dry fare characterizing legal writing, and the opinion was unusually celebratory of the case's funny bits. The court even threw this out: "the law does not reward humorlessness."[42] In the end, though, the court served up standard reasoning for law and humor disputes, sharing a ride through the case facts to evaluate whether they contained sufficient incongruity to merit protection normally accorded a true joke.

3. Contract

Of all the laws that regulate humor through private civil lawsuits, the most unlikely are those governing contracts. Under standard legal understanding, a contract is an enforceable promise or set of promises that arises when one party accepts the offer of another. Leaving aside that anodyne definition, the notion of being legally bound is a little scary to most people. As release theory instructs, humans sometimes process fear by making a joke. Cartoon 1-5 reflects this process, with a depiction of widely shared anxiety about what will happen to one's life after the contract trap is snapped?

Anyone who has made a contemporary consumer purchase or has confronted a terms-of-use contract on the Internet can also appreciate a crack about the ridiculous complexity of modern contracts that consumers are asked to embrace. How many sentient beings carefully read all contract terms before clicking "I agree"?

In the law and humor realm, one obvious place where contract law touches humor is in joke delivery businesses—joke book contracts, comedians' employment contracts, television comedy writers' contracts, and the like. These contexts yield interesting observations about when law protects against humor that crosses the line of propriety or good taste. Some contracts insist entertainers "keep it clean." Judging from the lack of

Cartoon 1-5 (cartoon 15—TCB-10562) Leo Cullum/The New Yorker Collection/The Cartoon Bank

cases on this subject, one might reasonably conclude that entertainers generally honor and courts generally enforce these provisions.

Even more insight into the law's attitude toward humor, however, comes from lawsuits about whether the law recognizes that a contract exists. The pattern is the same as for defamation and trademark suits: one party (the plaintiff) asserts that the other party (the defendant) violated the plaintiff's legal right. The defendant then argues that the law should not get involved because the crux of the matter was "just a joke" and violated no law. For contracts, this translates as "I made a joke, not an enforceable promise." Because contract law is so remote from anything comedic, the results of these breach-of-contract cases can be really interesting.

In legal jargon, the fight often hinges on whether particular communications are correctly perceived as a party's "manifestation of intent to be legally bound." A writing, an oral statement, or a non-verbal action can reveal the requisite intent to enter into a contract if a reasonable person would interpret it as such. Older cases feature business deals emerging from drunken promises uttered in a bar or scribbled on the back of an old receipt: Are these deals enforceable the day after? At least one court evaluating the legal effect of a drunken writing memorializing a real estate deal found the writing legally enforceable.[43]

Common (in fact, strangely common) cases raise issues on the periphery of standard contract law, wrestling with whether practical-joking employers or business owners act outside contractual terms imposed by an insurance agreement, an employment agreement, and the like. The facts can be unusual, featuring practical jokes and behavior such as an employer chasing an employee with a snake.[44]

A particularly bizarre example is *Woo v. Fireman's Fund Insurance Co.*[45] In that case, an oral surgeon (Dr. Woo) operated on an anesthetized employee from his office. In the course of the procedure, Dr. Woo temporarily implanted fake boar tusks in the employee's mouth, propped the employee's eyes open, photographed her, and shared the photos with office workers. After the employee/patient sued, Dr. Woo's liability insurance carrier refused to provide malpractice liability coverage for his antics. Astoundingly, the Washington Supreme Court found that Dr. Woo's actions were sufficiently consistent with his dental surgeon status as to fall within the scope of the liability policy. How did the court get to this conclusion? You guessed it: incongruity analysis. According to the court, Dr. Woo's attempt at humor took place as part of a dental procedure, and there was nothing unexpected or incongruent about interpreting the insurance contract to cover actions that took place during (or grew out of) that dental procedure.

Graphic illustrations of incongruity analysis appear in yet another group of contract cases, arising from extravagant or outlandish claims in advertisements or contests. The hacky-sack (*Martin*) case—which turned on a right to publicity claim—is one example of how an unrestrained ad can attract trouble. There are others. Reflect on a case from the Hooters restaurant manager who promised a "Toy-ota" to the best performing waitress. Did a contract breach occur when the manager provided only a small "toy Yoda" doll to the winning waitress? We do not have a definitive answer because the case settled.[46]

Two similar disputes resulted in court opinions citing related incongruity concepts: believability and exaggeration. One arose from a suit to collect a reward offered for the return of a missing laptop and the other arose from a defense lawyer's "million-dollar challenge" extended to anyone who might offer evidence supporting an alibi in a homicide case. Interestingly, both ultimately concerned a million-dollar reward offer. But in the laptop case, the reward notifications had first started as a $20,000 offer and the court determined that an ordinary reading of the context surrounding the offer made clear that it was not a joke, but rather a serious invitation for performance: return of the laptop.[47] In the homicide alibi case, however, the court rejected the contract suit, finding that framing the reward as a "million-dollar challenge" tapped into a hyperbolic, comic trope that is so enmeshed in common parlance as to render the offer unbelievable.[48]

For support, both these reward opinions invoked the mother-of-all advertisement joke cases, *Leonard v. PepsiCo.*[49] Now used throughout the United States to teach law students elementary contract law, *Leonard* arose from a promotional campaign encouraging consumers to collect "Pepsi Points" and redeem them for merchandise. As part of the campaign, Pepsi ran a television commercial suggesting one could redeem Pepsi Points for a Harrier Jet. The commercial ends with a teenager emerging from a Harrier Jet at his school, declaring, "Sure beats the bus." Next, the words appear: "HARRIER FIGHTER 7,000,000 PEPSI POINTS" followed by "Drink Pepsi—Get Stuff."

Resolving to obtain the jet, a young man (the *Leonard* plaintiff) created a scheme to raise the money needed to buy the requisite number of Pepsi points. He succeeded, presenting Pepsi with a $700,008.50 check and fifteen actual Pepsi Points. When Pepsi refused to produce the jet, the young man sued. In evaluating the fellow's insistence that the commercial was a serious offer, the court candidly acknowledged that it needed to "explain why the commercial is funny"[50] and hence not a legally enforceable offer. To that end, the court canvassed the commercial for incongruities, finding many: the suggestion that Pepsi reward merchandise can inject the drama of "military and espionage thrillers" into "unexceptional lives"; the "highly improbable pilot" represented by a teenager who "could barely be trusted with the keys to his parents' car"; the "exaggerated adolescent fantasy" of getting to school in a Harrier Jet; the mismatch between school transportation and a piece of military equipment designed to "attack and destroy surface targets," and the improbability that one could actually "drink 7,000,000 Pepsis (or roughly 190 Pepsis a day for the next hundred years . . .)."[51]

Tort and trademark infringement suits often have equally amusing facts. Also as with the contract suits, one can see how incongruity provides a useful test for figuring out whether an entity actually experienced the hurt that these legal theories seek to remedy. The tort and trademark cases rest on the following reasoning: if others interpret communications as reputational or property right violations, then the law should intervene even if the communications had comic elements. This similarity is striking since contract law operates in such a different—and naturally more dry—sphere.

Contract law provides government backup for parties who have created their own private world of rules. Are you yawning yet? Bear with me. "Freedom of contract" is the animating slogan in contract law. The idea here is, "Damn it, I should be able to make my own rules and the law should back me up once I make them." Huh? Here's a more formal way it is often expressed: contracting parties' privately created world of rules should operate even if it includes unusual or bizarre elements that would be incongruous in day-to-day life. The law shouldn't scoff at people's effort to arrange their joint concerns so long as their agreement is fair and doesn't run head-on into some kind of public policy—such as "surrogate mother-hood contracts are forbidden," "murder for hire is unlawful," and the like.

The catch with contract law, however, is that the law protects a contracted bargain only if the parties really intended to make a binding deal. When humor is part of the negotiating, one starts to wonder whether the parties were truly serious. In other words, the legal inquiry in most contract breach cases dealing with humor is, Did the defendant intend to be bound to the deal by law? If, for example, the defendant was simply ridiculing the defendant by pretending to enter a sham contract, the law may refuse to recognize an enforceable bargain. Or the defendant may have simply been making a comical effort to release anxiety or hostility—and for that reason should not be taken seriously.

These are just a few logical ways to evaluate whether a joke interferes with contract formation. Yet courts have generally still leaned on incongruity reasoning to decide whether a contract breach occurred. Why do they favor incongruity theory? Perhaps they instinctively perceive that incongruity notions are most consistent with contract law's preference for objective rather than subjective evidence of intent; that is, courts are using collective social judgments—not individual subjective judgments—to interpret whether something is too unlikely or bizarre to be worthy of legal enforcement. Yet the absence of discussion in contract cases about whether the defendants' actions suggested playful ridicule or chiding—common qualities of release or superiority humor—is revealing.

Incongruity reasoning has power independent of its overlap with the structure and purpose of legal rules. Perhaps a look at one more legal theory for regulating humor can help explain why courts find incongruity such a compelling analytical tool.

4. Workplace Humor and Harassment Claims

Workplace humor provides one of the most frequent and elusive contexts for indirect humor regulation. Unlike the previous three civil wrongs considered—trademark infringement, tort, and contract breach—regulation of workplace humor is more diffuse, with a less clear pattern. Jokes at work touch key parts of our economy and culture; they deserve serious attention.

Workplace joke cases have a variety of legal faces. Consider the dispute arising when prankster co-workers lowered the chair level of a woman who was rendered permanently disabled after she plopped too hard into her unexpectedly lowered seat. The court found that this type of gag was so condoned by management that the workers' compensation system provided the only available remedy for the harm.[52] A contrasting decision arose from horseplay at an office party that culminated when the CEO administered—in apparent jest—an electric shock to an employee.[53] Labeling this conduct "intentional," the court concluded that the employee could seek enhanced damages that would not be available under the workers' compensation system.

Moving from the strange to the even stranger: consider the workplace manager who indulged a fondness for scaring employees by sneaking up behind them. This routine went awry as the manager repeatedly performed the prank on an employee with an unusually sensitive startle reflex—causing the employee's mental health to deteriorate markedly. The employee unsuccessfully alleged employment discrimination, arguing that the managers' actions violated the Americans with Disabilities Act.[54] Although the court did comment on the manager's odd predilections, other complicating factors convinced the court to reject the discrimination claim.

Racist jokes also inspire discrimination claims, usually based on a hostile work environment theory. These employment discrimination claims rest on the notion that taunting humor can be part of a pattern that is so severe that the jokes' target experiences antagonistic working conditions not shared by employees who are not the butt of such jokes. The jokes often do not appear in isolation but are combined with other mistreatment. In most of the reported cases, the joker is ridiculing or belittling the victim. In one famous 2001 case resulting in discrimination liability, the jokes were savagely racist,[55] including jokes by supervisors of the defendant company of the following kind:

- Why don't black people like aspirin? Because they're white, and they work.
- What do you call a transparent man in a ditch? A n*gger with the shit kicked out of him.
- Did you ever see a black man on *The Jetsons*? Isn't it beautiful what the future looks like?

In upholding the large damage verdict imposing liability for racial harassment, the federal appeals court emphasized the overwhelming evidence of race discrimination presented by these jokes. Implicitly understanding that the "black/white" content of the jokes ensured they were particularly damaging, the court dismissed arguments that evidence of jokes targeted at other ethnic groups diminished the discriminatory effect of the black/white jokes.

This sensitivity to the racialized nature of the jokes is less common in more recent cases. Perhaps the humor is simply more watered down in recent cases or the racism is more undercover. The "jokes" are often puns—lame by any measure.[56] Currently, courts are generally unreceptive to these hostile work environment claims, setting a high bar for establishing discrimination and dismissing cases when the jokes were isolated or not accompanied by a repeated pattern of harassment. The discrimination laws are hard-wired against superiority humor, which ridicules, harasses, and humiliates. But courts just don't seem motivated to intervene and address the racism reflected by the jokes unless unadorned and repeated maliciousness accompanies attempts at humor.[57]

Although the legal theory for racial harassment overlaps substantially with that required for sexual harassment, results for sexual harassment plaintiffs are often favorable. Like U.S. federal racial discrimination law, U.S. federal sexual harassment law provides that sexual jokes can be so oppressive that they change the conditions of employment for the joke's target. For race discrimination, the jokes must be race-based; similarly for sex discrimination: the jokes must amount to discrimination on the basis of sex. As in the race discrimination cases, the standard of proof for sex discrimination is rigorous: courts demand more than an isolated joke to assign liability. The U.S. Supreme Court has admonished that Congress did not intend employment discrimination law to impose "a general civility code for the American workplace."[58]

Indeed, the Supreme Court has generally agreed with the sentiment reflected in Cartoons 1-6 and 1-7, declaring that "simple teasing, offhand comments and isolated incidents (unless extremely serious)" will not themselves suffice to establish a sexual harassment claim.[59] One wonders whether the advent of the #MeToo movement will ultimately inspire a shift in this approach. It may take quite a while, however, before effects are shown in published court opinions.

The situation appears friendlier for sexual harassment plaintiffs than race discrimination plaintiffs—so long as the jokes contain both sexual content and an apparent attempt to belittle. (Could it be that the predominant majority of federal judges—white males— are thinking of their daughters in deciding these cases?) Unlike racial harassment cases, in which courts often do not engage with the racialized substance of jokes, the sexual harassment cases have a lot to say about the humor's sexual content. As humor scholars would put it, the sexual harassment cases focus on both the superiority and release humor at issue in the case.

Two classic cases can illustrate. In *Harris v. Forklift Systems, Inc.*[60] the U.S. Supreme Court described a workplace where a supervisor frequently uttered quips to the plaintiff such as, "You're a woman, what do you know,"

"Sometimes a lick on the ear is just a lick on the ear—it doesn't always mean that all I'm interested in is sex."

Cartoon 1-6 (cartoon 21—TCB-38842) Michael Maslin/The New Yorker Collection/The Cartoon Bank

the two of us should "go to the Holiday Inn to negotiate [plaintiff's] raise," and congratulations on your success with the sale . . . "What did you do, promise the guy . . . some [sex] Saturday night?"[61] Although the Court did not characterize these taunts as asserting superiority or attempting ridicule, it found them sufficiently hostile and sufficiently "because of sex" to merit remanding the case for further consideration of sexual harassment liability.

In the second classic case, *Robinson v. Jacksonville Shipyards, Inc.*,[62] the district court evaluated a host of oppressive comments obviously designed to intimidate female workers with references to the smell and value of a woman's genitals: "Hey pussycat, come here and give me a whiff," and "she's sitting on a goldmine." Noting that "sexual joking" of this kind is likely to lead to the "stereotyping of women in terms of their sex object status," the court emphasized both the sexualized and belittling context for the jokes in finding liability.[63]

Subsequent cases show a similar distaste for explicit reference to gender or sex in jokes designed to disparage the plaintiff (who is usually, but not always, a woman). In one case, co-workers "laughingly" quipped that the plaintiff "used [her] miscarriage as an excuse to miss work," stating that

"Maybe zero tolerance is setting the bar too high."

Cartoon 1-7 (cartoon 19—TCB-43841) Lee Lorenz/The New Yorker Collection/The Cartoon Bank

plaintiff was obviously pregnant because her "tits were larger," and referring to the plaintiff as a "bitch on a broom."[64] Finding sexual harassment liability on the basis of these comments, the court said this humor reflected "barnyard type cruelty," sometimes based on the "misfortune of others."[65] Concluding that the law should punish the comments, the court responded to the statements as follows: "T'aint funny."[66] In a more recent case, a federal trial court also encountered no problem imposing liability for a joking barrage experienced by a female employee, citing the sexualized nature of cucumber jokes directed at the woman as well as post-partum quips about the plaintiff's belly and bra size.[67]

Nowhere is the focus on the sexual content of jokes more prominent than in the 2005 case of *Dick v. Phone Directories Co., Inc.*,[68] involving harassment of a plaintiff named Diane Dick. Part of the harassment featured punning on Dick's last name—with co-workers calling her "Ivanna Dick" and "Granny Dick"—as well as declaring that she had a "pussy." But the behavior went well beyond that—and included physical touching as well as taunting with a dildo. In analyzing these facts, the court made much of the "because of sex" requirement in discrimination law and highlighted that the plaintiff's theory of the case asserted that the perpetrators were motivated by sexual desire. Noting that most of the puns and jokes appeared designed merely to humiliate, the court concluded the plaintiff deserved a chance to prove that the conduct was also motivated by sexual desire.

The requirement that harassment in race discrimination cases rest on racially charged conduct is no less pertinent than the sex component of sexual harassment cases. Yet, as noted, a joke's racialized content usually does not feature prominently in race discrimination analysis. Race certainly is an uncomfortable topic in U.S. society—and jokes about race certainly can be classified as release humor, used to process anxiety about a taboo subject. But the case law on race tends to shy away from that analysis.

Highlighting the double standard is another set of facts reflecting courts' disparate treatment of race and sex discrimination cases. Equal Employment Opportunity Commission data comparing sexual and racial discrimination cases for the period 2010–2015 show more racial than sexual harassment complaints filed, but also that the EEOC found "no reasonable cause" to pursue the complaint in a much higher proportion of racial harassment cases. The statistics also reflect significantly higher recoveries in sexual harassment cases.[69]

Despite the apparent willingness of courts to think and write forthrightly about sex jokes, those inclined to deliver sexually harassing jokes do have a possible antidote against liability. Courts appear less likely to find a hostile work environment where the sex jokes take the form of wordplay infused with incongruity. In one case, the court found no liability for a wrongdoer whose jokes included a query about "how many wheels a menstrual cycle had" and an accusation that the male plaintiff needed a pap smear.[70] In another case brought by a comedy writers' assistant for the TV show *Friends*, the court found no liability flowing from graphic sexual quips pervasive in the workplace. The offending humor included alterations on an inspirational calendar in the plaintiff's work space, with the writers "changing . . . the word 'persistence' to 'pert tits' and 'happiness' to 'penis.'"[71] (The humor in these alterations presumably arises from the unlikelihood that an innocent inspirational calendar would feature human sexual parts.) The perpetrators also referenced the infertility of an actress on the show, joking that "she had 'dried twigs' or 'dried branches in her vagina.'"[72] These incongruous images, the court concluded, reflect the "creative process" necessary to create a television script and not a hostile working environment.

Finally are the many cases in which defendants avoided liability when the workplace jokes took the form of puns. These cases may be explained because (as with many race discrimination pun cases) the puns were not folded into a sufficiently vicious pattern of abuse. The courts did not mention whether it mattered to their decisions that the puns were feeble, downright silly, or both:

- jokes about President Clinton's ejaculate, including "a list of 'Ben & Jerry's New Presidential Ice Creams' containing word-plays on names of ice cream flavors, implying either sex or impeachment";[73]
- a reference to prosciutto ham as "prostitute ham";[74]
- a quip that by wearing a sleeveless shirt, the plaintiff was "enforcing [her] 2nd amendment rights . . . to bare arms";[75]
- a reference to rubber bands as "rubbers";[76]
- a statement in response to a request for a supervisor to put his "John Hancock" on a document: "I'll put my John on it, but not my cock on it";[77]
- a photograph of woman (with the plaintiff's face superimposed on the image) holding a gas pump in a suggestive way. Text on the photograph said: "Full Service Only" and "Pumping Ethyl."[78]

Most would agree this humor just doesn't work and is undeserving of favorable attention. It is nevertheless notable that—in both the racial and sexual harassment context—punsters seem to get a pass. Could it be that puns are just a touch more cerebral than the "barnyard cruelty" characterizing other harassing humor? Are puns easier on the ears of the well-educated lawyers who staff the U.S. judiciary than straightforwardly raunchy words? As artificial linguistic concepts, puns are an analytic step insulated from the sexual impulses, racial insults, and wounded feelings that discrimination law seeks to remedy. Perhaps one can more easily dismiss linguistic humor such as reflected in Cartoon 1-8 as mere abstract wordplay, which does not amount to a personal attack.

Another possibility: puns avoid legal trouble because of their kinship with incongruous jokes. Indeed, some theorists even characterize puns as a form of incongruity humor because they connect otherwise disparate phenomena. This chapter's end explores puns further. For the moment, we can at least be certain that the harassment cases conform to other indirect regulation cases in one key aspect: they target release and superiority humor for restriction and privilege incongruity humor.

5. Endnote on Indirect Regulation

Humor is laughing at what you haven't got when you ought to have it. . . . Humor is what you wish in your secret heart were not funny, but it is, and you must laugh. Humor is your unconscious therapy.

— Langston Hughes[79]

*"For the last time, Crawford, our firm is
'warm and fuzzy,' not 'touchy-feely.'"*

Cartoon 1-8 (cartoon 20—TCB-40418) Leo Cullum/The New Yorker Collection/The Cartoon Bank

If Langston Hughes is correct about the sources and motivations of humor, we should not be surprised that jokes get people into legal trouble. We must laugh, we don't always understand why we laugh, but we need the unconscious therapy. Pity then the poor judges and juries who must figure out when this sometimes unconscious therapy is deserving of a monetary penalty—and when it is to be forgiven and allowed to flourish.

The call to judges to rule on what is illegal humor is arguably "tough duty." First of all, the judges find themselves in the position of evaluating whether to bring a hammer down on apparent mirth-making. The task also involves disjointed logic: when considering whether to punish humor, the mindset of judges is a far cry from anything we naturally associate with laughter: property rights, contracts, reputational protection, discrimination, and the like. From this perspective, one can understand that courts evaluating these legal claims do not always appreciate that their decision implicitly includes a judgment about the merits or demerits of the humor involved in the case. Isn't it interesting, then, that courts evaluating whether humor is illegal are finding their way to humor theories developed by cerebral philosophers working wholly outside of any legal context?

B. THE FRONTAL ATTACK: PUNISHING THE JOKER, MUZZLING THE COMEDIAN, AND REGULATING THE PUNSTER

Maybe the contexts are idiosyncratic. Or maybe the examples are too isolated and erratic. But direct regulation—a frontal attack on humor—does not reveal the same themes about law's humor preferences that emerge from indirect regulation in contexts such as intellectual property, contract, employment discrimination, and defamation. That said, direct regulation demands our attention because it can have such a harsh effect on expression: direct regulation silences jokes before they can be told or at least severely restricts their circulation.

In surveying direct regulation, this section begins with criminal prohibitions on jokes in the United States. Not many of these prohibitions exist, but the choice of prohibited jokes reveals social and political values. Next is the related topic of muzzling stand-up comics—followed by the bizarre world of prohibiting puns.

1. Punishing the Joker

Criminal law prohibits conduct believed so harmful to society that statutes explicitly forbid it, and governments prosecute and punish it. A criminal conviction often comes with imprisonment, society's message that the offending conduct was so morally reprehensible as to merit taking from the offender one of the most precious parts of being human: liberty.

When prison time flows from joke-telling, the circumstances are usually special and the stakes grave. This typically involves the possibility of harm to a lot of people, including threats to national security. Courts have used a broad net in identifying assaults on national security and include within it any threat on the life of the president of the United States. In one case, a court found a national security breach when the apparent threat to the president was sent by postcard to "Ye ol' Whitehouse."[80] That said, courts do sometimes distinguish true threats against the president (which result in a conviction) from political hyperbole (which do not). Thus, the U.S. Supreme Court has held that the following statement by a draft protester was mere hyperbole protected by the Constitution: "If they ever make me carry a rifle the first man I want to get in my sights is [President] L.B.J."[81] Despite this precedent, cases are clear that an accused cannot escape conviction for threatening the president by simply asserting that the statement was meant only as a joke.[82]

After the terrorist attacks of 9/11, Americans and others have also become particularly touchy about anything that has to do with blowing up airports or airplanes. Although successful prosecutions for such jokes are rare, prosecutions resulting in acquittal still inflict significant consequences. In one instance, an American citizen of Palestinian descent and Muslim faith was sent to a bomb detection machine at an airport for careful inspection of two pieces of luggage. Suspecting she had been profiled, the traveler responded, "You already checked my luggage. Maybe I have a bomb in my purse."[83] Although ultimately acquitted for this quip, the traveler spent two days in jail and missed her father's funeral.

In another example, a frustrated United Kingdom air passenger tweeted: "Crap! Robin Hood airport is closed. You've got a week and a bit to get your shit together otherwise I'm blowing the airport sky high!" Although his conviction for this tweet was ultimately overturned, the tweeter incurred significant cost and hassle defending the matter. Despite authorities' repeated failure to secure successful convictions in these matters, the criminal prohibitions have successfully identified jokes of this kind as out of bounds in the collective understanding of air travelers.

Threat crimes are not confined to threats against the president, airplanes, and airports. Threats against private persons can also lead to conviction, even in the face of a "just-a-joke" defense. In one famous case, a man was convicted for writing the following rap on his Facebook page:

Did you know that it's illegal for me to say I want to kill my wife? . . .

It's one of the only sentences that I'm not allowed to say. . . .

Now it was okay for me to say it right then because I was just telling you that it's illegal for me to say I want to kill my wife. . . .

Um, but what's interesting is that it's very illegal to say I really, really think someone out there should kill my wife. . . .

But not illegal to say it with a mortar launcher.[84]

Although the U.S. Supreme Court reversed the man's conviction due to problems with the jury instructions, the Court made clear that " 'I'm going to kill you' is 'an expression of an intention to inflict loss or harm' regardless of the author's personal motive. A victim who receives that letter in the mail has received a threat, even if the author believes (wrongly) that his message will be taken as a joke."[85]

Joke threat cases take on special meaning in the context of behavior implicating U.S. civil rights laws. In one instance, an abortion protester was found to have violated the federal Freedom of Access to Clinic Entrances[86] statute for making intimidating statements to abortion clinic employees. After a court ordered the protestor to cease, the protestor continued the behavior, taunting the clinic doctor with the shout "[W]here's a pipe bomber when you need one."[87] The court refused to accept any suggestion that the statement was funny or hyperbolic, imposing a large fine and concluding that the doctor reasonably perceived the statement as a threat and not a joke.

With regularity, jokers prosecuted under these criminal statutes defend by pointing to free speech guarantees. Interestingly, this defense is not generally successful. Acquittal and reversed convictions appear to rest more on a sense that the conduct is simply not sufficiently reprehensible to support culpability.

One form of criminal landmine prevalent around the world does not present a problem for jokers in the United States: insult laws. At least ninety other countries—in Europe, the former Soviet Union, Africa, Latin America, Asia, and the Middle East—have a brand of direct regulation imposing criminal liability for insulting certain government officials. A classic form is the French Press Law of 1881, providing stiff penalties for insulting official entities like legislatures and courts as well as foreign chiefs of state, foreign ministers, and ambassadors of friendly nations. The French law fell into disuse but not before it served as a model for other laws around the globe. Moreover, while apparently moribund in several other countries, insult laws stand at the ready for punishing a particularly cutting joke or other insight into a political reality.[88] Indeed, the German government used such a law in 2016 to bring charges (ultimately dropped) against a professional German comedian who delivered jokes mocking the president of Turkey.[89]

For professional comedians, the intersection of law and humor sometimes provides a platform for making an ideological point about freedom of speech and sometimes enabling them to become First Amendment martyrs. As shown below, the United States boasts a few examples. Perhaps true to form—the most notoriously successful criminal prosecutions in the United States have not been for one-off jokes that poke at political matters but instead have resulted from American discomfort with naughty words, sex, and scatological topics. As explored below, however, this use of direct legal prohibitions to punish indecency and bad taste has arguably backfired.

2. Muzzling the Stand-Up Comedian

a. Fines, Punishment, and Supreme Court Opinions: Comedians as Outlaws Turned Heroes

Shit, piss, fuck, cunt, cocksucker, motherfucker, and tits. These words were the centerpiece of George Carlin's "Seven Words You Can Never Say on Television" routine, later known as "Seven Dirty Words" and "Filthy Words." The monologue repeats the seven words many times—with varying cadence, speed, rhythm, and timbre. In a 1973 version of the routine, he explored the possibility that other words might make the list:

> Twat is an interesting word because it's the only one I know of, the only slang word applying to the, a part of the sexual anatomy that doesn't have another meaning to it. Like, ah, snatch, box and pussy all have other meanings, man. Even in a Walt Disney movie, you can say, We're going to snatch that pussy and put him in a box and bring him on the airplane. Everybody loves it. The twat stands alone, man, as it should.[90]

The riffs expertly balance a friendly with a confrontational tone. While filled with high-spirited fun, the riffs were more than a linguistic frolic among off-color words. Carlin's monologue is a pointed critique of the authoritarian decision to mark certain words as off limits, with no reasoned explanation. Fabricating possible reasons for censorship, the monologue declares that dirty words "infect your soul, curve your spine, and keep the country from winning the war." His satire suggests that society needs to rethink the values reflected in its language prohibitions; words have no original truth: their meanings are learned and their power is granted by social—and as it turns out governmental—fiat.

About eighteen months after Carlin first recorded the routine, an afternoon radio host decided to play the monologue, first warning listeners that it contained language that some may regard as offensive. During that time, John Douglas, a board member of a group whose name speaks for itself—Morality in Media—was driving with his 15-year-old son. Douglas flipped through the radio and discovered the station playing the monologue. Choosing not to turn the dial to a station he might have found more appropriate for his 15-year-old, Douglas instead stayed tuned in and, about a month later, filed a complaint with the Federal Communications Commission (FCC). His complaint explained that his "young son" had been with him the day that the station played the Carlin monologue.

Upon receiving the FCC complaint, the station owner, Pacifica Foundation, defended by favorably comparing Carlin to satirists of the stature of Mark Twain and Mort Sahl. Unpersuaded, the FCC upheld the complaint, giving only a warning to Pacifica, but making clear that it would evaluate available sanctions (fines) if the agency received subsequent complaints.

Pacifica filed a court challenge to the FCC order, but the U.S. Supreme Court ultimately upheld the FCC decision. The Supreme Court explained that—though not obscene—Carlin's routine was indecent (grandiosely defined as "nonconformance with accepted standards of morality").[91] And because it had been broadcast during normal waking hours, the First Amendment did not prohibit restrictions against its broadcast. After all, the Court reasoned, the words of Carlin's monologue could penetrate listeners' ears without warning. This included children who might not yet know how to read: why Carlin's monologue could have "enlarged a child's vocabulary in an instant," the Court declared![92] The Supreme Court ended with rhetorical flourish, heralding as proper the "government's interest in the 'well-being of its youth' and in supporting 'parents' claim to authority in their household' justified the regulation of otherwise protected expression."[93] The bottom line here: the Constitution allows the FCC to regulate indecent broadcasts between the hours of 6 A.M. and 10 P.M.

Carlin's routine followed closely in the tradition of Lenny Bruce—who also found himself in repeated trouble for his profanity-laced monologues. The lineage between the two is not remote. Carlin shared the back seat of a police car with Bruce in 1962: Carlin had been arrested for failure to show the age identification needed to enter the club where Bruce was performing. Bruce was arrested on obscenity charges that night—accused of uttering such words as "fuck" and "tits."[94]

Like Carlin, Bruce recognized that words were his power—his means of tearing apart stupidity, hypocrisy, and oppression. Plying his trade many years before Carlin, Lenny Bruce faced even harder times than Carlin: blacklisted from performing in U.S. clubs because of his propensity to inflect his routines with indecent references, repeatedly arrested for his comedy, and tried as a criminal.

The odd thing about Lenny Bruce, however, is that despite his strident and unrepentant comedy, he didn't really advance U.S. constitutional law. This is especially surprising, since his run-ins with the law were not all local, reaching beyond simple scuffles with arbitrary displays of local morality. In their exhaustive overview of Lenny Bruce's place in the intersection of law and humor, law professors Ronald Collins and David Skover catalogue Bruce's troubles with Australian authorities among many others. But as Collins and Skover point out, "[T]he Bruce story is virtually absent from the recorded history of the First Amendment."[95] To be sure, First Amendment jurisprudence sometimes played a role in his criminal trials, with judges occasionally referring to free speech principles in evaluating whether Bruce should be convicted. But his trials did not advance the law. Bruce's much greater contribution flowed instead from his influence—as a counterculture icon—on Carlin and others.

Those who are "Funny on Purpose"[96] make their living in many realms. Their universe spans from performance (music, improvisation, stage, television, and film) and writing (books, articles, poems, web content, sketch comedy, and TV) to the visual arts (illustrations, comics, cartoons, and animation) and the digital realm (YouTube, podcasts, and social networking). Although just a slice of this robust creative activity, stand-up comedy has proven an important example of humor crashing up against the law. Around the world—from Estonia and Egypt to the United States—stand-up comedians are symbols of freedom of expression. It is difficult to ignore a real human being appearing live before other real human beings and daring to speak truth to power.

How wise was the U.S. legal response to avant-garde humor? Did official chains and gags serve their desired ends? The Lenny Bruce and George Carlin examples suggest that the answer is no. Legal prohibitions helped transport these comedians from clowning jokers to attention-getting social critics—and ultimately to free speech martyrs and cultural heroes. Reminiscing about the *Pacifica* Supreme Court case, George Carlin observed that "my name is a footnote in American legal history, which I am perversely kind of proud of."[97] Most constitutional law scholars, creative souls, and pop culture consumers would disagree that he is a mere footnote. Indeed, Carlin's Seven Dirty Words routine has enjoyed great longevity with a 5-star rating among iTunes customers—iTunes being a platform unknown for many years after Carlin first performed the monologue. Carlin's stature increased, not diminished, with attempted censorship: clearly a result intended by neither the FCC nor the Supreme Court that wrote *Pacifica*. But, alas, neither constitutional law on indecency nor generally accepted rules of decorum such as depicted in Cartoon 1-9 have not really changed since then.

b. Shaming by Self-Regulation: Beating Up on Each Other

A government's attempt to gag comedians can easily backfire. The result of oppressive regulation has ennobled stand-up comedians, galvanized their audiences, inspired defiance, and undermined the government's credibility and effectiveness. In at least one context, however, most comedians want the law to exert a strong grip: when other comedians steal their material. Yet here too the law fails them. The problem is not the reach of the copyright law, which clearly can encompass many jokes. When becoming victim to joke stealing, a comedian who has taken proper steps can successfully

Cartoon 1-9 (cartoon 23—TCB-125361/026315-313) Roz Chast/The New Yorker Collection/
The Cartoon Bank

sue the thieving rival. But, as an outpouring of scholarly studies and comedian testimonials document, copyright law simply does not provide a cost-
effective way to protect the tremendous effort required to write the dozens
of jokes in a single stand-up routine.[98]

So what do comedians do about this state of affairs? Answer: they take
matters into their own hands.

This vigilante approach takes many forms: personal confrontation, bad-
mouthing, reputation smearing, violence threatening, and shunning. In
other words, comics react to formal law's inadequacy with their own brand
of "outlaw" law—creating and enforcing a set of social norms regarding authorship and transfer of jokes.

Legal scholars have analyzed self-regulation in other trades, illustrated most prominently by informal rules for international trade. At one time, international regulation was sufficiently ineffective and undeveloped that merchants developed their own internal rules of trade, referred to as *lex mercatoria*, which proved a remarkably stable set of behavior-guiding norms. Stand-up comedians, it turns out, have taken a similar path.

The self-help system among comedians has not operated consistently. During the heyday of modern stand-up's precursor, vaudeville, and in the period immediately thereafter, comedians appropriated or refined each other's material with both regularity and impunity. During this time, comedians were using either stock jokes or jokes with fixed forms, such as knock-knock jokes, "rim shot jokes" (gags followed by the sound "ba dum tss"), marriage jokes, and the like. In this era, comedians asserted no propriety interest in the text of jokes. Comedians' unique imprints on their acts appeared instead through delivery, staging, and costumes—all of which are harder to rip off than words alone.

But as jokes became more original and the norm system for protecting their content developed, comedians began to invest more in developing new and personal joke text—with some even hiring their own writers. One cannot pinpoint whether the move away from standard jokes and forms inspired a more robust informal enforcement system or vice versa. Whatever its genesis, the relationship between informal law and artistic form for stand-up comedians is now well documented. Moreover, the informal enforcement system against joke theft has even created a new genre of stand-up gag: comical shaming. Here's a well-worn example from comedians who flourished in the 1940s and 1950s:

> One day Milton Berle and Henny Youngman were listening to Joey Bishop tell a particularly funny gag. "Gee, I wish I said that," Berle whispered. "Don't worry, Milton, [replied Youngman], you will."[99]

Unsurprisingly, more recent examples of comic retaliation and chiding are more vicious and usually . . . even more funny.[100]

Examples of shaming colleagues for joke-stealing are particularly hilarious in live stand-up acts. The in-person effect of the ridicule seems to elevate the comedy. Here's a 2006 transcript of a particularly clever tear-down by British comedian Stewart Lee of another British comedian Joe Pasquale. After a setup explaining how mainstream acts steal from comedians who are lower on the food chain, Stewart Lee declares that he has written a joke that Joe Pasquale would not be inclined to steal. Lee then reads the joke:

> Joe Pasquale goes into a bar.
>
> He says to the barman, "I'd like a pint of beer, please."
>
> And the barman says:
>
> "Why don't you just walk around the bar, pour yourself a cup of beer, and walk off without paying for it."
>
> ". . . after all, you are Joe Pasquale,"
>
> ". . . or perhaps send in someone else to steal the beer for you."
>
> "And then deny that beer can actually be owned."
>
> "You could say the very concept of ownership of beer is hard to understand . . . or better still . . . say it is YOUR beer and you brewed it at home in YOUR own house . . ."
>
> ". . . even though your home lacks the most rudimentary of brewing facilities."

Lee's timing in delivering this joke is extraordinary, and can be found on YouTube.[101]

Technological change now tests the effectiveness of self-regulation as well as whether formal legal mechanisms can effectively police theft of comedians' intellectual property. As in so many contexts, the Internet works outside of existing regulatory structures, challenges the status quo, and promotes evolution in expression. Nowhere is this more evident than in the work of comedian Josh "The Fat Jew" Ostrovsky. Known for aggregating jokes of others or simply reproducing others' material—often altered only by removing twitter handles and other identifiers of the original comedians—Ostrovsky disseminated this material through his own social media feeds. What was in this for him? Ostrovsky accumulated millions of followers in the process, which allowed him to establish sufficient fame to attract high-visibility gigs, sponsorships, and other lucrative promotional opportunities. According to *Rolling Stone* magazine, his methods have made him the target of considerable animus and attacks on the Web.[102] Perhaps in response, *Rolling Stone* suggests, Ostrovsky began to add original author credits to Instagram posts. But he has in the meantime built a reputation as a magnet for Internet followers and has thus become an attractive candidate for further promotional opportunities. Ostrovsky's success raises the question of whether informal shaming will continue to be adequate as comedians find that technology renders their creative work more open to use by others. Or, alternatively, will comedy itself evolve to take account of technology's new challenges and opportunities?

However it takes shape, comical self-regulation is a remarkable example of the relationship between law and humor. The development of an entire genre of stand-up shaming humor illustrates the creative consequence of law's inability to provide comedians with effective regulation. On the other hand, this genre shows how humor itself can regulate. Through its expressive power, humor's ridicule of the joke thief enforces legal and moral concepts of right and wrong.[103]

3. Regulating the Punster and the Rebellious Wordsmith

People have different reactions to puns. Some say they love them; some are more sheepish in their praise, offering something like, "I must admit I enjoy a good pun"; some are vaguely annoyed by them; and others despise them. (Caligula is reputed to have ordered an actor burned alive for making a cheesy pun.)

Why would one loathe puns so intensely? Here are adjectives sometimes used to describe those who utter puns: "self-serving, . . . self-promoting, . . . [n]arcissistic, effeminate, showy . . ."[104] (One could add tedious and pedantic to the list.) Ambrose Bierce viewed puns as a "form of wit to which wise men stoop and fools aspire." Dryden called puns the "lowest and most groveling kind of wit." But then again, our beloved William Shakespeare used them freely. Samuel Johnson hated them, but his esteemed friend Edmund Burke loved them. What can we make of all this disagreement?

If nothing else: puns are controversial. And where one finds controversy, one can usually find law.

In their linguistic form, puns have an innocent, sometimes even sweet quality. They bear none of the brash or unsettling characteristics of other forms of humor: puns contain no surprise, no punchline, no loud noises, no "ba dum tss" ending. Nor do puns generally depict another's misfortune. They also tend to be ephemeral: once the hearer resolves a pun's semantic twist, its comic force dissipates—and dissipates quickly.[105] One might say that their innocence springs from their limitations: some even assert that puns offer us "nothing but nonsense."[106]

Perhaps it's the sight gag that adds the extra smile to these cartoons, but even a pun hater like myself might nominate the two law-themed puns in Cartoons 1-10 and 1-11 as fine examples of innocent, cleverly amusing, and ephemeral wordplay.

This is not to argue that puns are always sweet. Nor are they always "nothing but nonsense." Sometimes they can deliver a powerful, coherent, and unkind message. The sexual and racial harassment material earlier in

"Counselor, please advise your client that, issues of personal safety aside, gravity is the law."

Cartoon 1-10 (cartoon 10—TCB-31076) Robert Mankoff/The New Yorker Collection/The Cartoon Bank

Cartoon 1-11 (cartoon 9—TCB-39380) Lee Lorenz/The New Yorker Collection/The Cartoon Bank

this chapter amply illustrates how puns can insult and lacerate feelings. Such ridicule can of course result in liability. For the most part, however, puns' unassuming form, their ties to cerebral wit, and their association with education and higher social classes help keep punsters out of trouble. In the trademark area, one line of cases suggests that a punster is more likely to encounter liability for mere obvious puns, and more likely to enjoy protection for clever ones.[107] On the whole, however, the U.S. cases have an "it's a pun, get over it" tone and often dismiss complaints that focus on them.

At bottom, puns are not a huge source of government regulation or legal liability in the United States. Not so in all countries. Remarkably, the People's Republic of China recently issued an edict forbidding punning. Through its media watchdog ministry, China demanded that radio and television authorities crack down "on the irregular and inaccurate use of the Chinese language, especially the misuse of idioms."[108] Citing the importance of language purity in preserving cultural heritage, the edict mandates communication only through standard Chinese and recommends harsh treatment for violators.

Why are puns such a lightning rod in China? As a tonal language, Chinese provides nearly limitless opportunities for jokes based on homophones. Chinese citizens sometimes use these homophones to make off-color references and political commentary that might otherwise be forbidden or captured through Internet censorship. The edict seeks to stifle this end run around speech restrictions and government criticism. Or so the theory goes.

Here are a few political puns that help illustrate what Beijing may be targeting:[109]

Smog the People: A reference to widespread problems with smog in big Chinese cities and a pun on Mao Zedong's slogan "serve the people."

River Crab: The Mandarin word for a real-life creature that inhabits riverbeds is also a homonym for the word "harmony." Chinese officials use the word "harmony" euphemistically to describe government censorship—as in completely eradicating or "harmonizing" non-compliant Internet posts from the reach of human knowledge. As such, stories about river crabs metaphorically relate to official censorship and social control mechanisms.

Grass-mud Horse: A mythical creature that symbolizes defiance of Internet censorship. The choice of the name for this creature comes from its homonym—a slang term for "your mother's vagina." When used for its slang meaning, this profane term would not survive the censors' knife. As a reference to a mythical creature, however, the Grass-mud Horse more easily slips through the filters. In fact, fables about the struggles between the River Crab (censorship) and the Grass-mud Horse (defiance) are common.

Other totalitarian governments have inspired similar wordplay by those making under-the-radar political and legal critiques. Humor scholars have paid careful attention to a handful of regimes—particularly contemporary Egypt,[110] Turkey,[111] Russia (as well as the former Soviet Union),[112] and Germany during the Third Reich[113]—and have determined that both puns and other word jockeying help ensure that jokesters avoid the censor's knife. Russian and German jokes are particularly rich in puns and linguistic somersaults that circumvent censorship bans.

In Russia, popular tropes for eluding government censorship come from a brand of obscenity called "mat." An underground or street language, mat is rooted in sexuality. Historically associated with lower classes as well as males, mat is now a powerful tool for both genders in all walks of life. The Russian language is flexible and possesses a grammar that arises from inflection and experience rather than formal rules. (Linguists call this a "synthetic grammar.") As a shining example of these qualities, mat—in all of its scatology and lasciviousness—serves as an adaptable vehicle for "linguistic theatre, verbal performance art."[114] Like puns in China, mat excels at tweaking the sensibilities of authorities: President Vladimir Putin even signed legislation outlawing swearing in movies, theatre productions, and concert performances.[115]

Official attempts to suppress mat have inspired various morphs in humor forms. Attempted suppression has even transformed mat *itself* into a joke: the outlawing of mat together with its linguistic flexibility has made it an even more entertaining part of conversation.[116] The flexibility of mat and the Russian language also allows speakers to push the censorship envelope through puns playing on the similarity between mat and non-obscene words. For example, "watch the eggs!" apparently also means "watch the testicles."[117] The expression "I don't believe it!" can be used as a near pun for "Fuck off!"[118]

A parallel development occurred in Hitler's Germany, when underground gallows humor mocked repressive policies.[119] Consider the following pun-like joke from the era:[120]

Whaddaya got for new jokes?

Three months in Dachau.

When conceived within social and cultural contexts that suppress free expression, humor takes on an especially furtive quality. The first (most obvious) reason for this is pure survival. Take, for example, jests about censorship during the Third Reich. These had to be discreet, whispered, and oblique in order to avoid the regime's wrath. Consider especially the experience of comedian Werner Fink, who became "a master of ambiguity . . . and was forced to adopt a number of tricks in order to conceal political messages in harmless packaging."[121] Fink even founded an association with a name desirable to Nazi brass, "Fighting Association for Harmless Humor," which he used as a mantle for his Nazi slogan parodies.[122] Apparently the German audiences became highly sensitized to coded jokes and could find extra amusement in observing joke tellers deftly crossing boundaries by stealth. Comedians in the Soviet Union similarly masked their legal critiques, as they were required to submit their performances to an official "department of jokes" for preclearance.

In Nazi Germany, the Soviet Union, modern-day Russia, and elsewhere, political joke-telling usually has taken place orally in informal settings, featuring puns or other linguistic artifice so as to avoid government detection.[123] For those in repressive regimes, linguistic humor provides an invaluable under-the-radar mechanism for communicating funny commentary. Although not nearly so crucial for insulating jokers from legal problems in open societies such as the United States, linguistic humor does tend to ensure that these jokers avoid liability. As such, linguistic humor provides an unlikely connection among different societies, which possess radically contrasting government forms, languages, and cultures. In all these diverse contexts, wordplay often insulates joke tellers from legal regulation.[124]

C. THE UNUSUAL CASE OF HATE SPEECH

One type of joke does prompt freedom-loving individuals to yearn for legal restriction. These are jokes that are so vicious in their libelous slur on a particular group that they rise to the level of hate speech. Hate speech makes us ashamed of our fellow humans. As tolerance-embracing Americans, we scorn hate speech. A dilemma arises, though, because American law loves freedom of expression even more.

Very few hate speech restrictions are constitutional. The U.S. Supreme Court has condoned just a sprinkling of regulation—generally through the criminal process—when hate speech is truly intended to terrorize another or when it is "directed to inciting or producing imminent lawless action and is likely to incite or produce such action."[125] These state-of-mind requirements are notoriously hard to prove. And when someone expresses hateful messages through comedy, prosecutors find the state-of-mind requirements even harder to establish. Without sufficient proof, the U.S. Constitution forecloses legal liability for the vilest racist slur or the most frightening burning cross—even a cross that blazes outside an

African American family's home. In other words, U.S. constitutional law seems to have accepted a proposition frequently repeated by comedian Ricky Gervais, "offense is the collateral damage of freedom of speech."[126]

It would seem, then, that effective joke-censorship laws may be missing precisely at the time and the circumstance when many would welcome them. What's a free society to do? The question of whether to regulate hate speech presents one of the most difficult dilemmas for constitutional law. On one hand is the expressive value of speech and its contribution to self-governance, truth discovery, and individual autonomy. On the other hand is hate speech's assault on human dignity. In free societies that cherish tolerance, should hate speech be allowed to flourish? Is it simply enough to say that by allowing hate speech, government is "modeling" tolerance for its citizens' benefit by tolerating the intolerant?

For those who struggle with the complex values at work in government censorship, these are powerful dilemmas. At present, however, they are dilemmas that U.S. constitutional interpretation has resolved in favor of free expression: courts generally decline to prevent hateful messages from assaulting the personal dignity of their many victims.

But government censorship is only part of the story. When considering controls over hate speech, one must consider informal ways that individuals are discouraged from—and sometimes even prevented from—expressing themselves. Ridicule, shaming, boycotts, and other forms of cultural regulation can have powerful silencing effect. In the humor context, one of the most horrific examples of silencing in recent memory is the January 2015 *Charlie Hebdo* murders.

An iconic French satirical magazine, *Charlie Hebdo* features political cartoons, polemics, and jokes. The magazine tends to target religion, taking an equal opportunity approach by mocking Catholicism, Judaism, Islam, and other religions. Repeatedly attracting controversy for its irreverence, the magazine has been subject to hate speech lawsuits, firebombing, vandalism, and hacking. Many of these clashes appeared as a response to the magazine's depiction of the Prophet Muhammad in a variety of satirical cartoons. The violent January 2015 attacks occurred at the magazine's Parisian headquarters. Two Islamic shooters killed eleven people (including the magazine's editor-in-chief) and injured eleven, the apparent motive for the attack being vengeance for the insult to the prophet.

Charlie Hebdo's satire operates on the fault line between acceptable and non-acceptable humor. One can reasonably debate whether the Muhammad cartoons constituted hate speech. One could also debate whether the freedom to create such cartoons is requisite to true democracy. Certainly many found no humor in the cartoons and others found them unnecessarily disrespectful. Nonetheless, free speech is a key component to democratic debate. Part of democratic debate is searing satire, which, the argument goes, is particularly crucial for "spreading truth and attacking fools and knaves."[127]

For complicated cultural and political reasons, French authorities chose not to apply the country's hate speech laws to *Charlie Hebdo*. In the law's absence, a lethal non-legal force—the armed gunmen—sought to silence those who created the cartoons. Key to understanding the dynamic between humor and censorship is the world's heartwarming response to the *Charlie Hebdo* tragedy. The response was spontaneous, yet cohesive: the battle cry "Je suis Charlie" was heard from remote precincts as groups came together to protest the attack and world officials created an impressive display of diplomatic solidarity. Conceptualizing the murders as an attack on artistic freedom of expression, protesters as well as government officials held up pencils as a memorial to the victims. The pencil trope took off in cartoons from an array of international artists and joined the pen as a symbol of the importance of humor in a democracy—such as France, which embraces a national slogan reflected in Cartoon 1-12 pronouncing dedication to liberty, equality, and fraternity.

Cartoon 1-12 (cartoon 7 TCB-141351 / 030072-313) Christopher Wyant/The New Yorker Collection/The Cartoon Bank

It is hard to say how much force cartoons such as these had in expressing the world's disgust with the *Charlie Hebdo* killing. Surely they had a galvanizing effect as the protests developed and provided an artistic outlet for the world's grief for the victims. What is not clear, however, is whether the cartoons had any influence on those who committed the murders or those who might be tempted to engage in similar violence.

In a sense, the *Charlie Hebdo* story is a tragic example of a larger controversy: the "political correctness" debate, which has played out across the world for decades. On the question of whether society should tolerate humor that disparages a particular group, one view holds that offensive jokes teach hatred, validate intolerance, and perpetuate unfair stereotypes. The targets of disparaging humor often belong to a group lacking political and economic power. Vilification of these groups occurs "in jokes, insults, ribbing, and public humiliation disguised as humor."[128] On the other hand is the view that—in the interest of inclusiveness—societies should not encourage their citizens to become brittle, boring, and thin-skinned. To involve courts in regulating insult in the form of jokes, the reasoning continued, is truly silly.

Although U.S. courts have become involved in political correctness debates in various ways, the most famous political correctness controversies in the country have played out largely on college campuses with the introduction of "speech codes," which were often broad enough to prohibit derogatory jokes. Opponents of these codes spoke of free speech, identity politics, and suppression of the rich, candid dialogue among diverse segments of our culture. While controversies about speech codes have now died down, the core questions remain: Are American humor sensibilities often hypersensitive and sanitizing? Alternatively, is American humor too often vulgar and disrespectful of others? Which is worse?

D. HUMOR'S PUSHBACK ON LAW: CENSORSHIP HUMOR

Both creative cartooning in the wake of the *Charlie Hebdo* killings as well as the clever self-regulation jokes by stand-up comedians illustrate an important dynamic: humor need not be a passive victim of formal and informal efforts to silence its voice and undermine its potency. Humor can fight back. This potential is beautifully illustrated by a genre of humor currently flourishing in many expressive outlets: comedy that mocks and capitalizes on censorship itself. Not only does this comedy have power-restricting potential, but one might argue that we are living in the golden age of censorship humor. Since the days of George Carlin and the Seven Dirty Words, American entertainment has experienced a surge in parody and mockery of censorship. Perhaps even more powerful is a related comedic strain, "unnecessary censorship" humor, which capitalizes on censorship's comic potential by creating censorship's effect when no official mandate requires it.

The intuition that censorship can be funny no doubt goes way back. We know it goes at least as far back as the first reality TV show—*Candid Camera*—when Alan Funt observed that an audience laughed harder after hearing a bleep than it did when hearing an unedited clip containing an off-color word. In other words, when a *Candid Camera* victim blurted something taboo, the laughs were less than they were when a bleep concealed the taboo language. The difference between censored and uncensored tracks was so marked that Funt even bleeped out innocent language—and expressions like "Oh God"—which would have never met a censor's ax.

Contemporary mirth makers have made considerable use of Funt's remarkable observation. Using censorship's ability to enhance laughter, modern comedy uses a full array of censorship tools: strategically placed censors' black bars . . . digitalized mosaic blurs or pixilations that obscure body parts, crude gestures, and the like . . . typographical symbol strings called grawlixes (#@%**X^!) . . . asterisks replacing letters in a word (e.g., sh*t) . . . acronyms (e.g., *WTF*) . . . and euphemisms (what the flip is that?). Creatively deploying these tools, would-be comedians have filled our culture with content that taps censorship's comic potential.

Representing a humor-type rooted in asserting superiority, many censorship jokes simply ridicule the censor. Military censors have traditionally provided ridicule's target. Recall Captain John Yossarian from Joseph Heller's *Catch-22*. A wartime censor of service personnel's letters to home, Yossarian fought boredom and indulged a mischievous spirit by sometimes slashing one word only (e.g., the article "the") from a personal letter or slashing all words but one in another letter (e.g., the article "the"). Topping off these playful indiscretions, Yossarian signed a pseudonym at the end: "Washington Irving," "Irving Washington," the name of his unit chaplain, and the like.

Cartoon 1-13 is a military censorship example in the same tradition.

Totalitarian regimes provide a similar target for censorship ridicule. As the above discussion of puns illustrates, comedians plying their trade within totalitarian regimes do not always enjoy the liberty of indulging irony and satire directed toward the government. But—as reflected in Cartoon 1-14—that does not stop others.

This mockery of censors is reflected in a number of satirical outlets. In one example, the news satire website *The Onion* reported that the U.S. Central Intelligence Agency discovered that it had been inadvertently using "black highlighters," rather than highlighters in a transparent color that enhances the text that it covers. According to the gag, the use of "black

CLEARED BY THE U.S. MILITARY

Cartoon 1-13 (cartoon 8A TCB-31031/010272-313) Robert Mankoff/The New Yorker Collection/The Cartoon Bank

"Sometimes I just want to curl up with a good book and burn it."

Cartoon 1-14 (cartoon 8B TCB-133318/004264-313) Zachary Kanin/The New Yorker Collection/The Cartoon Bank

highlighters" had the entirely unintended effect of concealing—rather than emphasizing—crucial parts of politically sensitive documents.[129]

The other form of censorship humor—based on fabricated or unnecessary censorship—tends to be less overtly political. Alan Funt's extra bleeps in *Candid Camera* provide early contemporary illustrations of unnecessary censorship humor. An outpouring of additional examples now appears throughout electronic media today: television and the Internet are spilling over with fabricated censorship jokes. ABC network's late-night show *Jimmy Kimmel Live!* has run a weekly feature "This Week in Unnecessary Censorship." The Jimmy Kimmel segments feature benign television show or news program clips that originally aired without censorship. The clips are displayed with a censoring twist through pixilation and/or a bleep in spoken text, implying something risqué has just been spoken. Hearing the bleep (and/or seeing the pixilation), the audience erupts in laughter as it interprets the clip's context and privately speculates on the potentially salacious words or images that would have required censorship.

Permeating Internet and TV entertainment, censorship humor has made its way into *New Yorker* cartoons. Examples are spare, but Cartoon 1-15, created by the late (great) Charles Barsotti, is particularly intriguing.

On one hand, Cartoon 1-15 presents straightforward ridicule of censorship: the message being that censorship renders the cartoon absurdly lacking in content. But wait, could the stealthy figures in the picture themselves be censors? This would add an ironic twist: the censors' words themselves are censored, leaving the censors unable to communicate. The cartoon presents an enigma: Is it a joke mocking censorship or is it simply a joke using unnecessary censorship as its medium?

Now we come to the central puzzle with censorship humor: how is it that something so core to U.S. beliefs—the evil of stifling freedom of expression—could be funny? In part, the answer is easy. Comedians in these examples are protesting the wrongheadedness of suppressing speech. But other ideas from humor scholarship suggest a more nuanced explanation. Two particularly apt humor theory concepts hold that humor is enhanced (1) in the presence of a "benign violation" and (2) when the audience is invited to participate as a comedic co-author.

Humor practitioners and scholars observe that norm violation is a frequent ingredient of humor. Thus, censorship humor's frolic into the realm of "naughty" helps account for the humor's allure.[130] A refinement of this observation posits that an audience enjoys naughty humor more if the violation is benign.[131]

Applied to censorship humor, benign violation reasoning would go like this: human experience shows that comedy often operates as controlled danger. Once a joke spills into real danger or a serious code violation,

Cartoon 1-15 (cartoon 8—TCB-124968) Charles Barsotti/The New Yorker Collection/The Cartoon Bank

the joke is no longer funny. A censored joke keeps an otherwise unfunny joke in the funny domain. The joke obliquely reflects a real violation and thus stimulates by depicting danger. Censorship strikes out the juicy, truly dangerous stuff. As such, the censorship controls the danger and thereby creates a medium ripe for laughter. The censorship renders the violation benign to the listener—the danger having been "bleeped out" (metaphorically and literally).

The concept of "audience as co-author" works in similar fashion. When a joke transgresses a norm, the participants may vicariously perceive that they are breaching the norm themselves. The audience enjoys that perception, if in fact the audience receives the cue that a joke is under way. Building on this cue, censorship enlists the audience to become the joke's co-author because the audience needs to fill in the omitted content. In writing its own version of the joke script, the audience receives a reward from its own insight in identifying what had been censored.[132] Of course, this solipsistic reward system does not operate where censorship is secret or stealthy. Where the censorship is obvious, however, the joke is co-constructed and both sides are happy. The audience enjoys creatively participating in writing the joke and the joke teller enjoys having the audience serve as co-conspirator. Complicity is fun.

At least two dynamics can magnify the joint fun created when the audience acts as a joke's co-author. First is the human tendency to assume that something negative (naughty or illegal) prompted the censor to edit.[133] Second is the sense of community created when the audience successfully intuits the humor's censored components. The audience and joke-teller see that they share membership in a common culture, which enables them to grasp precisely what images or words were censored from the joke.

Although theories of ridicule, benign violation, and joke co-authorship may explain the cognitive and emotional processes that allow censorship humor to amuse, the puzzle of why censorship is funny is still not fully solved. Censorship is serious business; it kills the currency of thought and communication. Censorship's power easily evokes fear, anxiety, and anger. Isn't it strange—even bizarre—that censorship can inspire laughter? Given that humans resist being gagged and hold censorship as a generic evil—how on earth do we get pleasure from it?

This question beckons a curious answer: humans might actually *like* a touch of censorship. Supreme Court opinions interpreting the First Amendment's free speech protections reveal occasional insights about censorship's potential value. The relevant opinions emerge in highly charged contexts, such as patriotism[134] and arguments about protecting our children from filth.[135] For some justices the important social values animating these topics rank higher than the value of freedom of expression.

Even if we don't embrace this balance of values, our common sense can still embrace the wisdom of occasionally restricting human discourse. The whole notion of government by rule of law suggests that boundaries are crucial for civilized society. Censorship can educate about where to draw the line between proper and improper. For individuals, boundaries grant comfort by imposing structure, ensuring predictability, and simplifying life. Censorship boundaries reinforce the virtues of silence, self-restraint, and leaving unpleasant words unspoken. Most important for generating humor—charting the line between what is and what is not appropriate to communicate fuels the alchemy that creates comedy. By demarcating an area of impropriety, censorship establishes the territory that jokes can probe and tweak.

The idea that we like censorship has scary potential. But let's not get ahead of ourselves. Two closing—and potentially mitigating—thoughts need considering. First, appreciating the occasional value of censorship does not mean we want more of it. Understanding censorship's benefits is not the same as advocating that the law try harder to enforce good taste and suppression of ideas. Second, humor is mysterious. Analysis can only gesture at an explanation of why we laugh—whether we are laughing at censorship or anything else. This understanding of the nature and wonder of humor's mystery—particularly its tendency to work by incongruity and contradiction—is a quality not only useful to celebrating law's effect on humor but is important to all contexts in which law regulates humor. The enigmatic nature of humor is equally important for the topic of the next chapter, Chapter 2, as well: humor about the law. Although jokes that riff on law and the legal process can often be understood as social critique, their popularity cannot be fully explained with rational analysis. Don't worry, though—that adds to the fun.

CHAPTER 2

✺

"About"

Humor About Law

Here's a piece of Americana for you:

Q: How many lawyer jokes are there?
A: Only three. All the rest are documented case histories.[1]

Are you surprised that a chapter on humor about law begins with a lawyer joke? I'm guessing not. Jokes about crafty lawyers, money-grubbing lawyers, and proliferating lawyers are a time-honored tradition in American comedy. Why are there so many lawyer jokes? People—even lots of regular people—find themselves in situations when they really need a lawyer. Lawyers can be enormously helpful to all sorts of folks, especially those in need of a forceful voice on their side. Lawyers are key to the administration of justice and serve to ensure that we enjoy government by rule of law. In other words, the volume of degrading lawyer jokes seems out of step with the real status of lawyers in the world.

To understand this paradox, one might start with the idea that comedy works by blending apparently incompatible perspectives. In the last chapter, we saw courts unconsciously tapping into this observation when searching for incongruities to decide what humor to protect. Professional comedians using censorship humor make full use of anomaly in the comic process: they harness contradiction to create humor by jumbling together the good (poking fun and laughing) with the bad (muzzling and punishing). This same theme of incongruity and incompatibility appears in humor about law—whether humor is taking shots at lawyers, judges, juries, legal texts, or the legal process generally. Nonetheless, incongruity plays a more complicated role in humor about law than in other contexts when law and humor join. In fact, incongruity works double duty in humor about law. For nearly all jokes, incongruity provides the jokes' structure and content. But for jokes about the law, incongruity also works below the surface to inspire the comedy. Our culture's inconsistent views about the merits of lawyers, law, and the legal process help both to create the conflict that produces the jokes and to enhance the jokes' amusing content.

Inconsistent views? Doesn't almost all humor about lawyers, judges, and the like have a satirical tone? The answer is yes: satire is the dominant genre in jests about law. To some, this trend might suggest that society holds a clear view that law and the human beings involved in the law, at best, are a necessary evil that require ridicule to keep them in their place. Many scholars who have analyzed law jokes concluded that the jokes are a paradigm of superiority humor, designed to show disdain and distinguish legal actors from higher human life forms. While the jokes' surface suggests this is true, the matter is more complex.

Americans do not categorically hate lawyers, law, legal institutions, or the legal process. Here is the evidence: American culture is utterly fascinated with the legal system, and that fascination springs from something other than pure disgust. Without legal themes, fictional television and digital entertainment would wither and die. Mystery novels would have no raw material. Sure, Americans may have passed a golden age of unquestioningly celebrating beatific lawyers (Sir Thomas More), brilliant trial lawyers (Perry Mason), involuntary icons (Atticus Finch), and champions of the underdog (Clarence Darrow)—but those images linger, even if many specific figures have faded from memory. And the lawyer-as-crusader image may be on the rise. Consider the photographs of young lawyers with laptops at JFK airport helping those affected by President Trump's selective immigrant ban in the early days of his presidency. Some have attributed the immediate spike in law school applications as an empathetic response to these images, which editors chose for the opening pages of hard copy newspapers and websites.

Additional evidence of esteem for law exists. Repeatedly in contemporary times, even when lawyers have been ridiculed and the market for legal jobs shrank precipitously, polls show that as many as 69 percent of U.S. parents would be delighted to have their children become lawyers.[2] One wonders what all those parents are thinking. It can't just be about money, since some lawyers do not make much and word is out about that grim reality. It can't be just about knowledge: buckets of other professions offer participants the prestige and satisfaction of deep expertise. It could be about power: lawyers sometimes hold the lofty position of understanding how the big wheels turn and make their way close to the action. But it could also be about the moral role of lawyers: the public holds stealth admiration for lawyers, implicitly understanding that lawyers provide a backbone for our social order. Whatever the reason, people tend to act according to their true sentiments when it comes to their children: if they would be quite happy for their kids to be lawyers, they must not really think that lawyers break bread with the devil.

Those who have paid attention to the matter point out that the Shakespearean line—"First thing we do, let's kill all the lawyers"[3]—comes from the mouth of a cad who was afraid of lawyers' work as freedom fighters and guardians of justice.[4] "Kill all the lawyers" is not a call for mass homicide, but an understanding that lawyers can be the enemy of evil. Whether for Shakespeare or for modern citizens, lawyers are opinion leaders, statesmen, and occasionally guardians of the rule of law. Who can speak truth to power? The answer has persistently been "our lawyers."

A similar conflict between esteem and disapproval appears with U.S. attitudes toward legal rules. Take, for example, constitutional protections for the criminally accused. In contemporary times, these sometimes appear—at first glance—as technicalities obstructing well-deserved punishment for those responsible for injecting violence and fear into modern life. Yet these constitutional protections feel far more precious when one personally confronts abusive law enforcement.

Folded into conflicting attitudes about rules are mixed feelings about legal language. For example, U.S. citizens often celebrate the august spirit reflected in the Preamble to the U.S. Constitution. Contrasting with this admiration, however, one also encounters satirizing critique of its language:

> The Preamble uses the expression, "We the People." This is fatuous. Who else are "We" if not the people? The periwigs? The quill pens? Paul Revere's silverware? . . . and phrases such as "establish Justice," . . . and "secure the Blessings of Liberty to ourselves and our Posterity" don't clarify anything in the main text. They are just prattle—blah, blah, blah.[5]

And then there is an analogous tension appearing in views about government's proper role in the lives of U.S. citizens and in managing the economy. Consider debates about the wisdom of extensive consumer protection laws. On one hand are those who favor "command and control" government monitoring to avoid the harms threatened when profit motives blind business to unsafe consumer goods. On the other are those who cite the paralyzing effect of regulation on innovation and efficiency. For this debate, citizens generally take one side or the other. Yet the deep disagreement over these matters preys on our minds, creating a tension providing rich raw material for comedy.

Split attitudes also characterize American views of legal procedures. One hears cries of doom over the tort litigation crisis: overuse of our court system for remedying minor personal injuries, class actions that enrich lawyers but fail to benefit true victims of harm, and the like. The increase in personal injury litigation has caused a proliferation of warning labels, providing a rich trove of raw material for jokes about lawsuit stupidity:

- On a Sears hairdryer: Do not use while sleeping. (damn, and that's the only time I have to work on my hair.)
- On a bag of Fritos: . . . You could be a winner! No purchase necessary. Details inside. (the shoplifter special?)
- On a bar of Dial soap: "Directions: Use like regular soap." (and that would be how??? . . .)
- On some Swanson frozen dinners: "Serving suggestion: Defrost." (but, it's "just" a suggestion.)
- On packaging for a Rowenta iron: "Do not iron clothes on body." (but wouldn't this save me more time?)
- On most brands of Christmas lights: "For indoor or outdoor use only." (as opposed to . . . what?)
- On a child's superman costume: "Wearing of this garment does not enable you to fly." (I don't blame the company. I blame the parents for this one.)
- On a Swedish chainsaw: "Do not attempt to stop chain with your hands or genitals." (Oh my God . . . was there a lot of this happening somewhere?)[6]

Contrast this ridicule of tort litigation's consequences with the strong public reaction against mandatory arbitration clauses. Slipped into many consumer contracts, these clauses foreclose traditional litigation in courts for consumers suffering physical and/or financial harm unless consumers opt out of the clauses within a very short period after purchasing a service or product. Almost always, complex documents describe the opt-out mechanisms: documents that either physically accompany products or—even more burdensome on the consumer—are available online. In the end, these are documents to which consumers—even lawyer consumers—rarely pay much heed. Although the U.S. Supreme Court has upheld these waiver clauses, public outcry has increased, reflecting the view that the clauses with hidden opt-out mechanisms trick Americans into giving up important rights. What kinds of rights? Rights to full use of the traditional complicated mechanisms of our judicial system, professionally staffed by judges and lawyers and guided by formal rules of substantive law and procedure. The public says they hate the litigation crisis with its complicated legal procedures, but they are hell-bent against forfeiting those procedures when they might be needed for personal protection.

So it appears that U.S. attitudes are conflicted: when it comes to lawyers, law, and the legal system, we grudgingly embrace some aspects of the law and hold other aspects in the pejorative. This tension comes out in the comedy about law. Starting with Freud, humor theorists have long held that comedy provides a vehicle for resolving internal conflict. Viewed in light of evidence about conflicted attitudes toward lawyers, law, and the legal process, law jokes may be more than just an emotional outburst or an exercise in asserting superiority over a scoundrel profession by pummeling everything associated with law. Rather, the jokes are a mechanism for working through society's ambivalence about legal matters. That's not to say that humor about law is routinely refined with subtlety. To the contrary, the satirical, sometimes vicious tone of this humor generally reflects an unqualified negative attitude. Satire plays a starring role in humor about the law. Real sentiments give footing to expressions of strong distaste for all things legal. Yet the satire also springs from contrasting views about its subject. Our jokes are biting because something has a hit a nerve: legal matters displease us, but we care deeply about lawyers, law, and the legal process.

Consider the following parody of a law faculty meeting—showing on one hand the professors' careful attention to proper procedure (a good thing, right?) together with a ridiculous inclination for overusing it. Imagine forty or so smart lawyers in a room who have grown to expect people to take notes as soon as they start speaking. The result is often brimming with farcical self-importance:

> [Following the Law School Curriculum Committee report, a] motion was introduced to substitute potato chips for corn chips at the next faculty meeting. A vote was taken. The Faculty was evenly divided. The Dean then offered to cast a tie-breaking vote. The hypothetical question was raised that if the Dean were to cast a tie-breaking vote, what would he vote for? The Dean replied that he would vote for corn chips. A substitute motion was introduced to disempower the Dean from casting tie-breaking votes. The Dean ruled the motion out of order. . . . A faculty member demanded to see a verified copy of the original motion regarding potato chips. However, the original motion had become a paper plane and last been seen flying out the window.[7]

An interesting inquiry is whether lampoons such as these act as an agent of change—spurring agents on the inside and outside of the legal system to modify institutions and behavior to eliminate the causes for this scorn. Such is the perennial debate about satire. Does it—in the end—simply amuse or placate? Or does it act as a catalyst for action, with powerful wit causing others to rethink their approach and change reprehensible behavior? Only by diving into the weeds can we get insight into the possible effect of humor about law. The mother lode of law-related humor—lawyer jokes—provides a logical place to start.

A. LAWYERS

In the form of movies, television shows, and novels, popular culture depicts lawyers as forces of good and evil. Occasionally, one sees portraits of lawyers as complex human beings—with mixed motives together with glimmers of brilliance combined with blind spots in their vision. Lawyer humor does not generally reflect this nuance. No ambiguity exists: lawyers come off badly in lawyer jokes. By contrast, in fictional depictions of lawyers—as well as news coverage that features real-life lawyers—one can occasionally find profound and flattering messages about a lawyer's ethical character and commitment to the moral standards required by his or her relationship to clients and the administration of justice. Sometimes this is depicted as self-righteousness, but other times it comes off as leadership or "moral pluck."[8] Humor about lawyers shows no such subtlety, and—as in Cartoon 2-1—is occasionally on the slapstick side of the humor scale.

"Damn thing's supposed to be attorney-proof."

Cartoon 2-1 (cartoon 35—TCB 51550) Danny Shanahan/The New Yorker Collection/The Cartoon Bank

The much revered analysis—and wonderful compendium—of lawyer jokes by Professor Mark Galanter submits that lawyer jokes reveal and reinforce a "jaundiced view of law."[9] While surely accurate, this characterization tells only part of the story: society's views about lawyers, law, and the legal process are more schizophrenic than the face of the jokes suggest.

In evaluating why lawyer jokes carry such negative messages, I first note observations that point away from some kind of inherent flaw in the character of U.S. lawyers. Most prominently are those who attribute the harsh quality and large quantity of U.S. lawyer jokes to heightened expectations about the role of law in U.S. government. The idea here is that American culture celebrates its rule of law with aplomb, and as a consequence, law carries a lot of responsibility. This thereby sets an unreasonably high bar for achievement and standards of conduct for the mortals who serve on the front lines of the rule of law: lawyers. According to one humor scholar from the United Kingdom, lawyer jokes are a "uniquely American phenomenon because no other country is so rooted in the sanctity of law."[10] Professor Galanter agrees that the tsunami of lawyer jokes is unique to the United States.

For Galanter, one can find an important explanation for this in variations between a common law system (such as in the United States) and a civil law system (such as used in much of Europe and the rest of the world). The consequent differences result in fewer lawyers and "larger contingents of judges" in civil law systems.[11] Not only do difference in the lawyer populations account for fewer lawyer jokes outside the United States, but variations in lawyer roles also have an influence. With common law systems, litigating lawyers participate aggressively in an adversarial process; in civil law systems, lawyers facilitate an inquisitional process, with judges more actively engaged in steering investigations and participating in questioning. In the end, lawyers serve a more dominant, agenda-setting role in the U.S. system, thereby capturing a greater slice of the public's imagination. Americans tend to have heightened expectations about what law can do: an attitude fueled in part by attempts to use courts as instruments of social change. This heightened expectation, of course, brings with it a greater risk that the key agent moving the system forward, lawyers, will disappoint those who feel the effects of their work.

And disappoint they do. "In no other country are those who practice law so reviled."[12]

Why do other technical professions not inspire such vicious humor? One theory is that lay people believe that the human-made rules that govern their lives should be easy to understand. The idea here is that since people make legal rules, they should also be able to make them easily understandable to other people. U.S. law, of course, hopelessly fails this expectation.[13]

By contrast, many lay people view the technicalities of medical science as beyond their grasp and therefore a less appropriate target for ridicule.

Aggravating these factors are irritating personality traits that appear regularly among those in the legal profession. Let's start with vanity. Swarmy, self-promoting advertisements—with individual lawyers forming the centerpiece—are now common in most states. On a more sophisticated level, many members of the profession understand that they should be sensitive about projecting their proper image. To this end, they solicit the advice of actors, public relations specialists, and others on the topic of how lawyers and the legal profession might rise in the esteem of others. This self-regarding orientation also appears in the myriad cultural-legal studies published in legal journals on the topic of lawyers and the legal profession. Reinforcing these images are the popular culture depictions of slick lawyers in well-cut suits as well as schleppy overworked government lawyers— both caricatures presenting an "I'm-the-man, now-listen-to-me" demeanor. Consider this gag exam question:

The proper attire for male attorneys to appear in municipal court is:

A. Slacks and a sport shirt

B. An Italian silk suit and alligator shoes

C. Striped slacks and a swallowtail coat

D. A Columbo raincoat[14]

Not only are these vain images unbecoming, but they also frame lawyers as appealing targets for jokes. Vain people are fun to ridicule: teasing and poking are more satisfying when the perpetrators of a barb provoke a reaction or at least know that they are hitting the target where it hurts.

Adding fuel to the impulse to ridicule lawyers is their combative nature. To the extent that lawyer jokes can be characterized as superiority humor, the satisfaction gained from a sharp barb may be heightened when the target of the joke is ambitious and quarrelsome by nature. As Aristotle told us, humor is handy for pointing out the failures of others.[15] When the "others" are full of themselves and foment conflict at the expense of others, the humor has more sizzle. Piercing the armor of a pugnacious person not only has a special thrill but also enhances dominance. These are common themes in lawyer jokes:

There was a small town with just one lawyer and he was starving for lack of business.

Then another lawyer moved to town and they both prospered.[16]

What profession is your boy going to select?

I'm going to educate him to be a lawyer. He's naturally argumentative and bent on mixing into other people's troubles, and he might just as well get paid for his time.[17]

And finally, lawyers tend to have good verbal skills: law school admissions tests screen for this talent and law schools refine it through classroom Socratic questioning and oral advocacy training. Many lawyers are quiet introverts, but those who are not tend to be loquacious and more bombastic than others. Even the introverted lawyers have honed their oral abilities. This lawyerly facility with words enhances both the incentive and challenge for the comedian.

These various observations about lawyers reflect complex strands in U.S. society and government. These do not, however, combine to create routinely subtle and complex humor. Many are just straightforward commentary on the general worthlessness of lawyers:

> Q: What is the definition of a shame (as in "that's a shame")?
> A: When a busload of lawyers goes off a cliff.
> Q: What is the definition of a "crying shame"?
> A: There was an empty seat.[18]

Instead, lawyer jokes fall quite easily into stable, caricatured categories. This joke quality is not unique to lawyers: clarity and fixed forms are more common for jokes than for other genres of humor. Although cultural contexts inspiring jokes may be intricate, jokes themselves do not usually share this quality. A joke is generally a "short humorous piece of oral literature,"[19] often encapsulating one prejudice or adverse sentiment in lampooning a subject.

In the hands of legal scholars, the taxonomies for sorting lawyer jokes have proliferated. Here are three dominant categories: (1) lawyers as crafty and cunning enemies of truth and justice, (2) lawyers as money-grubbing vultures, and (3) lawyers as a proliferating breed. One has to assume that each of these categories reflects some kind of shared social perceptions of lawyers. Why else would they gain currency? Jokes are particularly potent when they convey a thinly concealed message that would, without the cover of humor, become snagged in self-censorship's filter. Humor thus enables expression of sentiments that polite communication would avoid. Throughout the three categories of lawyer jokes is an unfortunate truth: as much as Americans need them and view them as a crucial part of life in a free society, lawyers are a profession for which most citizens bear serious ill-will.

1. Crafty and Cunning: Disloyal Lawyers as Allies of the Devil

The message of this category of crafty and cunning lawyers is that lawyers are bad people. Looking at just one website featuring lawyer jokes, one hears a clear message: jests compare lawyers with sharks, leeches, gigolos, toxic waste, attack dogs, dead skunks, manure, vampires, nuclear weapons, bottom-feeding fish, and more.[20] These distasteful images telegraph that lawyers are unworthy human beings—a message also captured in Cartoon 2-2.

Along similar lines are the many jokes associating lawyers with the devil:

> The devil visited a lawyer's office and made him an offer. "I can arrange some things for you," the devil said. "I'll increase your income five-fold. Your partners will love you; your clients will respect you; you'll have four months vacation each year and live to be a hundred. All I require in return is that your wife's soul, your children's souls, and their children's souls rot in hell for eternity."
>
> The lawyer thought for a moment. "What's the catch?" he asked.[21]

> A man died and was taken to his place of eternal torment by the devil.
>
> As he passed raging fire pits and shrieking sinners, he saw a man he recognized as a lawyer snuggling up to a beautiful woman.
>
> "That's unfair!" he cried. "I have to roast for all eternity, and that lawyer gets to spend it with a beautiful woman."
>
> "Shut up," barked the devil, jabbing the man with his pitchfork.
>
> "Who are you to question that woman's punishment?"[22]

"I shot a man in Reno, just to watch him die. After that,
law school was pretty much a given.

Cartoon 2-2 (cartoon 29—TCB 40288) Danny Shanahan/The New Yorker Collection/The Cartoon Bank

These are blunt references to evil. But the dynamic they reflect is more complicated than pure hatred and evil. Many subtle contradictions and anxieties lie at the root of the apparent disgust for lawyers. A look at cartoons and jokes dealing with the theme of untrustworthiness helps to tease out these sentiments.

Starting with a basic joke:

Q: How does a lawyer say, "Screw you"?
A: "Trust me."[23]

And another:

Two lawyers camping in Alaska spotted a ferocious grizzly bear. The first lawyer quickly opened his suitcase, pulled out a pair of running shoes, and started putting them on. The second lawyer looked at him and said, "Are you crazy? You'll never be able to outrun that bear!" "I don't have to," the first lawyer said. "I only need to outrun *you*."[24]

What's going on in these crude jokes? Clearly they reflect something about a propensity toward betrayal of other human beings. One wonders why lawyers invite others to believe that they are prone to betray. A partial explanation may come from the lawyerly role of representation: the notion that lawyers have a fiduciary obligation of zealous advocacy for today's client and the possibility that, within the confines of the conflict of interest rules, the lawyer may represent someone tomorrow for whom today's client holds deep distaste.

Another possibility for the feeling of betrayal comes from the psychology of dependency. In a society that places so much emphasis on law, those who identify with and inhabit the United States have an increased need for the expertise of specialists who understand law's complexities. With this dependency on experts arises a tension between the need for lay persons to trust lawyers with their important personal affairs and the accompanying resentment that any person should be forced to rely on another—whether it be a professional lawyer or not. Elevating the tension is unfamiliarity: ordinary citizens rarely use the services of a lawyer and therefore lack experience interacting with them. Pollsters call this a "lack-of-exposure" or "negativity" bias.[25] Since most Americans do not visit lawyers much or at all, they get their portrait of lawyers from the depictions (good and bad) on television and in other popular culture. As a result of the negativity bias, the human mind credits negative information more heavily than positive information. The events that do prompt the average citizen's need for a lawyer tend to be inherently stressful: a home purchase, an arrest, and the death of a loved one. Lawyer jokes may therefore provide an outlet for venting that stress. The jokes might also serve as a preemptive strike against the discomfort of dependency, the possibility of betrayal, or the frustration of being submissive to another.[26] As the aphorism teaches: "Everyone hates lawyers until they need one."[27]

Complementing this theme of betraying others is a parallel idea represented in Cartoon 2-3 about lawyers betraying the truth.

And here's a commonly repeated joke:

Q: How can you tell when lawyers are lying?

A: Their lips are moving.[28]

Along with these gags about lying lawyers are jokes suggesting that lawyers are engaged in the hypocrisy of betraying the justice system they are sworn to uphold. As depicted in Cartoons 2-4 and 2-5, this humor shows lawyers

"Here it is—the plain, unvarnished truth. Varnish it."

Cartoon 2-3 (cartoon 30—TCB 41623) Richard Cline/The New Yorker Collection/The Cartoon Bank

in behavior that ranges from strategic and weaselly to outright violations of the law.

Here again, the explanation for this humor may lie in tensions and contradictions arising from the U.S. legal system. Some assert that those not trained in the law blame lawyers for corrupting our laws. Under this theory, the untrained do not fully grasp or accept the indeterminacy and political nature of law.[29] Those trained in law understand that it plays out on a landscape that is both ambiguous and contingent. But that reality has somehow not made its way into the popular imagination. As a result, notions of neutral legal principles, static truths, and crystal-clear rules provide the legal model for most citizens. However unrealistic, these notions are hard to dispel. When law fails to live up to these ideals, the front-line agents in the legal system—lawyers—are easy to blame. And here again, the adversarial nature of our legal system aggravates matters. If there is but one just and true answer to a legal question, the argument would go, lawyers should not be able to "argue both sides." Since they argue both sides of a legal issue as a matter of course, lawyers must be dishonest and duplicitous.

According to Marc Galanter, practicing lawyers vary in their attitudes toward the "divergence of advocacy from truth seeking" reflected in their

"Hey, don't blame me. I don't make the laws—I just circumvent them."

Cartoon 2-4 (cartoon 31—TCB 122120) Michael Maslin/The New Yorker Collection/The Cartoon Bank

"*If you want justice, it's two hundred dollars an hour.*
Obstruction of justice runs a bit more."

Cartoon 2-5 (cartoon 32—TCB 29804) Leo Cullum/The New Yorker Collection/The Cartoon Bank

professional roles.[30] While some lawyers urge their brethren to acknowledge the "knavery" that accompanies legal practice, others argue only for a noble path of honesty called for by the ethical requirement to serve the administration of justice.[31] Still others see their job as requiring a complex blend of spinning, hiding, and salient truth-telling—combined to ensure competent, zealous representation of client interest.

In many instances, these conflicting forces do little to complicate the lawyer-as-liar theme conveyed in Cartoons 2-6 and 2-7.

These straightforward depictions of the lying lawyer, however, present only one strand of comedy about lawyerly deceit. Other humorous portraits of dishonesty in law practice reflect more subtle inner conflict and competing perspectives. The 1997 Jim Carrey film comedy *Liar Liar* provides a highly caricatured illustration of a lawyer struggling with disharmonious impulses. The film begins with a high-priced, corrupt lawyer (Jim Carrey) who distorts the truth for the benefit of his clients and his own professional development. At this point in the film, the gags are only mildly amusing, fueled largely by the elasticity of Carrey's face and body. After his son makes a birthday wish that—for one day—his father cannot tell a lie—the wish comes true. The humor in the film immediately accelerates as the

"Is it right? ... Is it fair?' Get a grip Carlton—we're a law firm!"

Cartoon 2-6 (cartoon 33—TCB 122644) Leo Cullum/The New Yorker Collection/The Cartoon Bank

audience watches the lawyer struggle to maintain his composure as he continually blurts out the truth. Carrey's despair at his truth-telling impulse becomes the main part of the gag.[32]

Finally, the image of lawyer as liar merges with the image of lawyer as felon. Check out these two entries in "The New (Legal) Devil's Dictionary":

> *Conviction*, n. (1) If you're a crook, the law's way of telling you to slow down. (2) Something you believe with all your heart, mind, and strength—for the purpose of this litigation, anyway.
>
> *Criminal Lawyer*, n. A grammatical redundancy, like "tiny infant" or "sweet sugar."[33]

2. Money-Grubbing Vultures

Business people who work on putting together deals often work for a percentage of the transaction's value. Physicians are reimbursed for specific services performed. Lawyers, however, are often paid by the hour. This

"O.K.—let's review what you didn't know and when you didn't know it."

Cartoon 2-7 (cartoon 34—TCB 47739) Lee Lorenz/The New Yorker Collection/The Cartoon Bank

model, it turns out, lends itself to some abuse. Legal ethicists document such practices as time inflation (billing 90 minutes for 60 minutes of work), inventing hours that simply were not worked, billing for overhead (using markup pricing when lawyers' fees are already out of sync with the labor theory of value), billing two clients for one task performed, billing for recycled work, performing unnecessary work, charging high lawyer rates for work that can be done by unskilled workers, and billing for preparing a bill.[34] Perhaps most striking are the stories about billing for personal expenses: items such as dry cleaning a toupee and purchasing running shoes (billed under the label "ground transportation").[35] Adding to this image is the contingency fee practice among personal injury lawyers. No wonder then that humor and, more generally, popular culture portray predatory greed in the legal profession.

> A newly deceased lawyer protested to St. Peter that, at 52, he'd been too young to die.
>
> "That's strange," St. Peter replied. "According to your billable hours, you're 89 years old."[36]

In addition to dishonesty in actual billing practices, lawyer lampoons focus on the notion that lawyers work only for economic gain, unwilling to take action without the expectation of recovering a fee.

Adding to the mercenary sting of this attitude is the reality that events requiring lawyering usually involve misfortune. Lawyers—even those struggling to eke out a living—therefore appear to be opportunistically benefiting from other's troubles. Cartoon 2-8 illustrates the money-trumps-justice message.

Much lawyer humor depicts the ability of a client to pay as paramount to lawyers' decisions to share their expertise with those in need. This is a subject of derision because, after all, justice should be a right, not something for which a U.S. citizen is billed. "Justice like love should be given freely."[37] This expectation comes into conflict with the need for lawyers to feed their families, pay their mortgages, make their car payments, and otherwise make a fair living. But one does not see this message reflected in stock lawyer humor such as Cartoon 2-9.

Multiple surveys suggest that the public thinks lawyers charge more than they are worth. One comparison with the medical profession is telling: "'Sure, lawyers are expensive, but so are doctors. They don't get the same reputation because insurance pays a lot of our medical bills.' No wonder why it's easier to see doctors as noble."[38] Also, the message does not come through that the investment in developing lawyerly expertise in a

"You have a pretty good case, Mr. Pitkin. How much justice can you afford?"

Cartoon 2-8 (cartoon 36—TCB 40228) J. B. Handlesman/The New Yorker Collection/The Cartoon Bank

*"My fees are quite high, and yet you say you have little money.
I think I'm seeing a conflict of interest here."*

Cartoon 2-9 (cartoon 38—TCB 34205) Leo Cullum/The New Yorker Collection/The Cartoon Bank

highly complex area is long and expensive. Rather, the message is confined to the straightforward sentiment, depicted in Cartoon 2-10, that lawyers worship at a holy money shrine.

Through contingency fee arrangements and hourly padding in billing practices, lawyers have not done themselves a favor. Yet one wonders whether the venom reflected in lawyers-as-economic-predators jokes is merited. Perhaps the reason lies in the clash between unreasonable expectations and lawyerly disregard of the somber role they hold in society.

3. Proliferating Lawyers

Q: Why do behavioral scientists prefer lawyers to rats for their experiments?
A: They multiply faster.[39]

For many years, the reality of stacking lawyers in cases reflected the common joke-narrative of the multiplying legal profession. Law schools acted as cash cows for universities, churning out volumes of students.

"He's illuminating something called 'The Book of Billable Hours.'"

Cartoon 2-10 (cartoon 37—TCB 45345) Lee Lorenz/The New Yorker Collection/The Cartoon Bank

"A pod of attorneys to see you, sir!"

Cartoon 2-11 (cartoon 40—TCB-33123) Mick Stevens/The New Yorker Collection/The Cartoon Bank

Running a law school generally entailed low capital expenditures (a few big classrooms, a little heat and lighting, and the school is off to the races!) and low operating costs (one relatively well-paid professor for a hundred or so tuition-paying students). Students perceived law school as the path to prestige and affluence. Thus, the attraction was mutual: students wanted law schools and law schools wanted students. As a consequence, the law schools increased enrollments and graduated an ever-increasing crop of students for many decades. Supply was plentiful, increasing the incentive for firms to add more lawyers to a legal matter (and bill more time). As suggested in Cartoon 2-12, this added to the sense that the abundance of lawyers was in fact a scourge.

Nonetheless, the depictions of an excessive supply of lawyers became overwhelming. The reproducing lawyer trope is a mainstay of lawyer humor, having long evoked the image of rat or cockroach infestation and dovetailed with themes of lawyers as corrupt, greedy, and lacking in moral fiber. Cartoons 2-13, 2-14 and 2-15 are just a few of many examples.

"I'm afraid you're retaining lawyers."

Cartoon 2-12 (cartoon 13—TCB 124660) Matthew Diffee/The New Yorker Collection/The Cartoon Bank

"They're cheaper in bulk."

Cartoon 2-13 (cartoon 42—TCB 121801) C. Covert Darbyshire/The New Yorker Collection/ The Cartoon Bank

This theme might recede. Starting in 2007, the story of the expanding legal community is no longer accurate. The market for legal services contracted dramatically during the recession that hit that year and has not rebounded with the rest of the economy, thus leading many to conclude that the legal profession has itself started to restructure and permanently contract. Perhaps consequently, law school applications dropped precipitously and law schools responded by reducing their class sizes. So, for the present time, U.S. law schools have hatched fewer new lawyers ready to enter the legal market. With fewer lawyers, one shouldn't be surprised that the too-many-lawyers narrative would recede.

But then again, the theme may rebound. Law school applications are now on the upswing. The need for lawyers may stay constant or even increase in the United States. Most U.S. lawyers are holding fast to a labor-intensive model of lawyering. Moreover, even if the country is entering a time of deregulation (with fewer laws to decipher), lawyerly skill and expertise are needed for dismantling as well as creating legal apparatus.

ATTORNEY
SIX-PACK

Cartoon 2-14 (cartoon 43—TCB 30465) Leo Cullum/The New Yorker Collection/The Cartoon Bank

"Would everyone check to see they have an attorney? I seem to have ended up with two."

Cartoon 2-15 (cartoon 41—TCB 34221) Michael Maslin/The New Yorker Collection/The Cartoon Bank

4. The Future of Lawyer Jokes

Consider the following lawyer joke, frequently occurring in scholarly studies, collections, and speeches:

Q: What's wrong with lawyer jokes?

A: Lawyers don't think they're funny and other people don't think they're jokes.[40]

A subtext of this joke is that most agree that lawyer jokes are really not funny. In the words of one scholarly study, law jokes fall into the category of "nonjokes, bad jokes, and near-humor."[41] That said, they apparently perform an expressive function, a function that the legal profession does not particularly relish: disapproval of how lawyers fail to meet expectations. In this way, lawyer jokes are what French philosopher Henri Bergson might describe as a means to ridicule deviations from established norms.

But one wonders whether lawyer jokes are an overblown rhetorical device, which no one really accepts as an accurate depiction of the profession. One might reasonably conclude that Americans do not believe lawyer jokes in the same way they embrace the truth of a joke belittling a politician they despise or a racist they wish to minimize. So why do the jokes continue to flourish? Perhaps the jokes tap into anxiety and animosity about how lawyers systematically default on their duty to society.

The structure of our legal system and the moral role associated with the "good lawyer" paradigm suggest that the conditions that have inspired lawyer jokes will remain: high-level expectations about how lawyers should act, the natural resentment inspired by dependency on expertise and fear of betrayal, irritation about common personality characteristics of lawyers, and occasional dereliction in lawyer performance.

Experts laud humor for its capacity to help individuals resolve their internal conflicts and process their fears. Perhaps, then, lawyer jokes will continue to serve that function and may unfortunately remain a key part of our culture. Yet, as one humor scholar has pointed out, "Not all humor reduces anxiety and not all anxiety-reduction is beneficial. Humor can help us cope with problems or deny them, inform or misinform."[42] Taking as a given that lawyer jokes come in part from authentic and accurate perceptions that lawyers do not perform their function properly, one should ask whether lawyer jokes can effect change. Will the jokes alter how the legal profession operates? At least some scholars take the upbeat attitude that lawyer jokes can have a self-correcting effect on the legal profession and can serve a pedagogical role in teaching ethics.[43] A look at humor about judges, juries, and the legal process may shed further light on the question of whether these jokes really can effect change.

B. JUDGES

Even if not prepared to admit it, Americans are of two minds when it comes to lawyers. The same love-hate attitude is true for American re-action to judges as well—although popular understanding of this ten-sion may be more upfront and conscious. On one hand, we embrace the Anglo-American tradition of holding judges in high esteem. We put them on high benches, dress them in flowing black robes hiding their street clothes, call them "Your Honor," and let them conduct most of their work in secret. We embrace severe sanctions for disobeying judges (civil and criminal contempt of court) and require that their judgments be protected by iron-clad finality principles. Yet we also speak of black robe disease, which infects judges with vanity, self-importance, and the expec-tation of unqualified respect. We ridicule our judges for taking themselves too seriously.

But humor about judges is not nearly as shrill or pointed as that leveled at lawyers. Maybe we cannot help but retain a measure of respect for those on high benches with black robes. Or, maybe, we do not want to lose our all-too-important hold on the rule of law. Most citizens likely understand on some level that when it comes to enforcing legal principles within the context of specific disputes, judges are working on the front lines of gov-ernment by rule of law. Whatever the explanation, one easily observes that jokes and other humor about judges are kinder than lawyer jokes, often taking judges on their own terms.

That said, one need not look far to observe American comedy having light hearted fun at the expense of judges. Gags like Cartoon 2-16 are abun-dant and easy to find.

Frivolity aside, cartoons generally chronicle a two-track outlook: a hat-tip to respect yoked with negative (tame, but unmistakably unflattering) images. Cartoons 2-17 and 2-18 depict a dominant trope: the vain judge.

> How many judges does it take to change a light bulb? Just one; he holds it still and the whole world revolves around him.[44]

Complementing the vanity theme is the judicial self-importance stereo-type. The connection between vanity and self-importance emerges in the following story, which may or may not have roots in a real event:

A distinguished member of the Boston bar was arguing before the full bench of appellate judges. The president judge stopped him, remarking brusquely, "That is not the law, counselor."

"I beg your honor's pardon," the attorney replied suavely. "It was the law before your honor spoke."[45]

Some judges might already have thought they were special human beings before they took the bench. Others who are not naturally narcissistic likely find it hard to resist internalizing years of heightened pandering from others. Self-important or not, a judge's rules of decorum require a proud bearing (serious affect) befitting the office of jurist. Thus the gag in Cartoon 2-19 arises from an incongruous blend of sensuality and the judicial patrician image.

Along with vanity and self-importance comes infallibility. Like the judge in Cartoon 2-20, judges themselves generally project a regard for themselves as infallible. And the public generally goes along with the fiction.

Mr. Schneider stood up in court. "As God is my judge, I do not owe my ex-wife any money." Glaring down at him, the judge replied, "He's not. I am. You do."[46]

"Recess is over, Your Honor."

Cartoon 2-16 (cartoon 12—TCB 29630) Mick Stevens/The New Yorker Collection/The Cartoon Bank

*"This court, featuring the unique judicial stylings of the
Honorable Jay Rallwell, is now in session."*

Cartoon 2-17 (cartoon 46—TCB 89571) Michael Maslin/The New Yorker Collection/The
Cartoon Bank

*"Before we begin today, may I say that both my client and I were
astonished that Your Honor was not nominated for the Supreme Court?"*

Cartoon 2-18 (cartoon 49—TCB-30220) James Stevenson/The New Yorker Collection/The
Cartoon Bank

"Your Honor, has anyone ever told you what a wry, sensuous mouth you have?"

Cartoon 2-19 (cartoon 47—TCB 43024) Michael Crawford/The New Yorker Collection/The Cartoon Bank

"And don't go whining to some higher court."

Cartoon 2-20 (cartoon 45—TCB 40329) Al Ross/The New Yorker Collection/The Cartoon Bank

Judges are, of course, human and fully capable of stumbling, but they have a difficult job and—absent misconduct—the United States has generally determined that we should not question their judgment and should embrace their integral contribution to government. But this embrace also requires an act of faith: once a case has made its way through the appeal process, the U.S. litigation system equates judicial decisions with truth. We all know in our heart that decisions do not necessarily equal unassailable truth: courts, even the highest court in the land, occasionally make horribly wrong decisions. But we do not lightly admit this. Why? For emotional and intellectual reasons, we want judges to be final. This helps to ensure that society is ruled by law (not force or other undue influence). Finality also helps to put a stop to litigation: Do we really want to devote huge chunks of our gross national product to litigating the same topic repeatedly? As Justice Jackson said of the U.S. Supreme Court, "[W]e are not final because we are infallible, we are infallible only because we are final." From the humor such as appears in Cartoons 2-21 and 2-22, many clearly believe that judges actively cultivate an appearance of infallible justice.

Perhaps to reinforce our struggle to accept judicial finality, Americans customarily indulge the myth that judges act only with dispassionate reason. Highly respected thinkers argue that law is inextricably entangled with emotion and that emotion often supports the principled administration of justice.[47] That sentiment, however, has not taken hold in lay American culture. As a consequence, the image of a judge showing a glimmer of grumpy humanity—as in Cartoon 2-23—is incongruous and worthy of a smile.

"If you please, Mr. Justice, would you mind not saying, 'Of course we could be wrong'?"

Cartoon 2-21 (cartoon 63—TCB 79852) Al Ross/The New Yorker Collection/The Cartoon Bank

"Let justice be served. Pass it on."

Cartoon 2-22 (cartoon 64—TCB 80616) Robert Weber/The New Yorker Collection/The Cartoon Bank

"Do you ever have one of those days when every-thing seems unconstitutional?"

Cartoon 2-23 (cartoon 65—TCB 35520) Joseph Mirachi/The New Yorker Collection/The Cartoon Bank

Occasionally a theme of corruption and bias comes through in the judge jokes:

> A lawyer passed on and found himself in Heaven, but not at all happy with his accommodations. He complained to St. Peter, who told him that his only recourse was to appeal his assignment. The lawyer immediately advised that he intended to appeal, but was then told that he would be waiting at least three years before his appeal could be heard. The lawyer protested that a three-year wait was unconscionable, but his words fell on deaf ears. The lawyer was then approached by the devil, who told him that he would be able to arrange an appeal to be heard in a few days, if the lawyer was willing to change venue to Hell. The lawyer asked: "Why can appeals be heard so much sooner in Hell?" The devil answered: "We have all of the judges."[48]

All this talk of dispassion, reason, and infallibility does not negate the possibility that—as Chapter 3 vividly displays—some judges have the impression they are not only funny but are the master of ceremonies for funny.

Finally, any overview of humor about judges would be deficient without mention of the laudatory riffs on Supreme Court Justice Ruth Bader Ginsburg (RBG). Starting around 2013, this octogenarian became a cult figure—particularly for young females. Reflecting this youthful enthusiasm were funny RBG attire and other paraphernalia offered for sale on the Internet, RBG Internet memes going viral, a tumblr account featuring permutations of her persona, a best-selling book (*Notorious RBG: The Life and Times of Ruth Bader Ginsburg*), a book of her workout routines published by her personal trainer, *Saturday Night Live* routines, and a parody rap video playing off the rapper, the Notorious B.I.G. Where's the humor here? Incongruity, again, provides a major explanation: a petite Jewish grandmother with a larger-than-life impact on legal progress juxtaposed with a 300-pound rapper with the nickname Biggie and rigorous workout routines.

C. JURIES

Jury trials in the United States occur in both criminal cases and civil cases between private persons. Required by the U.S. Constitution for non-petty offenses (which are those punishable by more than six months imprisonment), jury trials occur in state and federal courts. For federal courts, jury trials are also constitutionally required in some civil cases. The result is that juries are an important part of U.S. legal institutions and are commonplace in American life. One recent study concluded that approximately 154,000 jury trials occur in the United States each year. High-profile jury trials regularly grip the nation's imagination and provide frequent grist for television drama. Given the importance and pervasive occurrence of jury trials, one would expect them to attract many jokes. But humor does not always bear a relationship to society's most important and repeated events. Such is the case here: jury jokes are not that common.

To be sure, jokes, comedies, and cartoons about juries do appear throughout American culture. The prevalence of jury humor compares with judge humor—both falling well below the standard set by lawyer jokes. Humor about civil juries—as opposed to criminal ones—is especially sparse. This is particularly interesting because the civil jury has proven to be a prominent subject for serious popular dramas, with novels and movies invoking several character types for individual jurors, including the angry crusading juror, "the bribed or intimidated juror . . . the planted juror in a big tobacco lawsuit, the juror in mid-vendetta or love affair, and the juror out of his league or over his head."[49] Nonetheless, given the jury's importance in U.S. law and history, humor about the institution deserves attention. (Remarkably, jury jokes also appear in India—which does not even include trial by jury in its legal institutions.[50] Apparently, the compelling notion of judgment by peers transcends cultural and geographic boundaries.)

One wonders whether the low numbers of jury jokes result from the status of the jury system as a "sacred cow" of U.S. government or simply from its status as a trustworthy method for reaching just and accurate verdicts. A look at an overview of the jury-joke world as well as past and present thinking about juries may provide some insight. The universe of jury humor presents four separate portraits of jurors: (1) the stupid juror, (2) the lazy juror, (3) the misbehaving juror, and (4) the juror who injects good common sense into an otherwise ridiculous situation.[51] Only the fourth portrait—the common-sense juror—dovetails with generally accepted wisdom about the function and value of the U.S. jury. When viewed as a whole, the universe of juror jokes reflects the same types of contradictions and conflict that appear in other areas when humor intersects with law.

1. Stupid Jurors

As recently as the 1960s, local jury commissioners held considerable power over the composition of juries in the United States. Commissioners would ask prominent citizens in a particular community to name other prominent citizens to serve on juries—the proffered theory for this system being that jury service required intelligence, knowledge, and morality.[52] In practical effect, however, the system enabled courts to empanel all-white juries, allowing them to circumvent long-established U.S. Supreme Court constitutional rulings prohibiting race discrimination in the jury system. In the mid-1960s, Congress and the U.S. Supreme Court enforced a standard that did away with this commissioner system: juries must be selected from a fair cross section of the community. Putting vigor in this new standard, the Supreme Court made clear that lawyers would violate constitutional guarantees when they exercised peremptory strikes during jury selection on the basis of gender or race.

An interesting question is whether the practice in the jury commissioner system of cherry-picking "intelligent, knowledgeable, and moral" citizens suppressed jokes about the stupidity or ineptitude of jurors. After all, if jurors were all intelligent, knowledgeable, and moral, there would be no raw material for jokes, right? The answer to this question is "no." Indeed, the long-standing popularity of stupid juror jokes supports observations that the jury commissioner system not only failed to ensure that the highest quality juries decided cases, but also reinforced unconstitutional discrimination.

One finds stupid jury jokes in collections from as early as the late 1800s:

> An illiterate jury having spent hours reaching a verdict, one of the jurymen was asked what the trouble was:
>
> "Waal," he said, "six on 'em wanted to give the plaintiff $4,000, and six on 'em wanted to give him $3,000, so we split the difference and gave him $500."[53]

Also during this era, philosopher Herbert Spencer offered up the following quip:

> A jury is composed of twelve men of average ignorance.[54]

Along similar lines, Mark Twain said:

> We have a criminal jury system which is superior to any in the world; and its efficiency is only marked by the difficulty of finding twelve men every day who don't know anything and can't read.[55]

Although one might read Twain as critiquing only the difficulty of finding jurors who have not had previous exposure to the facts of a case, scholars have read that quote as reflecting the pejorative narrative that jurors lack the mental capacity to think beyond their own preconceptions. The trope of jurors as naïve and silly occasionally appears in contemporary comedy.

A defendant was asked if he wanted a bench trial or a jury trial. "Jury trial," the defendant replied.

"Do you understand the difference?" asked the judge.

"Sure," replied the defendant," [t]hat's where twelve ignorant people decide my fate instead of one."[56]

Because few citizens actually serve on juries, the public's impression of juries comes largely from popular culture. Interestingly, the public instinctively distrusts the accuracy of popular culture's image of juries. The following modern joke is built on the implication that television depicts jurors in an unreasonably favorable light:

The only difference between TV juries and real juries is 50 IQ points.[57]

Finally are the many contemporary jokes mixing the image of the stupid juror with an image of citizens trying to avoid jury duty:

"I can't serve on the jury duty because . . . I am either senile or mentally incompetent. I forget which."[58]

"I'm being judged by 12 people too dumb to get out of jury duty!"[59]

2. Lazy Jurors

The avoiding-jury-duty narrative depicted in these last two jokes is part of a greater theme of jurors who can't be bothered to muster the energy to do a proper job sifting and weighing evidence. Some of the gags—such as in Cartoon 2-24—depict unadorned laziness after becoming empaneled.

The lawyer for the prosecution had finished his closing argument, and the judge, a pompous and long-winded individual, was charging the jury. He was in the midst of an unusually long and tedious address when he suddenly noticed that one of the jurymen had fallen asleep. The indignation of his honor was boundless. Rapping sharply on his desk he awakened the slumberer, who seemed not at all abashed at being thus caught napping. After glaring at him angrily for a few moments, the magistrate in his most sarcastic tone said:

"So that's the way you attend to your duty, is it? You're a fine specimen to have on a jury. Do you think your opinion will be of any value when I send you out to determine the fate of this prisoner?"

"Yes, sir," said the juryman quietly, "I think so."

"Oh, you do, do you?" shouted the exasperated judge. "Pray, tell me, sir, how long have you been sleeping?"

"I don't know, your Honor," was the reply. "How long have you been talking?"[60]

While the sleeping or irresponsible juror image is common, this category's more dominant theme remains the various attempts to duck jury duty altogether.

> JUDGE: Is there any reason you could not serve as a juror in this case?
> JUROR: I don't want to be away from the job that long.
> JUDGE: Can't they do without you at work?
> JUROR: Yes, but I don't want them to know that.[61]

The notion that everyone wants to avoid jury duty pops up as a theme outside the formal joke world as well. Take, for example, Tina Fey's *30 Rock* character, Liz Lemon, showing up for jury duty dressed as Princess Leia—under the theory that she'd never make it onto a jury in such a getup. Even

*"In a concerted effort to get home for the holidays,
we find the defendant guilty, as charged."*

Cartoon 2-24 (cartoon 51—TCB 75912) Henry Martin/The New Yorker Collection/The Cartoon Bank

the *New York Daily News* ran a story cataloguing mildly amusing excuses for getting out of jury duty:

- "I have a weak bladder."
- "Jury duty might interfere with my upcoming 'boob job.'"
- "I only trust one lawyer, and he is dead."[62]

An interesting twist on the avoiding-jury-duty motif appeared in the 1995 film *Jury Duty*, starring Pauly Shore. Shore played an unemployed man who seeks out jury duty as a source of income, room, and board. Pursuing this goal, Shore uses a variety of tactics to get himself off juries for short cases so as to secure a place on a jury where he would be sequestered for a lengthy period of time. How does he do this? He performs the outrageous stunts such as pulling a fake prosthesis from his arm during jury selection in an orthopedic malpractice case and feigning recognition of an embezzlement defendant. This tomfoolery succeeds in landing him a place on the jury in a lengthy homicide trial. Integrating a contrastingly favorable portrait of juries into the movie, the movie ends with Pauly Shore uncovering a plot to frame the defendant, ensuring that truth carries the day.

3. Misbehaving Jurors

Forms of juror misbehavior include engaging in private contact with key trial participants during the trial, inappropriate exposure to news accounts and other extraneous material during the trial, harboring actual bias against one of the case parties, prejudging case facts, making improper statements during the proceedings, and failing to apply the law as the court instructs. Each of these sins is reflected in U.S. jury humor.

For comedy drawn from real life, consider the "extrajudicial" tweets by comedian Steve Martin, sent while he was serving as a prospective juror. Using his Twitter handle @SteveMartinToGo, Martin tweeted:

"Report from Jury Duty: defendant looks like a murderer. GUILTY. Waiting for opening remarks."

When a follower tweeted back that he may get in trouble for the tweet, Martin replied:

"(I'm kidding) Shhhh . . ."

But then Martin started up again:

"REPORT FROM JURY DUTY: guy I thought was up for murder turns out to be defense attorney. I bet he murdered someone anyway."[63]

No word on whether Martin was actually picked for the jury or got in trouble with the judge.

A significant theme in misbehaving juror jokes are jurors who refuse to convict obviously guilty defendants. Consider the following joke as well as Cartoon 2-25:

> I was recently chosen as foreman for the jury I was on. We ended up acquitting the defendant. When we came back into the courtroom the judge yelled at us, "How were you able to acquit?" "Insanity," I replied. "All 12 of you?" he retorted.[64]

> Foreman of the Jury—"We find the culprit Not Guilty, but we recommend him not to do it again."[65]

*"Ask the judge whether we can find the defendant
not guilty and still execute him."*

Cartoon 2-25 (cartoon 52—TCB 44049) Peter Steiner/The New Yorker Collection/The Cartoon Bank

Similar jokes depict a jury that not only decides not to follow the judge's instructions, but refuses to enter a verdict at all:

> The jury was out for three hours in a very dramatic case. A husband had shot his wife's lover, but only grazed his arm. The jury returned to the jury box and everyone in the courtroom awaited the verdict with bated breath.
>
> The foreman of the jury, Mr. Tepperman, stood up. The judge asked the foreman whether they had reached a verdict.
>
> "Yes," shrugged Mr. Tepperman, "we decided not to butt in!"[66]

Here's a related anecdote from an opinion piece in the *New York Times*:

> I couldn't find the reference, but in school we were told that a very poor man whose family was starving stole a pig from a rich man. The jury said, "Not guilty if he returns the pig." The judge refused to accept the verdict, and the jury reconvened and returned with, "Not guilty and he can keep the pig."[67]

Refusal to convict in the face of obvious evidence and refusal to render a verdict are examples of jury nullification, a practice defined as the refusal of a jury to apply the law as the court instructed. Nullification has its critics and its defenders. On one hand is the view that jury nullification is a lawless travesty of justice, inviting chaos and anarchy. On the other hand are those who observe that nullification can correct flaws in the litigation system, flaws that might include an overzealous prosecution or crimes that are unpopular or outdated (and thus do not reflect public sentiment about what constitutes punishable, i.e., morally despicable, conduct). Sometimes the jury might simply ignore the letter of the law because of an equitable factor unique to the case—such as sympathetic facts about the defendant or damning facts about the plaintiff.[68] These jury nullification jokes are therefore iconic examples of humor providing a vehicle for reckoning with our legal system's messy contradictions.

Interestingly, the phenomenon of the hung jury, which occurs when jurors fail to agree on a verdict, does not usually make its way into the humor world. The hung jury topic reflects uncomfortable schisms in our nation, particularly those based on race. Scholarly studies have often tracked disagreements among jurors in criminal cases to racial differences among jurors—with issues of mass incarceration and tensions between law enforcement and the black community hanging in the balance.[69] Traditional humor shies from this delicate topic—although plenty of younger comedians are taking it on.

This is where the contradiction comes in: the misbehaving juror gags that do flourish—along with lazy and stupid juror jokes—are at odds with a long-held account of juries in American society. Americans are repeatedly taught that jury duty performs an important civil function not only for the jurors but also for the administration of justice itself. Only the fourth category of jury gags—the common-sense juror—fully displays and pokes at the edges of this conventional narrative about the importance of juries,

4. Common-Sense Jurors

Law, history, and theoretical analysis all depict the U.S. jury system in a relatively favorable light. To be sure, critics have identified flaws and failures, but the cultural account of the institution is generally quite positive and can take on a mythical quality. This rosy view may find its roots in thinking that gave rise to Alexis de Tocqueville's depiction of the jury as a crucible of democratic development in the United States:

> The institution of the jury raises the people itself—or at least a class of citizens—with the direction of society. . . . The jury . . . serves to communicate the spirit of the judges to the minds of all the citizens and this spirit, with the habits which attend it, is the soundest preparation for free institutions. . . . The jury contributes powerfully [to] . . . increase the natural intelligence of a people. . . . It may be regarded as a gratuitous public school, ever open, in which every juror learns his rights, enters into daily communication with the most learned and enlightened members of the upper class, and becomes practically acquainted with the laws.[70]

The two themes that emerge from Tocqueville's description—the jury institution as educator and the jury institution as a vehicle for ensuring that the public becomes engaged in self-governance—have not made their way into jury humor. Nor has another somewhat grandiose view that the jury system stands as "a symbol of popular assent to the law."[71] What has, however, emerged as a positive theme in jury humor is the notion that the collective wisdom of the jury provides an effective mechanism for identifying the best result for resolving a particular human problem.

> I was married by a judge. I should have asked for a jury.
>
> —Groucho Marx[72]

Another important theme in U.S. law and culture holds that juries act as an important check against judges and lawyers—two agents that dominate the trial process. The jury mechanism is often held up as protection against a local justice system that may be prejudiced against a party or infected with corruption. As stated in the U.S. Supreme Court decision extending the federal

"His logic certainly isn't my logic."

Cartoon 2-26 (cartoon 57—TCB 79666) Al Ross/The New Yorker Collection/The Cartoon Bank

criminal jury trial right to those prosecuted in state systems, "providing an accused with the right to be tried by a jury of his peers gave him an inestimable safeguard against the corrupt or overzealous prosecutor and against the compliant, biased, or eccentric judge."[73] In so holding, the Court noted the history of American confidence in community sensibilities and man-on-the-street perceptions reflected in the jury system: "If the defendant preferred the common sense judgment of a jury to the more tutored but perhaps less sympathetic reaction of the single judge, he was to have it."[74] Jury jokes reflect these views, particularly as they relate to overbearing or corrupt lawyers and judges.

Jurors' skill in penetrating lawyerly spin efforts appears in both cartoons and jokes. Cartoon 2-26 is a good example.

A noted criminal defense lawyer was making the closing argument for his client accused of murder, although the body of the victim had never been found. The lawyer dramatically turned to the courtroom's clock, and pointing to it, announced, "Ladies and gentlemen of the jury, I have some astounding news. I have found the supposed victim of this murder to be alive! In just ten seconds, she will walk through the door of this courtroom."

A heavy quiet suddenly fell over the courtroom as everyone waited for the dramatic entry. But nothing happened.

The smirking lawyer continued, "The mere fact that you were watching the door, expecting the victim to walk into this courtroom, is clear proof that you have far more than even a reasonable doubt as to whether a murder was actually committed." Tickled with the impact of his cleverness, the cocky lawyer confidently sat down to await acquittal.

The jury was instructed, filed out, and filed back in just ten minutes with a guilty verdict. When the judge brought the proceedings to an end, the dismayed lawyer chased after the jury foreman: "Guilty? How could you convict? You were all watching the door!"

"Well," the foreman explained, "Most of us were watching the door. But one of us was watching the defendant, and he wasn't watching the door."[75]

Common-sense juror jokes that depict jurors thinking for themselves—as opposed to listening to the judge or the judge's instructions—are a close cousin of jury nullification jokes. A classic example is this joke about a Tennessee jury evaluating the guilt of a man charged with stealing a mule:

As the proof developed in the trial, the evidence was rather overwhelming that the man in fact did steal the mule. But the proof also showed that the defendant was basically an honorable and decent fellow who was really down on his luck and desperately needed the mule to help him on his family farm.

After deliberating, the jury returned and the foreman announced the verdict: "Not guilty, but he has to give back the mule."

The wise and learned judge said, "Ladies and gentlemen of the jury, I must reject your verdict. It is an inconsistent verdict, and I must request that you resume your deliberations and return a consistent verdict."

The jurors looked at one another and then filed back into the jury room. Five minutes later they returned.

"Have you reached another verdict?" inquired the judge.

"Yes, we have, Your Honor," reported the foreman. "Not guilty and he can keep that mule!"[76]

This notion of the jury as counterweight to judge and lawyer is buttressed by the belief that American citizens possess an independent spirit allowing them both the capacity for introspection and a valuable aversion to the tyranny of being told what one must do. Cartoon 2-27 pays homage to this wisdom.

The depiction of the common-sense juror not only harmonizes with history, practice, and culture but is also supported by legal academic literature, which brims with jury behavior studies. The array of academic models is dizzying: they include schemes based on theories of social judgment, social interaction, Bayesian and algebraic models, stochastic models (integrating time measurement), story-focused models, and cognitive prototypes—just

"But in a larger sense aren't we all guilty?"

Cartoon 2-27 (cartoon 54—TCB 81917) Charles Saxon/The New Yorker Collection/The Cartoon Bank

to name a few.[77] The forces fueling this outpouring of academic energy are complicated but likely include the great stakes posed by civil juries for companies facing potentially huge punitive verdicts, the importance of criminal juries in evaluating whether a defendant's conduct calls for a loss of liberty, and the enormous attorney fee potential generated by steep jury verdicts. Interestingly, the academic models reflect more sophisticated and nuanced analysis than the historical celebrations of the jury system, yet they generally reflect the same upbeat perspective about juries.

Most significantly, studies highlight the beneficial qualities of group decision making, although they do not necessarily embrace the folk judgment that jury verdicts reflect "collective wisdom" per se. Instead, the studies suggest that the procedures followed in jury deliberations may in fact yield a result superior to that which individual decision making might have produced.

An outpouring of analytical studies provides an encouraging snapshot of the efficacy of jury deliberations, suggesting that jurors' exchange of information during deliberation can contribute to enhance verdict accuracy by

(1) improving the jury's recall of the trial evidence, (2) enhancing juror understanding of and adherence to the judge's instructions, and (3) improving jurors' ability to draw accurate inferences from evidence.[78] An empirical study by the American Bar Association within the last decade adds to this positive view by confirming that citizens continue to support and have confidence in the jury system.[79] This raises a question: Given the strength of the jury's pedigree as an institution and its continuing support among the American public, what accounts for the unfavorable images of lack of sophistication, bias, and bullheadedness appearing in the other categories of jury humor surveyed above?

> From this perspective, jury jokes (like judge and lawyer jokes) provide a mechanism to work through the incongruity that arises when comparing the importance of juries to the realities of their performance (performance that sometimes reflects bias, incompetence, parochialism, and dysfunction). Conflicting sentiments held by members of the American public supply the answer for why we can ridicule juries, but also hold them in high esteem. When asked to give the "right answer" about their view of the jury system, the average American would likely repeat the traditional praise: juries serve truth, democracy, and the like. And for those concerned about the relationship between race and law enforcement, the jury system may provide a corrective mechanism and an opportunity for those who actually have the benefit of jury duty to hear about alternative perspectives. If juries are truly drawn from a cross-section of the community, particularly in urban areas, the experience of jury service allows those from different walks of life to hear the thoughts of those from different backgrounds.[80]

With an eye on continuing these positive consequences of the jury system, we are willing to chuckle and dismiss occasional hiccups in the system. When compared to jokes about the "oligarchic judicial branch," jury jokes are even less numerous and even more tame. After all, "ordinary citizens" hardly invoke the type of resentment that might arise from confronting a vain, autocratic being such as a judge. As far as comparisons are concerned, however, lawyers land on the bottom. Research reveals no dead judge jokes, no dead juror jokes, but buckets full of dead lawyer jokes.

D. GENDER, RACE, AND SEXUAL ORIENTATION MEET HUMOR AND THE LAW

Full consideration of humor about participants in the U.S. legal system should probe questions of gender, race, and sexual orientation. Humor about female lawyers, judges, and jurors has notable trends—providing raw material for discussion. Humor about lawyers, judges, and jurors of color, however, is mostly lacking. And there are almost no jokes dealing with the sexual orientation of legal participants. Those that exist are predictable and (usually) viciously mean.

1. Gender

a. Female Lawyers

Over the past forty years, women have entered the legal profession in large numbers; at times, the ratio of women to men in entering law school classes is close to even. While this represents substantial progress, gender equality among lawyers is far from complete. Women face conscious and unconscious forces that prevent them from enjoying the same success as men in navigating a legal career. Jokes and cartoons about female lawyers don't tend to move the needle of progress on this issue. At best, the humor reflects double-edged cultural attitudes that celebrate the potential contributions of women in the legal profession but also risk reinforcing stereotypes and cabining women in limited roles. The past and current trends in this humor send plenty of mixed messages.

One early theme reflected in humor about lady lawyers focused, unsurprisingly, on sexuality. A number of factors could explain the source of the jokes. First, the women's sexuality theme provided a handy trope for releasing anxieties about sex as a general matter. Or a desire to cast female lawyers in an unprofessional light may have motivated the impulse to associate them with sex. After all, as late as 1873, the U.S. Supreme Court upheld prohibitions on women holding law licenses, stating: "The paramount destiny and mission of woman are to fulfil the noble and benign offices of wife and mother. This is the law of the Creator. And the rules of civil society must be adapted to the general constitution of things, and cannot be based upon exceptional cases."[81] A more refined explanation is reflected in the following cartoon: the early lady-lawyer gags sprang from the belief that the serious profession of law is inconsistent with a dominant social construction of women's identity: the ability to gratify male sexual desire. Check out Cartoon 2-28: dated but still telling, no?

The idea that the most important characteristic for a female lawyer is not professional merit but physical desirability also appears in the following joke:

> Three young women have all been working eighty-hour weeks for six straight years in the struggle to make partner in the law firm, and the cutoff date is fast approaching. Each one

"Do you know Kimberly, my attorney?"

Cartoon 2-28 (cartoon 59—TCB 33803) Edward Franscino/The New Yorker Collection/The Cartoon Bank

is brainy, talented, and ambitious but there's only room for one new partner. At a loss as to which one to pick, the senior officer finally devises a little test. One day, while all three are out to lunch, he places an envelope containing $500 on each of their desks.

The first woman returns the envelope to him immediately.

The second woman invests the money in the market and returns $1500 to him the next morning.

The third woman pockets the cash.

So which one gets the promotion to partner? The one with the biggest tits![82]

This same message arguably also appears in Cartoon 2-29.

An assumed inconsistency between the concept of "blonde" and the concept of "lawyer" is perhaps reflected in the following joke:

Q: What do you get when you cross a blonde with a lawyer?
A: I don't know. There are some things even a blonde won't do.[83]

"I'd like to have myself declared legally blonde."

Cartoon 2-29 (cartoon 58—TCB 22412) Leo Cullum/The New Yorker Collection/The Cartoon Bank

In some instances, this theme of an apparent incongruity between being an attorney and a true woman can be seen in jokes suggesting that a determined female lawyer is not capable of maintaining a healthy romantic and family life:

> The lawyer and her husband were having a late dinner one night.
>
> "I just don't understand," she said. "The law specifically states one thing, yet Judge Asherman made a point of disallowing—"
>
> "Honey," said her husband, "for once—just once—why can't we talk about something other than the law and a case you're working on?"
>
> "I'm sorry," she said. "What would you like to talk about?"
>
> "How about sex?"
>
> "Okay," she said. After a moment, she asked, "How often do you think Judge Asherman has sex?"[84]

These gags reflect the lose-lose knot for female attorneys: if a woman is sufficiently seductive, then she's not a fully performing professional; if she's the pit bull that competent legal practice requires, she fails as a true woman.[85] Query whether that is the message of Cartoon 2-30.

Other joke themes about woman lawyers complement this tension between aggressiveness and sexual attractiveness. A particularly common trope is the young she-lawyer, whether the lawyer is depicted as an ingénue or otherwise.

Is Cartoon 2-31 disparaging to female lawyers? Or is it just a harmless pun? Hard to say: it is not exactly hit-you-over-the-head insulting, but it certainly doesn't celebrate the strength, good judgment, and competency of women either.

How about Cartoon 2-32? Does it present a more favorable image?

By standard dictionary definition, "plucky" means courageous—surely an admirable quality for a trial attorney. But a patronizing message emerges as well—not to mention the suggestion that a perky and spirited demeanor might be a safe choice for young women trying to navigate the rough waters of sexuality and professional competency.

Cartoon 2-30 (cartoon 60—TCB 38582) Danny Shanahan/The New Yorker Collection/The Cartoon Bank

"Do you need more time to prepare, counselor?"

Cartoon 2-31 (cartoon 14—TCB 119472) Danny Shanahan/The New Yorker Collection/The Cartoon Bank

To be fair, the dominance of young female lawyer figures in U.S. popular culture has accurately reflected legal profession demographics. Prior to the 1970s, few women even attempted to enter the profession. This was followed by an influx of women into law school—an increase that evened out at the end of the millennium. With this development, one would therefore expect that, at least for a time, the women in the profession were indeed mostly young. But the image of the young, fresh-faced female lawyer has remained.

As it turns out, this continues to reflect the current reality. An unexpected wrinkle developed because experienced female lawyers started to leave the profession, so that a large proportion of female lawyers continued to be those who are right out of law school. According to 2012 American Bar Association statistics, women received over 47 percent of the law degrees and held 45 percent of the associate positions in law firms but comprised only 20 percent of the law firm partners (only 15 percent of the equity partners).[86] Statistics further document that a greater percentage of women than men leave all types of law practice after entering the profession.[87]

*"If it please the court, I'd like to act as my own
plucky young female attorney."*

Cartoon 2-32 (cartoon 61—TCB 122488) Paul Noth/The New Yorker Collection/The Cartoon Bank

The exodus of women is a matter of considerable concern to legal profession leaders. Some note bias that female lawyers encounter when they return to work after having a child: assignments change, as supervising attorneys assume that the maternal lawyer prefers not to take cases requiring travel. Others note unequal compensation for men and women. This is a disparity exacerbated by the underrepresentation of women who move laterally among law firms or corporations—lateral movement being an important factor that increases a lawyer's pay.[88] A more general source of women's departure from the profession is the tenacious (old-fashioned) culture in law practice that adheres to the assumption that a professional has a spouse at home who takes care of life's mundane errands and unforeseen complications.[89] Of course, many women manage to juggle these home tasks along with their professional duties. Nonetheless, those who "do it all"—serve as mother, wife, housekeeper, and lawyer without interruption for years—are not usually honored with awards or monuments for doing so. With the possible exception of parodies celebrating the Notorious RBG (Ruth Bader Ginsburg), these women are also rarely reflected in jokes or other humor forms.

Gender wars continue. Any suggestion that they are absent from the legal profession is dispelled by the persistence of glass ceilings and scandals about a sexist legal culture that bubble up. As recently as 2015, revelations appeared that a justice of Pennsylvania's highest court repeatedly shared with judicial colleagues misogynistic jokes about women, including such gems as the following:

> "Have you heard the joke about the domestic-violence victim who is urged by her doctor to just keep her mouth shut?"

> Photo of a topless woman captioned: "Dear Abby: I'm an 18-year-old girl from Arkansas and I'm still a virgin. Do you think my brothers are gay?"[90]

With developments like this, one can expect female legal professionals as well as contemporary consumers of humor about female lawyers to scrutinize the message carefully. Perhaps it will be some time before we can expect with frequency to see a classic disparage-the-lawyer gag—such as in Cartoon 2-33—where the lawyers' genders appear to reflect no special message or assumption. Men and women. They are just part of the same picture.

"Listen. It's at the quiet moments like this that you can actually hear the meter running."

Cartoon 2-33 (cartoon 39—TCB 43341) Leo Cullum/The New Yorker Collection/The Cartoon Bank

b. Female Judges

The number of women who serve as judges in the United States has increased slowly over the last several decades. As things now stand, the percentage of judges who are female has not broken 35 percent and will not do so any time soon. Interestingly, though, women are well represented as judges in the *New Yorker* cartoons as well as in popular culture dramas. In fact, several analysts have observed that female judges feature as prominently, if not more so, in television dramas and reality television shows as male judges.[91] Nonetheless, female judges are not well represented in jokes, comedy routines, and other forms of humor. To evaluate traditional humor about female judges, the *New Yorker* cartoons are an instructive source of data.

But it turns out that the gender message from the cartoons is ambiguous. Upon reviewing them, one often wonders: "I don't know if this advances the progress of women in the profession, but I guess it's funny." Viewing the various jokes as a whole, one sees an internal battle at work: if female judges are committed to formal legal principle, they are unduly rigid; if they show insight into the feelings of others, they are unprofessionally "familiar" in relating to litigants and subject to inappropriate emotional influence. Cartoon 2-34 arguably depicts this double-bind.

"What are you—some kind of justice freak?"

Cartoon 2-34 (cartoon 62—TCB 33227) Danny Shanahan/The New Yorker Collection/The Cartoon Bank

Whatever mindset one embraces, most will likely agree that humor highlighting a female judge's gender does not tend to reflect a progressive attitude. Other than that, the data are too thin to support definitive conclusions.

c. Female Jurors

Until the end of the twentieth century, comedy about female jurors had a predictable, pejorative theme, highlighting women as naïve, uncritical, confused, and preoccupied with trivial matters.

The following comes from a 1915 collection of jokes:

"Mabel, I'm drawn on the grand jury."

"So am I, Gertrude."

"Our responsibilities will be heavy."

"I realize that. What shall we wear?"[92]

The same theme appears in two cartoons from the period 1950–1970: Cartoon 2-35 and Cartoon 2-36.

The stereotype of the flighty female juror seems to have dissipated in contemporary U.S. culture, although it has not disappeared. Consider the following joke from a current website, reflecting a juror who is blinded by her sense of justice and confused about the difference between criminal cases (brought by government to vindicate criminal violations) and civil cases (generally brought by private parties to recover remedies for wrongs committed by another private party):

Mrs. Hunter was called to serve for jury duty, but asked to be excused because she didn't believe in capital punishment and didn't want her personal thoughts to prevent the trial from running its proper course. But the public defender liked her thoughtfulness and tried to convince her that she was appropriate to serve on the jury.

"Madam," he explained, "this is not a murder trial! It's a simple civil lawsuit. A wife is bringing this case against her husband because he gambled away the $12,000 he had promised to use to remodel the kitchen for her birthday."

"Well, okay," agreed Mrs. Hunter, "I'll serve. I guess I could be wrong about capital punishment after all!"[93]

The bottom line of this survey: humor about lawyers, judges, and jurors tracks general attitudes toward gender outside the legal world. Some progress, but more is needed.

*"I've already made up my mind. Will it be all
right if I go out and have my hair done?"*

Cartoon 2-35 (cartoon 56—TCB 95051) Robert J. Day/The New Yorker Collection/The
Cartoon Bank

*"I don't listen to the
evidence. I like to make up my own mind."*

Cartoon 2-36 (cartoon 55—TCB 46294) Perry Barlow/The New Yorker Collection/The
Cartoon Bank

2. Race

The story for race and humor about law is even more dispiriting. Traditional sources of humor about the law such as the *New Yorker* rarely mention questions of race. To the extent that systematic study of cartoon content exists, reports document that the underrepresentation of women and people of color is striking.[94] Plenty of incisive commentary about race and politics is offered, but the raw material of comedy is limited. The usual contexts for humor about law poke at lawyers, juries, judges, and civil proceedings but have little racial content. One initial explanation might be found in the relatively low numbers of minorities who have entered the legal profession. Only recently have the percentages of minority law students broken through the 20 percent ceiling. One could also speculate that general discomfort about racial issues and guilt regarding the tradition of slavery and institutional racism embossed on our history inspires professional humorists to tread lightly and to steer clear of racial contexts. To be sure, television and the Internet occasionally depict a few minority members of the legal profession in situation comedies and the like. We can also see a black judge or two in cartoons—or (as in Cartoon 2-37) a juror of color as an attempt to represent the "fair cross-section of the community" requirement in visual humor about jurors. But are we really reckoning with these issues?

Starting perhaps in the late 1980s and early 1990s, mainstream media started to take some risk on jokes about race and law. Particularly notable is Jackie Chiles, the lawyer for Kramer on *Seinfeld.* Chiles appeared to be modeled on the black trial lawyer Johnnie Cochran. Cochran was well known especially for his catchy phrases—perhaps most famously his rhyme during closing argument at the homicide trial of O. J. Simpson: "If the glove doesn't fit, you must acquit." The fictional Chiles was likewise known for colorful, often rhythmic zingers:

> Rugged? The man's a goblin. He's only been exposed to smoke for four days. By the time this case gets to trial, he'll be nothing more than a shrunken head.

> Yeah, that's going to be a problem. It's gonna be a problem for them. This a clear violation of your rights as a consumer. It's an infringement on your constitutional rights. It's outrageous, egregious, preposterous.

> That's totally inappropriate. It's lewd, lascivious, salacious, outrageous.[95]

The Chiles character on *Seinfeld* may have been a touch edgy then, but times have begun to change. Comments on race and law are now more common in popular culture riffs, reinvigorated by new media forms such

"Your Honor, we're going to go with the prosecution's spin."

Cartoon 2-37 (cartoon 53—TCB 36774) Mike Twohy/The New Yorker Collection/The Cartoon Bank

as Internet entertainment and cable television, which regularly present satirical and racially charged legal humor. These flourishing media routinely present incisive, funny, and sometimes lacerating routines about disparate treatment of minorities within the criminal justice system. Dave Chappelle has done a lot of creative work on the subject, contrasting racialized treatment of those accused of insider trading as compared with those accused of drug crimes,[96] parodying race issues in jury selection,[97] and the like. Key & Peele have often riffed on police harassment and brutality (e.g., freedom from oppression in Negrotown),[98] as have the late Richard Pryor (e.g., life with chokeholds),[99] Chris Rock (e.g., staying out of trouble during a traffic stop),[100] Larry Wilmore (e.g., racial profiling),[101] John Oliver (e.g., mandatory minimums),[102] and the television show *Boondocks* (police view black victim as a perpetrator).[103] And then there's Jay Z's *99 Problems, but a Bitch Ain't One.* The rap is certainly not slapstick, but it has playful twists (as well as accurate depictions of the incentives for drug couriers and police officers created by car search jurisprudence).[104]

One unfortunate place where race intersects with humor and the law appears in racist humor by judges. The 2005 scandal involving a Pennsylvania Supreme Court justice exposed racist jokes along with sexist jokes.[105] Striking even closer to the core of U.S. legal identity was a 2012 outrage over a federal court judge making a racist joke regarding President Obama.[106] The federal judge apologized for his actions, vaguely defending himself by noting the joke derived from his dislike of Obama, not Obama's race. In a manner similar to misogynistic jokes, racist jokes create enormously difficult conditions for persons of color navigating the justice system as lawyers, jurors, or litigants, more difficult than conditions confronted by those who are not the butt of such humor.

To the extent that professionally produced humor on race and the law exists, the humor tends to be confined to the criminal context and highly satirical. As explored at the end of this chapter, opinions differ on whether satire can effect social change. But whatever one's view on that debate, satire at least breaks the silence and gets issues into the public debate. It may be a long time before we see frolicky, light hearted humor about how law and race intersect. I look forward to that time.

E. THE LEGAL SYSTEM AND LEGAL TEXTS

Jokes about the legal system as a whole are revered in the United States. We usually celebrate them as important political critique. In fact, courts and legislatures have ramped up legal protections for this humor. Law has culture's back here. Within legal analysis, the law injects First Amendment principles with steroids when we are asked to protect a communication that criticizes government, including that part of government featuring legal process. Some might even call First Amendment protection of political speech a constitutional fetish. Fetish or not, this protective instinct is ours. Whatever one's opinion on how deeply Americans admire humor about our legal system, the end result is robust comical jabs about something we care about enormously. The contradictory strands of celebration and disappointment weave through this comedy to the same degree as with humor about lawyers, judges, and jurors—perhaps even more.

Cracks about legal texts (opinions, statutes, constitutional provisions), which are the muscular structure of law, have a different character from sallies at the specific human players in the legal game (lawyers, jurors, and judges). Comedy about legal texts usually derives from frustration about complexity, vagueness, and the difficulty of compliance with a byzantine legal realm. As earlier noted, the language of the Constitution is a frequent target. Here's a riff on its faults:

> If overspecificity is the Scylla of legal drafting, excessive vagueness is the Charybdis.
> I fear that [constitutional drafters] Madison and Morris have come to grief on the latter's

rocky shoals. Some of the vital provisions in their document are couched in terms so general that women and men can only guess at their meaning. What, after all, constitutes the "general Welfare of the United States," interstate and foreign "Commerce," the "Privileges and Immunities of Citizens in the several States," or a "Republican form of Government"?[107]

This satirical complaint reflects a quality of angst different from what one observes with comedy about the human limitations of lawyers, judges, and jurors. Yet, as an umbrella topic, humor about legal texts is aptly joined with jabs at legal actors. The end product is a message we've heard before: the humor suggests that Americans have a contradictory reaction to law. For the purpose of the legal process and legal texts, we should appreciate that humans generally love the structure and guidance provided by rules, even if they don't want to admit it. To have rules that provide comfort, you need them to provide a fair and thorough approach. Under the U.S. legal orientation, that means lots of rules. Lots of rules means frustration from having to navigate all of the rules. Legal drafters can avoid a rat's nest of complicated rules by using broad language such as "a Republican form of government" or the "general Welfare of the United States." But we've already seen that that too inspires frustration. As reflected immediately below, the complex structure of legal procedures presents a similar dilemma.

1. The Legal System

In a society with rampant litigation and a tangle of difficult rules that govern citizens' lives, one expects humor culture to include robust mockery of the legal system. And so it is with American humor. The comedy tends to focus separately on defects in the system itself and the complexity of legal rules that govern life in the United States.

When it comes to humor about the legal process, the spotlight is generally trained on litigation. It's as if Americans generally find the tomfoolery and complications in the legislative process to be something that is just accepted in life. That said, one does see a glimpse of vexation about what occurs in legislatures as a bill becomes a law—see Cartoon 2-38.

But it is lawsuits—filed in court, pursued by lawyers, supervised by judges, and evaluated by juries—that most catch the attention of American humorists. The straightforward legal jokes about the litigation system often suggest corruption and incompetence. Lawyers bribing judges, jurors who are paid off, undue influence on any participant in the judicial process available for compromise, all these are a focus of jokes and cartoons, such as

Cartoon 2-38 (cartoon 70—TCB 142327) Edward Steed/The New Yorker Collection/The Cartoon Bank

Cartoon 2-39. At the height of a political corruption trial, the prosecuting attorney attacked a witness. "Isn't it true," he bellowed, "that you accepted five thousand dollars to compromise this case?"

> The witness stared out the window, as though he hadn't heard the question.
>
> "Isn't it true that you accepted five thousand dollars to compromise this case?" the lawyer repeated.
>
> The witness still did not respond.
>
> Finally, the judge leaned over and said, "Sir, please answer the question."
>
> "Oh," the startled witness said, "I thought he was talking to you."[108]

> Taking his seat in his chambers, the judge faced the opposing lawyers. "So," he said, "I have been presented, by both of you, with a bribe." Both lawyers squirmed uncomfortably. "You, attorney Leon, gave me $15,000. And you, attorney Campos, gave me $10,000." The judge reached into his pocket and pulled out a check. He handed it to Leon. . . . "Now then, I 'm returning $5,000, and we're going to decide this case solely on its merits."[109]

"Objection."

Cartoon 2-39 (cartoon 50—TCB 136942)   Liam Frances Walsh/The New Yorker Collection/The Cartoon Bank

Here are two more joke examples:

A prosecuting attorney called his first witness, a grandmotherly, elderly woman, to the stand. He approached her and asked, "Mrs. Jones, do you know me?" She responded, "Why, yes, I do know you, Mr. Williams. I've known you since you were a young boy. And frankly, you've been a big disappointment to me. You lie, you cheat on your wife, you manipulate people and talk about them behind their backs. You think you are a rising big shot when you haven't the brains to realize you never will amount to anything more than a two-bit paper pusher. Yes, I know you." The lawyer was stunned.

Not knowing what else to do he pointed across the room and asked, "Mrs. Williams, do you know the defense attorney?" She again replied, "Why, yes I do. I've known Mr. Bradley since he was a youngster, too. I used to baby-sit him for his parents. And he, too, has been a real disappointment to me. He's lazy, bigoted, he has a drinking problem. The man can't build a normal relationship with anyone, and his law practice is one of the shoddiest in the entire state. Yes, I know him."

At this point, the judge rapped the courtroom to silence and called both counselors to the bench. In a very quiet voice, he said with menace, "If either of you asks her if she knows me, you'll be jailed for contempt!"[110]

After . . . years of assisting more senior attorneys at trial, a young lawyer was finally allowed to try a case on her own. Determined not to lose, she prepared furiously.

The trial went on for eight exhausting days. Finally, the case went to the jury, which quickly returned with a verdict in favor of her client.

Ecstatic, the attorney phoned the firm's managing partner, and the moment he was on the line announced, "It's me! The jury just came back, and justice has prevailed!"

The managing partner gasped, stammering, "Appeal at once."[111]

Another theme suggests law is steeped in general depravity that infects the entire trial process:

"You must have listened to so much law in the past week that you are almost a lawyer yourself now."

"Yes," said the juryman, "I am so full of law that I'm going to find it hard to keep from cheating people after I get back to business."[112]

The advantage of access to skilled legal counsel—not available to all—is another common point of contention:

The jury consists of twelve persons chosen to decide who has the better lawyer.

—Robert Frost[113]

Trial counsel are often viewed as hired guns for trials, demonstrating a ruthless approach, which sometimes ends in success. Even the most dignified and civil trial lawyers do not insist on the type of sportsmanship (depicted in Cartoon 2-40) that we demand of children and professional athletes.

Under the U.S. system, trials are billed as a "search for the truth," although more nuanced thinking suggests that the U.S. adversarial model aligns more with a search for a just resolution of a controversy, while the inquisitional system used in much of the world focuses more on truth-seeking. U.S. practice focuses not so much on what the ultimate truth may be but on whether parties have met their burden of proof needed to win a case. In civil suits, plaintiffs generally win if they are able to prove their case by a preponderance of the evidence. In criminal cases, the government wins if it is able to establish guilt beyond a reasonable doubt. "Preponderance of the evidence" and "beyond a reasonable doubt" are not standards that require definitive

"Good trial." "Good trial." "Good trial."

Cartoon 2-40 (cartoon 27—TCB 140413) Emily Flake/The New Yorker Collection/The Cartoon Bank

truth; they simply prescribe the necessary level of certainty about what the truth might be. One might say that the search-for-truth notion is unrealistic. Nonetheless, the idea that the adversary litigation system produces authentic facts is deeply ingrained in American legal culture.

A crucial component of this truth-seeking folklore in U.S. trial practice is cross-examination. Indeed, aggressive cross-examination has captured the public's imagination and has appeared throughout popular culture. Cross-examination of a key witness is often a trial drama's denouement: a witness turns out to be the perpetrator of a crime, a witness's character flaw is exposed or credibility impeached, and the like.

Trial lawyers learn that a skilled cross-examination must control witnesses, hog-tying them to a series of answers for which no alternative exists. How can this serve the search for the truth? If witnesses have more information to share or more explanation to provide, why not let them elaborate on their answers? Traditional practice often requires a leading question on cross-examination, for which "yes" or "no" is the only appropriate answer. When viewed in light of the accuracy-seeking goal, this notion that witnesses cannot explain their answers seems counterintuitive. Add this to the sentiment that witnesses do sometimes lie, then the whole process of allowing attorneys to persist in demanding only specific answers seems to the uninitiated to provide an environment for lies to flourish and for travesties of justice to occur. As illustrated in Cartoon 2-41, Cartoon 2-42, and the following joke, this impression often inspires comedy.

> A man charged with assault and battery insisted at his trial that he had just pushed his victim "a little bit." When he was pressured by the prosecutor to illustrate just how hard, the defendant approached the lawyer, slapped him in the face, grabbed him firmly by the lapels, and flung him over the table.
>
> He then faced judge and jury and calmly declared, "I would say it was about one-tenth that hard."[114]

A backstory puts these trial rules, including constraint on witness answers, in a more reasonable light, even if they don't ultimately justify the truth-seeking mythology. First, one must remember that the lawyer-witness

"The witness will confine his 'Knock knock' answers to 'Who's there?'"

Cartoon 2-41 (cartoon 26—TCB 142325) Paul Noth/The New Yorker Collection/The Cartoon Bank

"I knew the suspect was lying because of certain telltale discrepancies between his voice and non verbal gestures. Also his pants were on fire."

Cartoon 2-42 (cartoon 24—TCB 41390) Robert Mankoff/The New Yorker Collection/The Cartoon Bank

dance takes place in the context of the adversary system. The cross-examiner's goal is only to elicit specific information supplementing testimony on direct examination. Second, one must appreciate that the rules of practice and evidence give latitude to a judge—allowing the judge to moderate the evidentiary strictures mocked in American humor. After the strict questioning of cross-examination unfolds, the option remains for opponents to engage in redirect questioning of the witness—allowing the witness to supplement answers that had been restricted on cross. Moreover, in imposing restrictions on questioning, judges are often guided simply by the laudatory goal of efficiency: not wasting the time of lawyers and juries on the meanderings of a loquacious witness. Restrictions on questioning often derive from Federal Rule of Evidence 611(a) or its identical state court counterparts, which, quite pragmatically, instruct trial judges to "exercise reasonable control over the mode and order of examining witnesses and presenting evidence so as to: (1) make those procedures effective for determining the truth; (2) avoid wasting time; and (3) protect witnesses from harassment or undue embarrassment." Needless to say, humor does not tend to reflect this common-sense approach to controlling trial proceedings. Pragmatic common sense does not usually provide the inspiration for great jokes.

"Please direct your comments to the jury, counsellor, not the Greek chorus."

Cartoon 2-43 (cartoon 28—TCB 132410) Drew Dernavich/The New Yorker Collection/The Cartoon Bank

Accompanying the image of stupid, corrupt, or lying persons in the legal process are gags mocking a process brimming with ridiculous, histrionic displays. Cartoon 2-43 and a quip by H. L. Mencken provide two extravagant examples.

> The penalty for laughing in a courtroom is six months in jail; if it were not for this penalty, the jury would never hear the evidence.
>
> –H. L. Mencken[115]

In short, ridicule of the trial process taps into the same sense of contradiction evinced in other humor about law. We understand that we have a justice system that other countries model. We hold pride in the system, yet we mourn its faults. The jokes and cartoons allow us to process this incongruity. One resolution of this clash concludes that the system is not perfect, but it usually keeps things fair and honest:

> The judge asked the defendant, "Mr. Jones, do you understand that you have sworn to tell the truth, the whole truth and nothing but the truth?"
>
> "I do."
>
> "Now what do you say to defend yourself?"
>
> "Your Honor, under those limitations, nothing."[116]

And at bottom, it is a kooky legal system, but it is our system and it is the only system we have.

2. Legal Texts

Within the universe of humor about the legal process is a smaller genre: comedy about procedural rules. Complicated, sometimes byzantine, legal procedural rules bedevil the U.S. legal system and frustrate all those whose lives touch the legal process, whatever their power: judges, legislators, presidents, governors, lawyers, and laypersons. The rules often require highly technical legal knowledge, meaning that one must usually hire an expert (a legal professional) to decipher them and to navigate the legal system. Resulting vexations with the rat's nest of procedural rules provides grist for many jokes about criminal and civil procedural systems. Consider, for example, the many parodies about law enforcement stumbling over the specifics of the *Miranda* warnings, inventory car searches, and the like. YouTube has a very funny parody video, featuring the New York City police department's use of a new "Stop and Kiss" policy (as contrasted with "Stop and Frisk"—an approach to law enforcement endorsed in the U.S. Supreme Court's *Terry v. Ohio* decision).[117]

In the civil procedure context, one can find a lot of pedantic humor about procedural matters. Take, for example, a T-shirt featuring the face of an unpopular U.S. president, with the caption "Motion to Dismiss." Or a silly play on precise terms of a Federal Rule of Civil Procedure:

BY THE COURT: You may call your next witness.

BY DEFENDANT'S ATTORNEY: Your Honor, at this time I would like to swat [opposing counsel] on the head with his client's deposition.

THE COURT: You mean read it?

DEFENDANT'S ATTORNEY: No, Sir. I mean to swat him on the head with it. Pursuant to Rule 32, I may use the deposition "for any purpose" and that's the purpose I want to use it for.

THE COURT: Well, it does say that.

Quiet pause.

THE COURT: There being no objection, you may proceed.

DEFENDANT'S ATTORNEY: Thank you, Judge.

Thereafter, Defendant's Attorney swatted plaintiff's attorney on the head with the deposition.

BY PLAINTIFF'S ATTORNEY (THE VICTIM): But Judge . . .

THE COURT: Next witness.

PLAINTIFF'S ATTORNEY: . . . We object.

THE COURT: Sustained. Next witness.[118]

A curiously popular theme in civil procedure humor concerns the law of venue. Venue principles govern the specific geographic location within a single court system where a litigant may properly file a lawsuit. Venue is distinct from a related U.S. concept—personal jurisdiction—which is controlled by constitutional principles that restrict the ability of courts to exercise power over only those individuals with sufficient contacts with the state where a court sits. Unlike personal jurisdiction doctrine (which triggers high stakes of judicial power and federalism), venue is a more bureaucratic concept, is laid out by a statute or a court rule, and is designed to locate the most convenient place for litigation. Venue rules are not concerned with balancing and monitoring the high-stakes power struggles in U.S. federalism. Rather, venue focuses on systemic factors bearing on the efficiency of a court system, the likely location of evidence, and the parties' convenience.

Why is venue a lightning rod for jokes? Perhaps it a fun word to say—already part of the lay vocabulary, but perhaps a touch French and exotic sounding. Perhaps it is because venue law is so formalistic and dry. Reading about the law of venue is about as interesting as eating cardboard. But the underlying values and concerns—as well as the resulting laws—are certainly not any more ridiculously grandiose or complicated than other procedural rules. As procedural rules go, venue is relatively straightforward. Consequently, venue's status as a whipping boy for legal complexity remains puzzling. Apparently the concept reflects some kind of droll charm, as Cartoon 2-44 as well as various quips and jokes try to capture.

Useful pickup line: I'll teach you about jurisdiction if we change the venue to my place.[119]

Here's a joke—ubiquitous among law joke compilations—that combines lawyer and judge ridicule with a riff on venue:

An attorney passed on and found himself in heaven, but not at all happy with his accommodations. He complained to St. Peter, who told him that his only recourse was to appeal his assignment. The attorney immediately advised that he intended to appeal, but was then told that he would be waiting at least three years before his appeal could be heard. The attorney protested that a three-year wait was unconscionable, but his words fell on deaf ears. The lawyer was then approached by the devil, who told him that he would be able to arrange an appeal to be heard in a few days, if the attorney was willing to change venue to Hell. When the attorney asked why appeals could be heard so much sooner in Hell, he was told, "We have all of the judges."[120]

"Not another change of venue, Counsellor!"

Cartoon 2-44 (cartoon 72—TCB 36761) Ed Fisher/The New Yorker Collection/The Cartoon Bank

All of the gags about procedure provide an opportunity to riff on— maybe even show off about—knowledge of a legal technicality. They seem also to reflect irritation with complexity—a sentiment that is both understandable and deserving of respect for citizens of a government that is not designed for lawyers and experts but instead designed by the people and for the people. Take note, though, of an important observation that should moderate exasperation at procedural complexity: complexity usually does not spring from evil intent. Nor does complexity arise from incompetence in designing a procedural system. More likely, procedural complications result from admirable impulses to do right by other people.

To understand how benevolent intentions can give rise to complicated procedures, note first that legal training focuses extensively on the meaning of constitutional due process: one should not lose any portion of life, liberty, or property without notice and an opportunity to be heard. Procedural fairness not only serves accuracy but is also intrinsically valuable to a just society. As citizens, we not only want government to treat us fairly, but we take pride in being members of a society that even-handedly deploys well-considered procedures for all people.

When confronted with an issue or dispute that requires complex considerations for resolution, the lawyerly mind turns naturally to the best method for disposition. Lawyers know the value of procedure for minimizing bias, controlling emotion, and eliminating irrelevant facts. And, as they try to do right by a situation, those who design legal rules think hard about the appropriate steps to take for reaching an accurate conclusion. Lawyers reflexively lean on procedure to keep things honest. In other words, lawyers show care with complex procedures. Just as doctors sometimes overuse technology in service of medical treatment, lawyers sometimes overuse procedure in service of fairness and equality. The impulse is admirable, even if the end result is sometimes over the top.

Although complex procedures often mean more fees for lawyers, this may be more an ironic byproduct of well-meaning intentions than an intentional maneuver to ensure job security. Experienced lawyers understand how ad hoc, behind-the-scenes maneuvering makes victory possible, and that transparent, fixed procedures can prevent unfair advantage. As the technicians who usually design procedural systems, lawyers tend to understand how to structure procedures as a leveling mechanism. To be sure, however, the result is self-serving:

> To me, a lawyer is basically the person that knows the rules of the country. We're all throwing dice, playing the game, moving our pieces around the board, but if there is a problem, the lawyer is the only person who has read the inside top of the box.
>
> —Jerry Seinfeld[121]

Complementing procedural complexity is the tangle of laws governing day-to-day, out-of-court conduct, sometimes called "substantive law" or "rules of decision." This category of law can be as complicated as—if not more complicated than—procedural law. Examples of complicated substantive legal doctrines are legion, but it is tax law that most commonly appears in humor culture. One set of studies documents six decades of tax jokes in radio and television situation comedies. Consider the following opening from a 1944 episode of *Fibber McGee and Molly*:

> The Spanish used to burn people they didn't like. In England they once cut off ears for stealing a penny. Russia had the whip. But for sheer ingenuity in instruments of torture, America wins again. We refer to income tax Form 1040.[122]

As popular comedy has begun to evolve away from the formal joke or clever introduction in the last several decades, recent comic portrayals of the tax system are more situational and plot driven. But punchy zingers about complexity in the tax system still stand out. In a 1990 television episode of *Roseanne*, an Internal Revenue Service employee declares that "no human being can really understand" the tax laws: "We don't write the stinking laws. You got a complaint, talk to the idiots in Congress."[123] This focus on the federal tax code is reflected in *New Yorker* cartoons, with well over 200 income-tax cartoons appearing in the magazine since 1925. The complexity of the federal income tax system has seized the popular imagination.

As with comedy about tangled procedural law, benign explanations are available to explain substantive legal complexity—whether it occurs in tax law or another area that regulates life outside the litigation system. As with procedural law, complexity springs in part from a desire to be fair and to account accurately for the presence of specific circumstances to be considered in governing specific problems. To take into account the twists, turns, and nuances of life, general principles of law must have exceptions. The resulting exceptions—permutations on a general legal rule—may be characterized as justice or as loopholes. Sometimes complexity emerges not only from a desire to fine-tune law to life's complex realities but also from legislative compromise of competing interests. While most would agree that accommodating diverse interests in fashioning regulation is laudable, the end result is often not as logical or streamlined as it would be if only one side completely got its way.

Aside from causing confusion, loopholes and complexity also tend to selectively benefit affluent, powerful members of society. The first gain is for lawyers, who make a profession out of navigating this complexity. The other beneficiaries are those who can afford the lawyerly expertise that allows them to avoid unfavorable regulation. This is a common subject for jokes:

> Two well-dressed lawyers went to an expensive restaurant. They ordered two drinks and then got sandwiches from their briefcases and began to eat them. . . .
>
> Waitress: Sorry, Sir! But you can't eat your *own* food here. It's against the rules.
>
> The lawyers quietly looked at each other and *exchanged* their sandwiches and continued their meals.[124]

> A lawyer was on his deathbed in his bedroom, and he called to his wife.
>
> She rushed in and said, "What is it, honey?"
>
> He told her to run and get a Bible as soon as possible. Being a religious woman, she thought this was a good idea. She ran and got it, prepared to read him his favorite verse or something of the sort. He snatched it from her and began scanning pages, his eyes darting right and left. The wife was curious, so she asked, "What are you doing, honey?"
>
> He shouted, "I'm looking for loopholes!"[125]

In addition to the twists and turns in substantive legal rules, sheer volume is often quite daunting. The United States has a lot of law: case reporters, statutes, and regulations being the primary sources. Cartoon 2-45 shows that one can find comedy in observing how serious legal practitioners can be about the goal of mastering law's overwhelming tsunami of official materials.

Complexity, it turns out, is not an inevitable quality for an orderly society. For example, many Asian cultures tend to rely more on non-law modes of regulation—whether it is emphasis on honor, shaming, or conciliatory approaches to dispute resolution. Whatever one says about these approaches, they do not create a regulatory tangle.

Even within the realm of legal regulation, other non-U.S. cultures provide contrasting orientations that minimize complexity. Think about the Italian legal system: Italy has a unitary court system that adjudicates laws adopted by a single bicameral legislature. The principal sources of Italian law are limited: a Constitution, a Civil Code, and a Code of Civil Procedure.[126] Add to this simplicity a state of mind that contrasts dramatically with

"What burns me up is that the answer is right here somewhere, staring us in the face."

Cartoon 2-45 (cartoon 71—TCB 38948) Robert J. Day/The New Yorker Collection/The Cartoon Bank

U.S. governance. For the Italian mindset, the question about legal regulation is whether a prohibition exists. According to this way of thinking, one looks at the legal text and if there is nothing in the text that says that a course of action is forbidden, then it is presumed to be allowed. Contrast this with the typical U.S. legal orientation: to render solid legal advice, American lawyers strongly prefer to rest their advice on legal authorization rather than the absence of prohibition. It is not enough that the law lacks a provision condemning a certain course of action. Rather, well-grounded legal advice requires affirmative permission. Thus, the incentive is for U.S. legal materials to canvass all aspects of life, while Italian law need only point to specific prohibitions. No surprise that American legal materials fill vast libraries.

Adding to the volume and complexity of American law is the structure of the U.S. government. The United States has a robust system of federalism, meaning that power is splintered among many different units: fifty states, a handful of territories, and an overarching federal government that possesses technically limited but significant power. No wonder then that legal materials proliferate. Each of these units requires written rules.

Also contributing to the complexity is the common law system followed in the United States (as well as elsewhere in the world). As contrasted with the more minimalist civil law system for which governing law appears in a unified code, the common law system creates a substantial part of legal regulation through ad hoc decision making by courts over time. This system of court-made common law has virtues: it allows courts to tailor justice in conjunction with accommodating the specific equities of each case. The raw material in the process is the specific arguments developed by the lawyers who represent the adversaries in a particular case. In the words of Justice Harlan, common law rules are "forged between the hammer and anvil of opposing counsel" and are "wrought" to accommodate the precise facts of the dispute.[127] A downside of the specificity within which the common law operates is proliferating rules and parallel lines of cases governing the same subject matter, but not referring to each other. This all creates a lot of opportunity for jokes.

F. CAN SATIRE INSPIRE CHANGE?

Spilling over with flaws, legal participants, the legal system, and texts all inspire humor that tends toward ridicule and satire. Innocent amusement, jaunty frivolity, and hilarious mirth are largely lacking. Rather, it is the satirical art of "diminishing or derogating a subject by making it ridiculous and evoking toward it attitudes of amusement, contempt, score or indignation" that dominates.[128] One wonders whether the sharp edge that surrounds humor about the law may actually be an agent for change. Sometimes the humor has a dry charm. But can all this satire actually help the system improve?

A debate flourishes about the transformative power of satire. Some say that caustic criticism can prompt change because satire can have a powerfully shaming effect. On one hand, logic suggests that satire's sting causes its targets to rethink their decisions and change their behavior. Plenty of theorists believe that satire speaks truth to power, challenges assumptions, showcases new perspectives, generates conversation, and, accordingly, can change the course of history.[129] From this point of view, satire can act as a "social corrective."[130]

But another view holds that satire ultimately supports the status quo. Under this view, satire provides an outlet of angst and outrage about the state of the world. We laugh and delight at seeing a despicable part of life torn apart, disemboweled, and apparently relieved of its serious potential. But in the end, according to this view, satire acts as a bromide. One writer has argued that "anti-establishment comedy allows the public to disclaim with laughter any responsibility for injustice," but then simply go on with their lives.[131] In other words, satire replaces real protest. "At its most insidious; humor can put us into a nonserious frame of mind about matters we urgently need to take seriously."[132]

Even more critical is the view that American attitudes about humor are in need of a drastic adjustment. Some commentators observe that sharp-edged satire not only assuages our conscience but also can misinform and obscure problems.[133] With the advent of comical news reporting on news outlets such as HBO and Comedy Central, commentators persuasively suggest that audiences are not thinking critically about the issues but are instead simply whipped up to "a frenzy of proud identification with a smart and quick-witted host."[134] Skeptics also quote Jonathan Swift's suggestion that satire distracts us from our own failings: "Satire is a mirror in which people see every face but their own."[135] One wonders about the wisdom of the following 1785 poem by William Cowper:

> Yet what can satire do, whether grave or gay?
>
> It can correct a foible, may chastise
>
> The freaks of fashion, regulate the dress,
>
> Retrench a sword-blade, or dispatch a patch;
>
> But where are its sublime trophies found?
>
> What vice has it subdued? Whose heart reclaim'd

By rigour, or whom laugh'd into reform?

Alas! Leviathan is not so tamed.

Laugh'd at, he laughs again; and, stricken hard,

Turns to the stroke his adamantine scales,

That fear no discipline of human hands.[136]

The critique of satirical news sources is only one side of the story. Clearly popular comedy news shows have an important education to share. And whatever critique is out there, one cannot doubt that humor about law will surely persist. We simply need to think deeply about whether it makes a difference in improving how law works. Onward then to the internal workings of law: statutes, court opinions, court proceedings, and the like. As it turns out, there's tons of funny stuff here—*in* the law. This is not only (arguably) the most entertaining part of law's intersection with humor but also provides a window into the important question of how well law in the United States is working.

CHAPTER 3

༻

"In"

Humor in Law

L aw can get tedious. Even for a diehard legal Olympian, dry legal doctrine and routine legal proceedings can use spicing up. Hence we
observe the inclination of judges and lawyers to crack jokes during trials
and appellate arguments. After dedicated hours of deep dives into legal
doctrine, legal scholars distract and entertain themselves with empirical
studies of jokes cracked during Supreme Court arguments, funny briefs,
funny court opinions, funny statutes, and the like. Rarely just playful
jokers making their way through life, lawyers also use humor to advocate,
persuading others of a particular point of view. Judges also use humor to
make a point—particularly a point directed at a lawyer gone awry. Perhaps
the funniest material is inadvertently funny, something like a malaprop
uttered by a lawyer during court proceedings:

> District Attorney turns to question a witness: "All right, Mr. C., is it not a fact that this
> witness came into this Court here and admitted having sexual relations with you in open
> court, in front of the jury?"[1]

Funny lawyers, funny judges, funny laws—all make up the corpus of humor
in law. Americans tend to make laws that are broad in scope. Americans are
also litigious. The result is that U.S. legal proceedings traverse many topics
that arise in human civilization. Because the substance of law and the litigation process tend to canvass so many parts of life, no single common
thread emerges that connects the ways humor appears in law. Multiple
interlocking themes nonetheless present themselves. First is a theme borne
of tension: those steeped in serious and complicated legal work need an

outlet for expressing intellectual and emotional strain, and humor can provide a chance for release. Second, humor in law routinely juxtaposes light hearted with weighty matters. Because law and legal proceedings are generally shrouded with a serious decorum, the unlikely sight or sound of a funny bit has an unexpected element of surprise. This surprise heightens the comic effect of what might otherwise not have inspired a laugh. When a judge, lawyer, or juror's joke arises from losing patience or commitment to calm self-control, this glimmer of humanity adds to the comedy's sizzle. Another common theme arises from the tragedies of life that give rise to the need for statutes and lawsuits. Because law so often plays out on "a field of pain and death,"[2] humor in the law provides a welcome relief. Finally, in some instances, one frequently sees an element of ridicule or superiority motivating a legal actor's joke:

> THE COURT: Please begin.
>
> COUNSEL: Thank you.
>
> COUNSEL (TO WITNESS): Miss, while you have, you do have—you still—oh, you don't.
>
> THE COURT: That was a great start, Counsel.[3]

Together, these themes show the same dynamic illustrated in other intersections of humor and the law: superiority, incongruity, and release all combined to inspire a laugh.

A. FUNNY LAWYERS

Many lawyers are natural wordsmiths: witty, spirited writers and talkers. Making good use of these qualities, many are funny too. Studies testing for the personality characteristics of lawyers document that a large portion are introverts. No surprise there: introversion and long hours of mastering small details and filigreed analysis go well together. And, of course, introversion and a sense of humor are not exclusive. To be sure, extroversion ensures that someone is more likely to share humor with others, perhaps out of an enhanced need to connect often with others. With that need comes an inclination to deploy the lighter side of human communication to make sure those many connections occur. Humor helps establish human bonds and is therefore a powerful tool for a "people person." Yet the most successful comedy requires creativity and a deep understanding of the dark underbelly of life: both qualities associated with introverts. Moreover, even introverts (particularly introverted lawyers) are trained to deploy knowledge and skills in an outgoing way. For that reason, others may learn that introverted lawyers are funny.

The question arises, however, about when it is appropriate for (introverted and extroverted) lawyers to be funny when plying their trade—a trade that involves a variety of tasks. The universe of lawyer work includes hours of solitary document drafting and review, tooling away with colleagues doing background office tasks, rainmaking (client development), providing client advice, interacting with the media on behalf of a client, social justice advocacy, negotiating deals or lawsuit settlements, mediating, and appearing in court as part of traditional adversary litigation. Breaking these tasks into parts, we need little analysis to conclude that a judicious sense of humor keeps one sane while immersed in long hours of solitary tasks, works to bond co-workers, and often smooths the way for making connections with potential clients. Of course, humor can go awry in all of these contexts. Emailed jokes can be particularly treacherous. The following wise advice pertains to emailed jokes: "Dance like no one is watching; email like it may someday be read in a deposition."[4]

1. Advice Giving, Media Spinning, and Social Justice Advocacy

Other circumstances for when it is appropriate for a lawyer to use humor are more sensitive to context. The role of humor in providing client advice depends on whether the topic strikes a nerve. The therapeutic humor community of scholars offers plenty of anecdotes about the benefits of humor to improving well-being. That said, a lawyer might want to hesitate before joking about a living will—detailing the circumstances under which one wishes that heroic medical efforts should cease—to a terminally ill client. A wisecrack that breaks emotional or mental anxiety can be helpful in tense situations, but the circumstances under which most people visit lawyers range from serious to grave. An organic joke—emerging from the special circumstances of the dialogue—can be a great development. Nonetheless, most would agree that it is best to avoid injecting the process of giving legal advice to a bereaved relative or a recently arrested client with more than a light hearted laugh.

As for using humor in situations involving media coverage, the answer may depend on the type of media involved. A jest in the hands of a news outlet could be misconstrued or misused. Social media do not automatically get filtered through a third-party news outlet, yet a legal professional can easily lose control of his or her social media content, enabling others to take humor out of context or otherwise exploit it in unintended ways.

Humor in service of social justice advocacy generally takes the form of satire. As described in Chapter 2, the jury is out on the question of whether satire acts mostly just to assuage anger and pain or whether it can effect social change. Consider a classic case study, Jonathan Swift's 1729 essay "A Modest Proposal," in which Swift urged the Irish to sell their children as food to wealthy British persons. The subtitle of the piece is "For Preventing the Children of Poor People in Ireland From Being a Burden to Their Parents or Country, and For Making Them Beneficial to the Public." Here's an excerpt: "I have been assured by a very knowing American of my acquaintance in London that a young healthy child well nursed is at one year old a most delicious, nourishing, and wholesome food, whether stewed, roasted, baked or boiled."[5]

Swift's goal was to use absurdity to poke at British greed and British treatment of the Irish as well as to highlight poverty's grinding cruelty. The essay has been enormously influential in the field of rhetoric and literature, raising awareness of oppression among generations of students who were required to study its text. Importantly, modern satirists have paid homage by mimicking the essay's approach, using it to take on contemporary issues of oppression. Yet beyond this, one wonders how much Swift's essay—along with similar satirical rhetoric from lawyer activists—has changed the targeted social conditions.

2. Negotiation and Mediation

For the various places where lawyers might use humor, negotiation is a setting that has captured some academic attention. The negotiation and mediation literature builds on general research about positive contributions of humor in building connections and establishing community. Of course, the literature contains common-sense observations, such as the damaging effect of using humor at the expense of other parties; even well-meaning humor can make participants feel singled out and wonder at the true meaning of a joke.[6] But humor also boasts several positive contributions to advancing common goals in negotiation: helping to unseat parties from a stalled position, reducing anxiety, changing the tone of negative interactions, establishing group norms, and safely acknowledging (yet making light of) the various parties' vulnerabilities. From an adversary perspective, making a good joke can catapult a lawyer into the center of attention as a dominating force in negotiations. Social science literature focusing on corporate business behavior supports this observation, concluding that successful humor (a joke that inspires laughter) is quite effective in conveying confidence and promoting the aura of status and power. On the risk side, however, unsuccessful humor (a joke that falls flat) conveys lower competence, which can undermine perceptions of status and power.[7]

Issues of race and gender inject unique complications into the risk-benefit calculus. At least for gender, seasoned female attorneys often cite the upside of humor. For handling male adversaries who use sexism or condescension to diminish the status of female lawyers, practitioners note that humor can disarm without undermining the goal of promoting a useful working relationship with an adversary. A humorous retort's message might lacerate, but it is most effective when delivered in a breezy—not angry—manner. One report suggests that snappy "flash card" retorts to common put-downs are good to have at the ready.[8] For example, when referred to as a girl, a female lawyer might respond, "The difference between women and girls is that girls still think men are smart and know what they are doing."[9] The message here is that you touched a nerve, but you inflicted no damage—since it is you, not me, who has a problem.

For mediation, which focuses less on conquering an opponent and more on finding a compromise, humor can provide a light hearted, but important, vehicle for acknowledging the parties' painful histories, reframing a controversy, signaling upbeat possibilities, and fostering difficult dialogue.[10] The formats for mediations vary, but the basic premise is for parties to design their own conflict resolution, with the help of one or more trained mediators who are often lawyers. Mediation therefore differs from negotiation, which does not necessarily entail a third party (who could be an audience for a joke). It differs from arbitration and traditional litigation for which a resolution is imposed on the parties by an outside agent (arbitrator, judge, or jury).

Some lawyers hold that the risk that jokes might alienate one of the parties is too great to support humor in mediation. Many mediators, however, are huge humor proponents, citing the overlap between the mediation process and comedy creation. Some proponents do more than advocate cracking jokes during mediation. They argue that studying comedy methods and structure can enhance the mediation's efficacy. Take the example of improvisation. Because the comedic method of improvisation focuses on fostering intuition and creativity, some mediators suggest that improvisation training can create synergy among participants that promotes successful mediation.[11] Embracing another's suggestion and then adding to it (known as the "yes and" improv method) can show participants how keeping an open mind and working collaboratively can yield a fine product and hone one's ability to anticipate other people's reactions.

Another line of thinking points out the similarities between the structures of jokes and mediation. First, both have a foundation in conflict and incongruity. Next, both "play" with the conflict by exploring alternative resolutions. In mediation, either the mediator or the parties may generate these alternatives. This process is mirrored with jokes when the joke teller communicates the punchline, which is the part of the joke that initially appears incongruous with the setup. The similarity between mediation and jokes arises because both end with participants considering alternative resolutions to conflict. In mediation, this occurs with the parties' decision to accommodate diverse interests in a certain way, thereby experiencing the pleasure of reaching an agreement. With jokes, this occurs when the listener resolves incongruities—reconciling the punchline with the joke's setup, thereby experiencing the pleasure of laughter. According to this theory, both mediators and mediating parties benefit from thinking about joke structure, which provides a neutral invitation to open one's mind to alternative resolutions.

3. Adversary Litigation

By far, the greatest stash of funny stuff that lawyers do involves jokes—or sometimes even more elaborate shenanigans—in court papers and in litigation proceedings (or in the related adversary context of arbitration). Perhaps out of lawyerly caution, jokes' appearance in formal court papers is far less frequent than in heat-of-the-moment litigation exchanges. Although witty zingers do exist, the record on humor in court papers is mixed. A successful example comes from the "Monkey Selfie" case, *Naruto v. Slater,* in which the "next friend" of a crested macaque ape named Naruto claimed that Naruto held a copyright to self-initiated photographic images. Naruto had snapped the self-portraits while handling a camera owned by a primate scholar. When disputes over the ownership of the very funny snaps arose, an animal rights specialist joined the fray. In the motion to dismiss the complaint claiming that Naruto's copyright had been infringed, the defendants began:

> A monkey, an animal-rights organization and a primatologist walk into federal court to sue for infringement of the monkey's claimed copyright. What seems like the setup for a punchline is really happening. It should not be happening. Under [appellate precedent], dismissal of this action is required. . . . Monkey see, monkey sue is not good law. . . .
>
> Accepting Plaintiff's . . . argument would present the bizarre possibility of protracted family and probate court battles when the offspring of non-human authors scrum over the rights to valuable works.[12]

This is cheeky stuff for a court filing. One cannot tell whether it was the humor or the general ridiculousness of the claim that worked to the defendants' favor, but the court dismissed the case as the defendants had requested. The jaunty language may indeed have gone over well, since the court took the unusual move of publishing the motion's language as an introduction to its decision dismissing the case.

A contrasting example shows humor's potential to backfire when placed in a formal document. In this example, a lawyer submitted a petition for rehearing, trying to persuade a U.S. court of appeals to change its decision affirming a lower court's order. The rehearing petition began like this:

> Sometimes, in deciding a case, the Court ought to put itself "into the shoes of the attorney" before it. Consider the conversation that naturally flows from the Court's opinion here:
>
> LAWYER: I regret to inform you that the court of appeals affirmed.
>
> CLIENT: What reasons did they give?
>
> LAWYER: They said that they were persuaded by the trial judge's reasons.
>
> CLIENT: Hmm. What did they say about personal jurisdiction?
>
> LAWYER: Well, I just told you that they adopted the trial judge's reasons.
>
> CLIENT: But the judge didn't give any reasons. He made no findings or conclusions on jurisdiction. Remember? You were the one who told me that last year.
>
> LAWYER: Oh, yes. You're right. The Circuit affirms for "the reasons" given below, but there weren't any on jurisdiction.
>
> CLIENT: So what do we do?
>
> LAWYER: We move for panel rehearing.
>
> CLIENT: But how will that change anything?
>
> LAWYER: All institutions make mistakes. Panel rehearing's purpose is for overlooked matters like this. Trust the system.
>
> CLIENT: That's a little challenging right now.
>
> LAWYER: Have faith. The 5th Circuit has to tackle thousands of cases a year, so mistakes will happen once in a while, but the Court is conscientious about fixing them on rehearing.[13]

This approach to advocacy may be smirk-inducing for those who are not the object of a lawyer's subtle jab and who suspect that appellate courts have an unthinking orientation toward rubber stamping lower courts' decisions. The dialogue provides a creative way to express frustration over an order affirming "for the reasons given" by a lower court—when in fact the lower court *gave no reasons*. But as the object of this scorn, the U.S. court of appeals had a different reaction—lobbing back to the lawyer an equally pointed hypothetical dialogue. Tracking precisely the lawyer's style, the opinion began: "Sometimes, in litigating a case, lawyers ought to put themselves in the shoes of the judges before them." The opinion followed up with its own hypothetical dialogue:

JUDGE 1: I cannot imagine why they thought that was a good idea.

JUDGE 2: What's their argument?

JUDGE 3: They say that we made a mistake by not expressly addressing their personal jurisdiction argument.

JUDGE 2: That's silly. It goes without saying that there was personal jurisdiction here.

JUDGE 1: I agree. The company reached out to Appellee in Texas, traveled to Texas to negotiate the contract, and entered into a contract with a Texas corporation.

JUDGE 2: So what do you think we should do about their petition?

JUDGE 1: Deny it.

JUDGE 3: I agree. Deny.

JUDGE 2: Sounds right.[14]

One cringes to envision how the lawyer explained this opinion to the inquiring client: "And the court wrote a hypothetical dialogue because . . . ?" Rehearing petitions are disfavored and few are granted.[15] The petitions are generally just part of the grist of routine work cluttering an appellate judge's day. In this case, however, one might speculate that the appellate judges had fun drafting this order resolving the petition, perhaps even acting out of boredom with their cloistered professional lives, or boredom with their insular lot. By reason of ethics and decorum, appellate judges must minimize fraternizing with those outside the courthouse community and thus must seek ways to entertain themselves within the small community that constitutes their primary professional associates. Humor no doubt plays an especially important role in the many instances when an insular group of judicial comrades are judges' only playmates for the remainder of their professional lives.

Despite the risk that humor may rebound adversely, a comic approach in written advocacy promises many advantages. Levity can inject surprise into an otherwise dry brief, demonstrate creativity, unmask hypocrisy, display daring, invite the readers' personal connection with the text, generate a bond through shared amusement, and undermine the dignity of an opponent's position.[16] And, as in the case of negotiation and mediation, humor can also show confidence, status, and power. Perhaps because preparation of written expression allows lawyers a sober second thought about humor's potential downside, however, lawyers rarely inject it into formal documents.

Despite similar risks for oral humor, documented evidence of jokes within the courtroom is far more common. Attorneys take conflicting positions on the wisdom of light hearted jests in the courtroom. Arguments in favor of using courtroom humor mirror those for written briefs. The in-person context of the courtroom adds some additional benefits: humor can put the jury at ease in what likely feels like an unfamiliar setting, humor can seize an immediate opportunity for flagging an opponent's weakness or attempts to obfuscate, and humor can build trust when it is sensitively focused on the interpersonal dynamics of a particular courtroom. The unique downsides of courtroom humor derive in large part from the formality of the courtroom setting. If a joke falls flat, the austere courtroom setting amplifies the failure.[17] The presence of jurors also ups the ante. Because popular culture depicts court proceedings as somber, a joke can shatter that expectation and come off as unprofessional. Moreover, jurors introduce more persons into the important audience of a joke and increase the possibility that a joke will fail. One person's humor can be another person's offense. An attorney's witticism may appeal to the judge and part of the jury. But when a unanimous jury is required for an effective verdict, the downside of alienating just one juror is significant.

Published examples of humor in the courtroom likely reflect examples showcasing the most memorable stories. These examples generally show amusing, but calamitous, results. A publication bias may be at work with the available examples: those instances when courtroom levity provoked just enough mild amusement to win over an audience in court—whether before judge or jury—may make less interesting reading and therefore go unnoticed. Only the flashiest (possibly depicted in Cartoon 3-1), and most potentially devastating, examples might gain notoriety.

True or not, the apparently disastrous selections are striking. Here are three prominent examples:

> **The George Zimmerman "Knock-Knock" Joke**: In a highly publicized 2013 incident, George Zimmerman shot a black high school student—Trayvon Martin—under circumstances that Zimmerman claimed were self-defense. After much controversy and an extensive inquiry, Zimmerman was charged with second-degree murder and manslaughter. The shooting, the charging, and the lead-up to trial captured the public's attention. Apparently alluding to this media attention, George Zimmerman's lawyer made the following joke to the jury in his opening statement:
>
> "Knock knock."
>
> "Who's there?"
>
> "George Zimmerman."
>
> "George Zimmerman, who?"
>
> "Alright good. You're on the jury."[18]

What's the gag here? If you, honorable jury member, haven't heard of George Zimmerman, then there's a chance you might be impartial. This suggestion could insult the many jury members who quite understandably

*"The Court will allow the cape but will draw the
line at the wind machine."*

Cartoon 3-1 (cartoon 25—TCB 132928) Drew Dernavich/The New Yorker Collection/The
Cartoon Bank

had heard of George Zimmerman but also thought they would be able
to weigh the evidence without prejudice. It also suggested that the jurors
who did make it to the jury likely did so because of their ignorance. In
the end, however, the defense bounced back: the jury acquitted George
Zimmerman.

The *Roe v. Wade*[19] Joke: In this landmark abortion case before the U.S.
Supreme Court, the Texas attorney general represented the state, arguing
that the blanket Texas restriction on abortion was consistent with the U.S.
Constitution. His opposing attorneys were women. He began his argument
with a joke that bombed—inspiring several seconds of stunned silence: "It's
an old joke, but when a man argues against two beautiful ladies like this,
they are going to have the last word."[20] The attorney general ultimately lost.
Did the throwback to the 1950s joke cause this 7-2 ruling? Probably not.
But the attorney general certainly stained his legacy by including such a
gendered joke in a landmark women's rights case. In the words of one commentator, the joke amounted to "spoiled icing on the collapsed cake."[21]

The Supreme Court Plum Joke: In oral argument before the Supreme Court, a lawyer argued that the government should not be allowed to force private companies to pay for certain advertising campaigns. In doing so, the lawyer made a joke, directed toward Justice Antonin Scalia, that the justice should not buy green plums because they might give his wife diarrhea. The remainder of his argument was similarly off-kilter, including the statement that his client was not going to change its message so as to advertise something like "we want you to eat worms."[22] Some justices warned the advocate that he was not being clear. He ultimately lost his case in the Supreme Court. A malpractice suit followed and scholarly discussion ensued, but little more is known since the malpractice case settled without a written opinion.

As is usually the case with humor that backfires in formal settings, the jokes reflected strong qualities of release humor (e.g., the scatological reference to Scalia's wife's digestion) and superiority humor (e.g., jokes suggesting the jury was ignorant and that the opposing oral advocates were merely beautiful ladies). Perhaps for those reasons, they attracted many opinions from legal commentators. Legal commentary in traditional fora (such as law review articles)—as well as the Internet and blogs—also includes multiple other examples of what turned out to be grave mistakes by lawyers in the courtroom.

Exceptions exist, however, to the general observation that edgy quips by lawyers in court proceedings have an unwelcome effect. A salient example comes from the remarkable oral argument in the Supreme Court case *Barnes v. Glen Theatre, Inc.*[23] *Barnes* is a landmark decision that reckons with the scope of the U.S. Constitution's First Amendment protection of expressive conduct. In *Barnes*, a state law outlawed nude dancing and the Supreme Court grappled with whether this unconstitutionally prohibited expression. The oral argument in the case, featuring lots of riffs on nude dancing, was in fact so entertaining that it provided the script (not just the inspiration) for *Arguendo*, a comedy presented by the Elevator Repair Service troupe. The play follows the precise words of the oral transcript.

In *Barnes*, the state attorney general, Mr. Uhl, bore the task of justifying the public nudity prohibition, which the state had used to prosecute a nude dancing establishment. Even without theatrical enhancements, Mr. Uhl's argument at the Supreme Court was an unusually entertaining hoot as far as oral arguments go—lots of laughter reverberating in the marble courtroom, even with the muffling effect of red velvet curtains. In the Supreme Court, an oral advocate generally receives the courtesy of a few minutes of introduction—but in this case, Justice John Paul Stevens jumped in almost immediately with the suggestion that one could get in trouble with giving a public speech in a park while naked. The attorney general continued, feeding the growing giggles in the courtroom.

> Uhl: . . . He would get in trouble, Your Honor, if he walked into a public place such as a bar or a bookstore without his clothes on. . . .

When Justice Stevens interjected with an apparently ironic tone, "He can evidently sing in an opera without his clothes on," the attorney general responded with a suggestion that it would be ridiculous to insulate from liability all naked movement on stage.[24] When he asked about whether the First Amendment was "the 'good taste' clause of the Constitution," Justice Stevens made clear that he intended his suggestion that the prohibition could extend to go-go dancing but not to opera to be satirical.[25] Other justices joined the fray as well—speaking of sunbathing, "song and dance," and nudist colonies.

Attorney General Uhl did not need creative genius to inject the argument with entertaining release humor. The subject matter of the case did that work for him. But he rolled with the punches. If the justices were going to have a little fun, he would too—alluding, for example, to the pasties worn by the go-go dancers at issue in the case when he argued that the prohibition was "sufficiently narrowly tailored, just as the clothing on the dancers is narrowly tailored, to accomplish the state's interest in prohibiting public nudity."[26]

Attorney General Uhl won the case by a five-to-four margin. One cannot know whether Uhl's comic approach—playing part straight man and part comic partner—helped with the win. But the tape of the oral argument makes clear that he read his audience well. The justices wanted to have a little fun, and he obliged them. His choice of repartee—verbal jockeying about naked women—was characteristically male. But that approach had no unfavorable boomerang. At the time, Justice Sandra Day O'Connor was the only woman on the Court, and she ultimately backed his position.

Courtroom humor can carry reputational risk for an attorney, even when it apparently does not sully the case result. In one well-publicized case before a federal appellate court, an assistant U.S. attorney began her oral argument, quipping that she was a retiring "valley girl." The court warmly joked with the attorney, speaking with them about "going to Cal," being a "valley girl," and knowing the best places to eat. The public response was less favorable. The popular blog *Above the Law* ran a story entitled "When Humor in the Courtroom Isn't Funny." The story suggested prosecutorial privilege was at work: "I think it's a rare defense lawyer who would get that kind of reception from an appellate panel."[27] The blog post continued that the assistant U.S. attorney's joke translated to, "I am powerful enough to ignore the formality that is normally expected here."[28] While this comment reflects the characteristically ritualized rivalry between defense attorneys and prosecutors, it highlights an important downside of humor in a formal setting. Some humor—particularly "inside humor"—can come across as just a little too cozy.

This assistant U.S. attorney successfully deployed humor to connect personally with the judges. But an attorney cannot always count on judges to play along with her jokes. Indeed, one important landmine in using humor in the courtroom is the judge's ego and personal style. As one commentator has noted: "[I]f the jurist is stern, unsmiling and perhaps even tyrannical, to crack a joke could be considered a moral sin and result in a rebuke from his 'Honor the Humorless.'"[29] The judge could also just not like the joke or be squeamish about the possible unseemliness of humor in her courtroom. And then of course there is the possibility that the judge resents the lawyer's trying to steal the limelight.

"I'll handle the jokes, counsellor."

Cartoon 3-2 (cartoon 48—TCB 67654) J.C. Duffy/The New Yorker Collection/The Cartoon Bank

B. FUNNY JUDGES

People did sometimes stick things in my underwear. . . .

—Justice Steven Breyer

Oral argument in *Safford United School District v. Redding* (2008)

That's enough frivolity for a while. . . .

—Chief Justice John Roberts

Oral arguments in *National Federation of Independent Business v. Sebellius* (Affordable Care Act case, 2012)

Judges sometimes crack jokes or say things in jest during formal proceedings. Occasionally, as is likely the case with an unpretentious pragmatist like Justice Stephen Breyer, this humor is an unadorned statement that ends up evoking a laugh. The humor's inadvertent source adds to the chuckle. The contrast is the judge who has the impression that he or she might make an impact with others through his jokes. Justice Scalia displayed this inclination toward the end of his life. It was Scalia's nearly unbridled desire to capture the court gallery's attention with a clever crack that prompted Chief Justice John Roberts's scolding during the 2012 Affordable Care Act case, which Roberts apparently meant as a gentle "get hold of yourself."

Vast compendia of transcripts and written descriptions of reputedly comic remarks and dialogue in litigation proceedings are available. Many are remarkable for their decided lack of truly funny bits. Often the transcripts or descriptions reflect pedantic or tedious jokes. Sometimes the remarks do not make much sense, and it is hard to decipher why they are interpreted as witty. Why is this? Humor's success depends on tone of voice, facial expressions, or—even less tangible—the vibe in a room. These qualities are missing from cold transcripts and other written records. As with lawyers who indulge in humor, judicial humor appears in court proceedings, informal settings, and opinions. All of these contexts have garnered plenty of attention. Despite the tendency for powerful people to indulge considerable self-regard, the comic behavior of judges suggests that some may either be very bored with their jobs or possess an exaggerated sense that they are really entertaining others. See Cartoon 3-3.

1. In-Court and Extrajudicial Humor

Starting with court proceedings, one observes a range of humor types as judges navigate the challenges, potential tedium, and sense of entitlement

"The court of the city of New York is now in session. Today featuring the mildly humorous yet firm justice of his honor William T. James."

Cartoon 3-3 (cartoon 44—TCB 37009) Peter C. Vey/The New Yorker Collection/The Cartoon Bank

accompanying the insular world of judging. In the category of superiority humor, consider the dialogue of Supreme Court Justice Harold H. Burton from when he was a trial judge sentencing a convicted homicide defendant. When then-Judge Burton asked the defendant if he had anything to say, the defendant said, "As God is my judge, I didn't do it. I'm not guilty." To which Judge Burton replied, "He isn't, I am. You did. You are."[30] This may be fun to read (at least in the abstract), but the judge's quip does not exactly reflect a solemn humility that one might argue best befits one human being passing judgment on another.

Other examples show judicial attempts at humor that awkwardly stumble. Take, for example, the judge who resigned after making the following personal remark in a domestic violence case: "I've been married 45 years. We've never considered divorce, a few times murder maybe."[31]

A striking example of a judge forgoing restraint and joining jocular banter occurred in a Georgia state courtroom in 2016. Encountering a spirited homicide defendant in the courtroom, the judge, in his dialogue with the defendant, started to mirror the defendant's tone. One website described the judge-defendant duo as "among America's most legendary comedy teams."[32] The interchange is tawdry—but appealing to the sensibilities that celebrate the topics characterizing release humor and the incongruous picture of a judge stooping to a defendant's vulgarity. Here are some of the tamer (yes, tamer) parts of the transcript, which went viral on the Internet:

THE COURT: Okay. That's fine. You're going to be here on—let me tell you how this is going to work. You're going to be—

MR. ALLEN: You ain't going to tell me shit.

THE COURT: Listen.

MR. ALLEN: Suck my dick.

THE COURT: Shut up. Listen to me.

MR. ALLEN: Suck my dick, you fuckman.

THE COURT: Listen!

MR. ALLEN: Suck my dick.

THE COURT: You will be here in court on Mon—

MR. ALLEN: You'll be here sucking my dick.

MR. ALLEN: —I'll pull it out and jack on you.

THE COURT: Okay. Why don't you do that right now?

MR. ALLEN: Take off the cuffs.

THE COURT: How many hands do you have to do it.

MR. ALLEN: Take off the cuffs.

THE COURT: Come on—no. Jack off.[33]

Show this to any trial lawyer, and he or she will likely smirk or visibly stifle a giggle. In fact, most who understand anything about the legal process will at least secretly chuckle. Why is it entertaining? First, the defendant's audacity is remarkable. Accused of homicide, the defendant may have had little to lose, but the judge did possess the power to make what was left of his life significantly less pleasant. Also striking is how the judge—who is meant to be a dignified authority figure— descended quickly to the defendant's level. And the swear words! Why are humans so amused by profanity? Linguist Steven Pinker provides a persuasive account of the pleasure humans derive from swearing. According to Pinker, "taboo words, though evocative of the nastier aspects of their referents, don't get their punch from those connotations alone. Taboo status *itself* gives a word an emotional zing, regardless of its actual referent."[34] In other words, we like to hear naughty words simply because they are naughty. Adding the context of the courtroom clearly enhances the impact. Stories about cursing in the courtroom are reliable sources of fun:

COUNSEL: Your Honor, the defense would argue the People haven't proved the prior
conviction.

DISTRICT ATTORNEY: Oh, shit!

COUNSEL: That's a legal term?

THE COURT: One used quite often in law school.[35]

And then there is the comic appeal that arises when judges make incongruous statements. One cannot know for sure, but Justice Breyer's statement about having items put in his underwear prompted an outburst of
laughter probably because it was such an oddly indecorous confession
from a refined gentleman in a ceremonial posture—sitting in a black robe
on an elevated bench in the highest court in the land. This analysis doesn't
even account for the incongruity arising from the gravity of the task facing
Justice Breyer at the time, requiring him to pinpoint the meaning of the
U.S. Constitution as it applies to invasive searches of school students. The
case facts further suggest that the oral argument transported the justice
to his adolescent days, evoking unpleasant memories of dressing for gym
and being teased. The juxtaposition of adolescence and a brilliant jurist—
together with the honesty of his admission—is surprising and charming.

A small flurry of academic interest has focused on jokes by U.S. Supreme
Court justices. One legal academic calculated the number of times in one
term that each justice evoked enough of a reaction to prompt the court
reporter to note "(Laughter)" in the official transcript of oral argument.
And yes, this produced a study that received considerable attention from
the news media.[36] Reporting on this research with headlines such as "Who
Is the Funniest Justice?"[37]—the media declared Scalia (at seventy-seven
laughter notations) the funniest justice and Thomas, the least funny (at
zero). The result for Justice Thomas is not surprising, since he almost never
says anything at oral argument. As for Justice Scalia's success in achieving the
highest number of laughter notions, common perceptions about laughing
might lead one to conclude that a person's propensity to evoke laughter
relates to how funny a person is. Yet experts who have studied laughter suggest that the matter is more complex. The laughter for Justice Scalia's quips
may not have been a barometer of his comic potential.

Following through on the intuition of philosopher Henri Bergson about
the social qualities of laughter, neuroscientist Richard Provine conducted
path-breaking work on laughter's function. According to Provine, laughter
provides glue among people, giving a signal to others that invites them to
share in a social interaction. According to this now broadly embraced view,
laughter is not primarily a response to witticisms but is more focused on
sending cues to others: we laugh in order to show approval, to scorn, to
form a community, to express surprise, to show embarrassment, to smooth

over awkwardness, and—perhaps most interestingly—to prime others to laugh at us and with us.[38]

Stand-up comedians capitalize on laughter's priming effect. In fact, comedian Eddie Murphy has admitted that he transforms his sometimes involuntary deep belly laugh into a calculated laugh strategically integrated into his routine. Fellow comedians critique other comics for using the "pre-laugh" technique. Regarded as a cheap trick or a crutch, the technique relies on self-laughing that occurs before even beginning a joke; the purpose being to build suspense and encourage the audience to laugh once the joke is over.[39] Comedian Dave Chappelle is reputed to "goose[ ] the audience by dropping the microphone to his chest, bending over, laughing, and running upstage" after telling a joke.[40]

Further academic research supports the instinct that this artistry reflects. British neuroscientist Sophie Scott has studied and documented laughter's infectious quality. Based on her empirical work, Scott concluded that men and women are generally equal in their ability to create and interpret humor, but women are slightly more effective in making laughter contagious.[41] Her main point, however, confirms Provine's thesis: laughter is much more about social community than wit.

What does this thesis mean for interpreting studies about the laughter Supreme Court justices evoke? First, the empirical studies should be taken for what they are—in some cases, they are ironic (tongue-in-cheek), but they are never intended as a scientific barometer of judicial comic ability. Judicial humor comes in a variety of forms:

- Justice Scalia liked to tease and taunt.
- Chief Justice Rehnquist was known for his practical jokes.
- Chief Justice Roberts favors the ironic.
- Justices Kennedy and Kagan are known for one-line aphorisms.
- Some justices are more prone to visual humor, making funny faces or gestures.

A wisecrack accompanied by a comical look is more likely to elicit the transcript notation "(Laughter)" than one delivered with obvious sarcasm. Both, however, can derive from the same sentiment, meant to convey the same message. In short, racking up a high number of transcript laughter notations is not proof of a justice's comic talent.

But the scientific backdrop does suggest that a justice's propensity to inspire laughter may display an inclination to make social connections. That social connection may concern the advocate immediately before the Court or the audience in the courtroom gallery (members of the Supreme Court bar in the front center, followed by case parties, journalists, and tourists in back center, and with law clerks in chairs flanking the courtroom sides). Or the justice may be reaching out for connection with fellow justices— whether by referencing an inside joke or not. Buttressing this notion that the laughter reflects the justices' impulses as social beings, rather than something hilarious about the facts and law of a particular case, are the studies' observations that many laughter-evoking comments during oral arguments tend to be self-deprecating or at least focusing on the Supreme Court's foibles as an institution.[42]

Finally worth noting on the topic of U.S. Supreme Court oral argument humor is the disconnect between in-court and out-of-court displays of wit. Justice Breyer's humor scores for in-court jokes are not stellar. But he has often displayed little fear or restraint in communicating a dry wit and a good sense of timing at law school and book tour events. Particularly salient evidence emerged during his appearance on the National Public Radio game show *Wait, Wait . . . Don't Tell Me!*, featuring host Peter Sagal and other funny celebrities. Here is the dialogue with Justice Breyer about the various studies done on joke-cracking during Supreme Court arguments:

> MR. SAGAL: Speaking of laughter, something else we wanted to ask you about: We found that there have been two studies, two distinct studies, one by the New York Times, one by an independent court observer. These were studies of who is the funniest member of the Supreme Court. And the New York Times study compared a period of time. They found that, looking at the transcripts, they looked for the words "laughter" after comments by justices. You had 28 big laugh lines. Scalia—
>
> JUSTICE BREYER: Well—
>
> MR. SAGAL: Scalia only had 25. The other guy, different period of time, Scalia had 77; you only had 45.
>
> JUSTICE BREYER: Well, I'm not sure—they must not have much to do with their time, but the—(laughter)—being sort of the most humorous of the Supreme Court justices is like being one of the shortest tall people. (Laughter.)
>
> MR. SAGAL: So, I mean, you don't feel a rivalry? You don't like consider—
>
> JUSTICE BREYER: No.
>
> MR. SAGAL: —arguments; you don't read the briefs and go, oh, wow, I can riff on that principle? (Laughter.)
>
> JUSTICE BREYER: No.
>
> MR. SAGAL: I'm going to kill with—
>
> MR. ROCCA: Oh, yo momma contest; I love that.
>
> JUSTICE BREYER: That's the reporters' invention.
>
> MR. SAGAL: Now, be that as it may, you must have enjoyed yourself a little bit with the case this week over the famous "Bong Hits for Jesus" banner. I mean, compared to the dry contractual issues that you sometimes have to deal with, please tell me you looked forward to that argument a little bit.

JUSTICE BREYER: Yes, I looked forward to it a little bit. (Laughter.)

MR. SAGAL: Okay. (Applause.) Did you—I have not read the complete arguments—did
    you in fact engage in any drug humor at all, just a little bit?

JUSTICE BREYER: I don't engage in any direct humor.

MR. SAGAL: No, no—

JUSTICE BREYER: Humor is a matter for other people to judge.

MR. SAGAL: I understand. Okay, so it's not up to you.

One thing I've always wondered about the Supreme Court, considering the deliberation
    that goes into the actual important decisions that control our legal framework, how
    do you go about ordering lunch?

JUSTICE BREYER: (Chuckles.) This is a very sensitive topic. (Laughter.)[43]

Current trends in cognitive science point to social cooperation as the primary function and explanation for the human capacity for reason.[44] This insight helps to explain why humans have surpassed other animals in myriad
ways while at the same time routinely exhibiting irrationality in the face of
their rational powers. More narrowly, the reason-cooperation connection
supports the hypothesis that judges make jokes more to bond with others
than out of an irrepressible impulse to express cerebral wit or to show off
comic talent. That said, the judicial inclination to make jokes can go awry.
A judge's jokes can immediately derail litigation, set up a judicial decision
for later nullification, or even get a judge into ethical trouble.

In almost all reported instances, a judge's humor is simply a wisecrack
that ultimately causes no reversible error. Yet even jests that are clearly
harmless can prompt distracting or expensive litigation. In one case, a
judge quipped that he had child care issues that had arisen and that he was
going to have to pay his entire salary to have other judges "babysit" during
jury deliberations. On appeal, the defendant argued that the comments
suggested prejudice because the judge had a financial incentive to stall
the trial. The court of appeals paid attention to the claim but dismissed
it, stating that it was "obvious that the judge was not actually paying his
colleagues to help him out and that his comments were intended to be
humorous."[45]

A closer call on whether error arose from a judicial joke occurred in a
criminal fraud case. Here, a defendant moved for a new trial—partially on
the basis of a judge's remark to the jury that the defendant's co-conspirator
(who had vomited outside the courtroom before his testimony) was going
"directly to prison" if he "pukes on my carpet." Observing that "it would
have been better had the judge said nothing" about the co-conspirator's
physical condition, the appellate court reasoned that the jury was likely not
made more sympathetic to the co-conspirator's testimony as a prosecution
witness, since the jury knew that he had already pleaded guilty to the fraud

himself and was simply cooperating with the prosecution in hopes of reducing his sentence.[46]

Perhaps even more notable is a first-degree murder case in which the judge uttered a number of jests (if you can call them that) during the jury selection and trial. Here are some examples:

- The judge described members of the jury pool who were not picked for the jury as having "escaped" and referred to the empaneled jurors as "you lucky people."
- The judge explained to empaneled jurors that breaks would occur because "it gets tiresome just sitting here, for all of us."
- The judge remarked that a drawing shown to the jury "won't win any art prizes."
- The defendant's former girlfriend testified and was asked to identify the defendant. Apparently she had sex appeal. When she pointed to the defendant who was sitting next to the defendant's trial counsel, Harrington, the judge said, "Harrington, you wish."[47]

The court of appeals took a dim view of the judge's conduct, agreeing with the defendant that the "judge's remarks were inappropriate for a first degree murder trial," but was unable to provide relief for the convicted defendant. Noting the nearly impossible standard imposed for a court's post-conviction review, the appellate court reluctantly concluded that the outcome of the trial would not have been different if these comments had not been uttered.[48]

Speaking of juries and mistrials, check out this randomly bizarre turn of events from a medical malpractice trial. Let's start first with the defendant: a punk rock drummer turned OB-GYN doc. What happened to this fellow? During jury selection in a suit claiming that he was negligent, a prospective juror collapsed, struck his head, and lost consciousness. Someone called emergency medical personnel but in the meantime summoned the punk-rocker turned OB-GYN to help. Consistent with the Hippocratic Oath, he did just that—working with a nearby nurse to use a defibrillator and manual CPR. The prospective juror originally was not breathing and had no pulse—but started to revive nicely by the time the emergency folks arrived at the courthouse. What happened next? The judge declared a mistrial, concluding that the jury's impression (presumably now quite favorable) of the defendant would amount to "incurable" bias. When the OB-GYN punk rocker heard the news, he reacted: "No good deed goes unpunished."[49]

Moving on to courtrooms on a different continent, Australia provides a great foil for evaluating jokes in U.S. courtrooms. As a culture that takes humor very seriously, Australia has a rich academic literature on law and humor. Australian scholars and judicial ethicists share particularly focused analysis on when humor should be encouraged in court proceedings. Few of the examples listed above would pass the comedy bar that Australians set. Nonetheless, the consensus position holds that "appropriate judicial humour enhances core values by promoting procedural justice, maintaining legitimacy, or relieving tension."[50] So, for example, an Australian judge's self-deprecating joke relevant to the circumstances is generally deemed not only appropriate but potentially helpful. Statements such as, "Sorry, I'm confused already," and "I'm sorry, I'm getting my hearing aid later this week," can communicate to others in the courtroom a sense of judicial humility and shared enterprise that can increase accuracy in the proceeding as well as the perception of fairness.[51] By contrast, an Australian judge's jokes made at the expense of a litigant or defendant are rarely deemed acceptable, particularly given a judge's hierarchical position in relation to other courtroom participants. The propriety of a judge's playful jabs directed at a lawyer are far more context dependent, varying according to such factors as whether the judge is delicately trying to harness or discourage unacceptable attorney behavior, whether the judge's joke was particularly sarcastic, whether it occurred outside the presence of the jury, and whether the lawyer and judge have a close relationship.[52] Most people have experienced a situation where they are not part of a particular in-group and observe those who are part of the in-group enjoying cozy and funny repartee with each other. In those instances, one can naturally feel a sense of alienation and unfairness about being an outsider. The Australian analysts see an offense to justice arising from such circumstances.

Although negative consequences of judicial humor in the United States are rare, they can occur. For example, in the eleventh hour of a state robbery case, a judge asked the prosecutor to participate in a practical joke played on the defense counsel, during which the judge told the defense counsel that a panoply of rebuttal witnesses would be called, and the prosecutor reluctantly went along with the gag. After the defense counsel rose to object and argued for several minutes about the prosecutor's bad faith, the judge finally advised him to "sit down and relax" because the rebuttal witnesses were part of a "put on."[53] Under pressure, the trial judge later granted a mistrial on account of the joke but denied the defense motion to disqualify the judge from presiding. An appellate court, however, did disqualify the judge from participating but nonetheless allowed the retrial to proceed. Later, on habeas corpus review, the federal court of appeals characterized the judge's antics as a "hoax"—but reluctantly concluded that law allowed no further relief for the defendant.[54] (It is unclear whether the appellate court chose the word "hoax" with precision. In the world of professional practical jokers, a "hoax"—which simply seeks to trick without taking account of possible consequences—has a lower position on the joke hierarchy than a prank, which is regarded as a well-planned ruse designed for specific lessons and with special care to avoid unintended results.)

Aside from the effect of judicial humor for the parties and the fate of litigation, ethical consequences hang in the balance. The *Model Code of Judicial Conduct* is ambiguous when it comes to humor. The relevant canons and rules speak generally of fairness, impartiality, and avoiding abusive, discourteous, or intemperate behavior. Unless a judge's jokes are bullying, highly offensive, or cruel—disciplinary entities avoid imposing sanctions.

The behavior that does merit sanction tends to be outrageous—although nearly all the offending behavior is out of court. Sexual harassment and related misconduct provide a particularly popular mode for humor leading to professional discipline.[55] A hearing panel on judicial qualifications found that a Kansas state court judge committed at least fifteen incidents of sexual harassment, including (1) telling a court employee that the judge's wife's obstetrician offered to add "an extra stitch" to the wife after childbirth in order to ensure the judge's later pleasure, (2) mentioning to female attorneys that their legs rubbed together, and (3) asking another female attorney whether she would return from vacation pregnant.[56]

A more wide-ranging scandal involving sexualized jokes that entangled a Pennsylvania Supreme Court justice was also based on out-of-court behavior. The Pennsylvania Judicial Conduct Board charged Justice J. Michael Eakin with a myriad of violations of the Pennsylvania Constitution, as well as ethical canons relating to general impropriety and extra-judicial conduct conflicting with judicial duties. Justice Eakin had participated enthusiastically in two email chains that could be easily described as a caricature of NSFW (not safe for work). Participants in one chain included golfing buddies, and the other chain included a larger group of judges, prosecutors, and private attorneys. Some of the emails were sent from Eakin's state-owned computer; most displayed racy humor—digital clips, lewd jokes, and sexualized images. Not all simply riffed on men having sex with women. Justice Eakin's emails (both sent and received) contained a potpourri of content—including racist and homophobic jokes. While these facts are themselves remarkable, the circumstances surrounding the controversy raised the stakes, including blackmail involving another justice as well as a related scandal that brought down the state attorney general. Justice Eakin was removed from the bench.

2. Humor in Opinions

Whether in or out of the courtroom, aberrant judicial joke-telling offers a colorful, if scandalous, portrait of how powerful people can use and abuse humor. Humor in actual opinions is usually less offensive but still controversial. Eye-catching, witty opinions have upsides and downsides. On one hand, entertaining opinions can assuage the losing side's pain (or appropriately tamp down the winning side's glee), add a clarifying edge to an opinion's reasoning and holding, and serve as a "social corrective" that uses satire or sarcasm to "sanction wrongdoers and to deter others from engaging in similar conduct."[57] From a judge's personal perspective, funny and "flamboyant expression can enhance . . . [a judge's] visibility, and [that] visibility can help in winning promotion" to a higher court.[58] On the other hand, opinions with witty jabs risk alienating not only their targets but also others who disapprove of an opinion's intemperate frivolity or lack of decorum.[59]

While the topics and the language in the humor-laced opinions do not tend toward the unsavory or off-color, their tone frequently reflects what communications scholars identify as "differentiation humor": satire, mockery, and sarcasm that the joke teller uses to distinguish himself or herself from the object of scorn.[60] In a well-known example, U.S. Court of Appeals Judge Richard Posner expressed exasperation with lawyers for ignoring "apparently dispositive precedent." Not satisfied with simply using words to compare the lawyers' strategy to an ostrich burying its head in the sand, Posner's opinion included not one, but two, photographs: one of an actual ostrich (head buried) and the other of a suited man (also with head buried). The opinion stated: "The ostrich is a noble animal but not a proper model for an appellate advocate."[61] Needless to say, this ridicule got the bar's attention: lawyers around the United States characterized Posner's approach as bullying.[62] To be sure, the satire likely had some of its intended regulatory effect: one has to assume that a lawyer would not lightly choose to omit discussion of possibly binding precedent when arguing before Judge Posner in the future. One wonders, however, whether the cries of bullying regulated Posner's own comical regulatory instincts.

Another federal court of appeals judge, Alex Kozinski, has written numerous satirical opinions that are well known for prompting cries of foul. Kozinski's lacerating prose was so effective in skewering a copyright suit by Mattel, challenging a parodic song about Barbie, that the media reprimanded his opinion as being "too funny."[63] Among the many zingers in his opinion, Kozinski described the dispute as follows: "[I]f this were a sci-fi melodrama, it might be called Speech-zilla meets Trademark Kong."[64] Reporting on Kozinski's prose, one reporter said that if he were making up this quote "it would be called satire."[65] The reporter added: "Sadly, our court system is not set up to figure [out] when people are just kidding. Law is based on painstakingly literal determinations of meaning. 'I was just pullin' his leg, your honor,' is seldom a well-advised legal defense."[66] In another case—called Kozinski's "greatest hit"—the judge disposed of an antitrust action against movie theaters with an opinion that "obliquely" contained

207 movie titles.[67] This opinion received better reviews than Posner's ostrich opinion and Kozinski's Barbie satire: several legal professionals celebrated Kozinski's brilliance, writing ability, and encyclopedic knowledge of movies—although one strand of Internet commentary declared him "self-indulgent."[68] Others observed that if Kozinski had ambitions for promotion to the Supreme Court, his eye-catching opinion style may not have helped promote his cause. Nor—as it turns out—did his out-of-court behavior. Kozinski retired precipitously in 2017 amid allegations of inappropriate sexual misconduct (much of which was allegedly directed at female law clerks). Upon his retirement, Kozinski issued an apologetic statement through his lawyer, explaining that he "had a broad sense of humor and a candid way of speaking."[69]

Posner, Kozinski, and other lower court judges are well known for edgy, caustic humor. Whether it be by reason of his station or his talent for attracting attention, Justice Antonin Scalia outshone them and likely garnered the most attention for judicial jocularity of any judge over the last quarter century. As his career on the bench evolved, Justice Scalia's clever choice of words, often dispatched to ridicule a colleague, increased. Toward his life's end, his filter seemed to disintegrate, his sarcasm enhanced, and his wit blared full blast. Insults reached a crescendo at the end of his life. Fond of clever turns of phrase, Scalia inflected his opinions during the last several terms he sat on the Court with particularly derisive references to colleagues' opinions, describing them with such terms as "argle-bargle," "jiggery-pokery," "tutti-frutti," and "pure applesauce."[70]

Not all who knew of Justice Scalia's tendencies disapproved his aggressive intemperate name-calling, wise cracks, and colorful references to food. In the last years of his life, Justice Scalia had not only referred to applesauce in his professional work product, but he referenced broccoli and fortune cookies as well. All three food substances—applesauce, broccoli, and fortune cookies—appeared at an ad hoc memorial that appeared outside the Supreme Court building following his sudden death.[71]

He had a particular distaste for efforts to recognize the rights of those who did not identify as heterosexuals—a distaste he often expressed with facetious barbs, wordplay, and unsavory images. In an opinion dissenting from the majority's recognition of a fundamental privacy right in same-sex sexual intimacy, Justice Scalia used a majority opinion statement about privacy as a springboard for theatrical imagery. Scalia noted the majority's observation that "laws prohibiting sodomy do not seem to have been enforced against consenting adults acting in private." Scalia added: "The key qualifier here is 'acting in private.' . . . I do not know what 'acting in private' means; surely consensual sodomy, like heterosexual intercourse, is rarely performed on stage."[72]

Subsequent Scalia opinions dealing with homosexual rights evidence a similar tone. Dissenting from a Court decision declaring unconstitutional a state provision excluding homosexuals from legal protection, Justice Scalia began his opinion with a characteristically showy salvo: "The Court has mistaken a Kulturkampf for a fit of spite."[73]

Scalia's later dissent in the case recognizing a constitutional right to same-sex marriage indulged the same sniggering tone. In the crescendo of this dissent, Justice Scalia declared that "what really astounds" him about the majority "is the hubris reflected in today's judicial Putsch."[74] Moving on to quote the text of the majority opinion, he characterized the majority opinion's "profundities" as "profoundly incoherent." Next Scalia reproduced the following quote from the majority opinion: "The nature of marriage is that, through its enduring bond, two persons together can find other freedoms, such as expression, intimacy, and spirituality." He snapped back with the following:

> (Really? Who ever thought that intimacy and spirituality [whatever that means] were freedoms? And if intimacy is, one would think Freedom of Intimacy is abridged rather than expanded by marriage. Ask the nearest hippie. Expression, sure enough, *is* a freedom, but anyone in a long-lasting marriage will attest that that happy state constricts, rather than expands, what one can prudently say.)[75]

Many consumers of his language, including other judges, agree that Justice Scalia often crossed the line. California Supreme Court Justice Stanley Mosk wrote an article highlighting a dissent typical of Scalia's hyperbolic prose, in which Scalia referred to his colleague's "bulldozer of social engineering," "psycho-journey," and "ludicrous" notion, as well as a "jurisprudential disaster."[76] In a gracious but stinging slap, Mosk suggested that his "best hope is that lawyers who may be tempted to speak in such a manner to a judge or to opposing counsel do not look to Supreme Court opinions for guidance."[77]

Do these opinions from Posner, Kozinski, and Scalia display our opinion leaders at their best? Or are they—as Aristotle described humorous expressions—humans showing themselves in a "worse than average state," manifesting what Aristotle regarded as the "ridiculous," the "ugly," and the "painful"?[78] One thoughtful scholar queries whether judicial opinions should showcase the dark underbelly of American humor. After all, biting judicial jokes have been shown to travel the same path as other satirical caricatures that fueled unfortunate forces in history:

> Discrimination against African Americans was fueled by the minstrel show, gender discrimination was justified by reference to the comic female . . . shrew, the Chinese were

debased with the likes of Charlie Chan, transvestites and trans-gendereds find their isolation from civic life exacerbated by . . . images of the hilarious dress-wearing man, and
gay men have been harassed with the comic figure of the queer.[79]

Despite the harsh words for some judicial comedy, other attempts at
amusing opinions are less mean-spirited. The opinions' jesting tone appears
motivated primarily by a creative impulse—which may be encouraged by
the reality that a judge does indeed have a captive audience for her comedic
efforts. One notable example is a 2008 dissent from a U.S. Supreme Court
order denying review (technically named a dissent from denial of petition
for a writ of certiorari) in which Chief Justice Roberts took issue with the
Court's decision not to review a case dealing with the concept of probable
cause to arrest within the context of a Philadelphia drug bust. Although not
slapstick funny, the opinion parodied *Dragnet*-style rhetoric. Here's how
the opinion began:

> North Philly, May 4th, 2001. Officer Sean Devlin, Narcotic Strike Force was working
> the morning shift, undercover surveillance. The neighborhood: tough as a three-dollar
> steak. Devlin knew. Five years on the beat, nine months with the strike force. Devlin
> spotted him, a lone man on the corner. Another approached, quick exchange of words,
> cash handed over. Small objects handed back. Each man then quickly on his way. Devlin
> knew the guy wasn't buying bus tokens. He radioed a description, and Officer Stein
> picked up the buyer. Sure enough, three bags of crack in the guy's pocket. Head down-
> town and book him, just another day at the office.[80]

Finally, while most judicial opinions avoid off-color references, sometimes the case's particular subject matter presents an irresistible opportunity for judges to enter a low-lying swamp. Justice Scalia's words
confronting his sentiments on homosexuality are an example. Other lower
court examples abound—most of which are either scatological, silly, or
sexual in a juvenile way.

Here is one gem, arising from a lower court appeal from an armed robbery conviction, in which the defendant challenged the trial judge's failure
to order him a second competency hearing. (It doesn't take too much legal
knowledge to conclude that if a defendant argues "you should have checked
again whether I had lost my mind" as the centerpiece of his appeal, the evidence of guilt must have been overwhelming.) During pretrial proceedings
and at the beginning of trial, the defendant had been painfully clear that he
did not care for the public defender assigned to him. Taking the cue, the
defender asked to withdraw. When the judge refused the defender's second
request to withdraw, the defendant (in the words of the appellate court)
"managed to get out of his pants and expose a key portion of the lower part

of his anatomy to the judge and jury. He then began to urinate in the presence of the jurors."[81] The court of appeals was so captivated with this image that it chose to begin its opinion affirming the conviction (and rejecting the basis for the appeal) with the following paragraph:

> While the public's perception of lawyers seems to reach new lows every day, parents—we are told—still encourage their children to enter this profession. But the parent who happens to read this opinion may not be so quick to urge a loved child to become a lawyer after learning how the defendant in this case expressed his extreme personal dislike of his lawyer. Likewise, the would-be lawyer raised on the hit television series, *L.A. Law*, to believe a law degree is that golden ticket to a glamorous career of big money, fast cars and intimate relationships among the beautiful people may think twice before sending in his or her law school application when word of this case gets out.[82]

While the facts are remarkable and the court's presentation is clever, one wonders whether the court's decision to tee off on the sad facts in this case (1) appropriately made light of the defendant's attack on the profession of "attorney-at-law" or (2) degraded the level of court dignity necessary to reinforce the rule of law.

What possesses judges to write these wacky opinions? Some commentators say it is childish egotism—fueled by black robe disease, press attention, and a rise in the mystique of "pop judging."[83] Published compilations of humorous opinions preserving these judicial bursts of creativity for posterity no doubt encourage the practice. (A leading compilation boasts 717 pages of self-described "humorous, extraordinary, . . . clever and witty opinions . . . dating from 1256 A.D. to the present.")[84] From this perspective, attempts at comedy in opinion writing breach judicial protocol and impartiality norms. More forgivingly, one can view the opinions as salve for the tedium and insular world of judging. Court session after court session, boring argument after boring argument, term after term—one can use a little levity. Other commentators are even more upbeat, arguing that humor is a particularly apt tool for judges to use in reining in misconduct by softening the job of sanctioning attorney and litigant breaches and sending a deterrent message to others.

How might judges accommodate the impulse to write funny opinions and yet keep the practice in a positive light? One answer is for judges to use more "identification humor" in their work. Identification humor stands at the opposite end of the spectrum from differentiation humor: identification humor seeks to unite rather than alienate and divide. Identification jokes celebrate shared experiences, observations, and values—with the effect of enhancing mutual understanding.[85] This overlap between a government official and citizens could help promote the rule of law by ensuring that citizens are invested in the law's message. Recognized as particularly constructive by one legal scholar, an excellent example of identification humor appears in a case evaluating whether federal law preempts a county ordinance regulating household products. In navigating the issue, the court peppered the opinion with the italicized names of well-known household products.[86] The result was a bit "punny" for some tastes but, nonetheless, served the purpose of building bridges with those affected by the opinion. One might also say that Judge Kozinski's movie title opinion performs a similar function, inviting readers to perform a *Where's Waldo?* type exercise, searching for partially concealed, yet familiar references to shared popular culture.

C. FUNNY LEGAL INSTRUMENTS

Legal instruments are often part of private law: when both parties to a transaction or legally regulated relationship are private individuals or institutions, and the role of government is generally restricted to enforcing legally recognized obligations arising from the transaction or relationship. Perhaps because private persons do not generally conduct their affairs on a public stage and perhaps because society is less interested in the affairs of a "person on the street," humor arising from person-to-person interactions reflected in formal legal instruments does not make its way into scholarly studies. Two contexts, however, have yielded some funny raw material that has ended up in the public domain: contracts and wills.

1. Contracts

Unless they become subjects of litigation or must be approved by a regulatory entity, contracts are, by definition, private affairs that do not generally fall under public scrutiny. The discrete, individually tailored quality of contracts reflects their function: a contract is a private set of rules negotiated by parties who wish for the law to back up their deal if it ultimately disintegrates. Issues arise, however, from the many occasions when the parties to the deal are not equal. In some instances, the private rules of a contract are imposed, forced, inflicted, or pressed upon an individual by a powerful entity. In that case, the one-sidedness of the resulting contract can sadly distort human relationships—but can also inspire a chuckle. The chuckle arises because the contract farcically reflects a sad reality: one side to a contract is able to drive over the other side with wide tires.

In other instances, contracts are the products of negotiations between parties possessing something approximating equal bargaining power. The contracts of prominent sports figures and rock stars can fall into this category—the crowd-drawing power of sports figures or stars roughly matching the financial strength of the corporate entity with whom they negotiate. With stars and sports figures sometimes being a finicky lot, their contractual terms can prove amusing. Here are some examples:

- In a contract with the Chicago Bulls, Michael Jordan insisted that a provision reflect that—anywhere, anytime—he could play basketball, including pick-up games, exhibitions, and the like. This is apparently an unusual concession. Speculation is that some owners were concerned with injuries resulting from extracurricular activities. Apparently, he is the only player general manager Jerry Krause gave this provision to. I suspect other professional athletes have a lot of limits put on their activities to prevent injuries.
- The Houston Astros promised pitcher Roy Oswalt a bulldozer if they won the 2005 National League Championship Series. The Astros won and the team gave Oswalt a Caterpillar D6N XL as promised.
- Van Halen's rider required concert venues to provide the band with a bowl of M&M'S but no brown ones. This provision was quite ingenious. Van Halen's show was a huge production that used 850 par lamp lights and at the time most venues weren't used to them. If the band arrived and there were brown M&M'S in the bowl, it showed that the venue may not have read the contract carefully enough and they would do an additional check to make sure everything for the show was put up properly.[87]

Perhaps it is our feeling of superiority over spoiled, vain celebrities that makes these contracts so rib-tickling. Perhaps, too, amusement arises from the incongruity of such whimsical contract terms making their way into a solemn deal. Or, maybe, it is just our understanding of humanity's shared foibles: everyone has an idiosyncratic weakness, and some people are simply fascinated with heavy equipment or disgusted by brown food.

The fame of contracting parties behind these comical provisions suggests that one of the contracting parties may have concluded that commercial advantage supported disclosure. Bulldozer and brown M&M'S provisions provide fuel for lighthearted chit-chat—with its accompanying free word-of-mouth publicity.

Sometimes, however, confidential constraints prevent full disclosure of a party's identity—although we might learn a stray, captivating contract detail. So, for example, the Internet tells us that someone insisted on a contract provision requiring another contracting party (perhaps the "party of the second part") to attest that she (the "party of the first part") is a "sexy bitch."[88] Even without knowing who the contracting parties are, one may find this amusing. Why is that? Possible answers:

- Reference to sex and profanity: release humor, check!
- Appearance of a naughty term in a formal, legally enforceable instrument: incongruity humor, check!
- Our sadness about someone for whom such an arguably demeaning description is so important: superiority humor, check!

Here's another similar (and even more famous) example: blending a salacious context with allegations that the "party of the first part" was none other than the president of the United States, the confidentiality contract signed by Stormy Daniels and the attorney for Donald Trump has provided fodder for both giggling and punctilious ridicule by contract attorneys. For most who are legally trained, the contract is a paradigm of bad form. Let's start with the observation that the first page of the contract is numbered "Page 0." Page zero? Moving on: the contract's title (Non-Disparagement Agreement) spells "non-disparagement" wrong. Sifting through the remainder of the contract, one finds a mother lode of inept word choices, illogical constructions, and bad grammar. The section enumeration is wacky: there's even a section 3.0.1.1.2! Even for lawyerly sensibilities, the redundancies are ridiculous: "separately and further" and "undertakings and obligations" are examples. And then there's all the language trying to prevent Stormy Daniels from making public photos, tapes, and other "property" that document her liaison with the president. Trying to hog-tie her from sharing this "property," the contract uses the following verbs: *sell, transfer, turn-over, assign, deliver, divest, convey.* As one lawyer-blogger suggested: "Hey, why not add a few more?"[89] The blogger also described the contract as a "dumpster fire"—"the most flamboyantly dreadful contract I can recall seeing."[90]

Finally—when it comes to contracts—the humor world contains a fair bit of (superior) facetious jests about formality and complexity in the contract instruments. Cartoon 3-4 is just one example from the world of visual humor.

Verbal jokes about complex contracts abound:

The professor of a contract law class asked one of his better students, "If you were to give someone an orange, how would you go about it?"

The student replied, "Here's an orange."

Cartoon 3-4 (cartoon 69—TCB-67854) Roz Chast/The New Yorker Collection/The Cartoon Bank

The professor was outraged. "No! No! Think like a lawyer!"

The student then replied, "Okay. I'd tell him, 'I hereby give and convey to you all and singular, my estate and interests, rights, claim, title, and advantages of and in, said orange, together with all its rind, juice, pulp, and seeds, and all rights and advantages with full power to bite, cut, freeze and otherwise eat, the same, or give the same away with and without the pulp, juice, rind and seeds, anything herein before or hereinafter or in any deed, or deeds, instruments of whatever nature or kind whatsoever to the contrary in anywise notwithstanding. . . .'"[91]

2. Wills

A will is a legally recognized document whereby people transfer their worldly wealth to beneficiaries after their death. Generally, the wealth is tangible, although financial wealth and intellectual property (rights to license fees, for example) can be transferred as well. Wills also take on other solemn legal matters, such as appointing guardians for minor children, selecting executors of estates, and setting up trusts for beneficiaries. Any person over the age of majority and who is of sound mind can legally draft a will. As an instrument that reckons with death, loyalties, family, and love, a will can evoke powerful emotions.

These matters are both grave and central to the human condition. It is not surprising then that wills provide grist for cartoons and other comedy—as well as actual vehicles for funny revenge. The sober contexts in which wills are most relevant magnify any humor that arises. The potential for anxiety—and thus need from comedic release—in these situations may not be mysterious, but it is compelling nonetheless. For those familiar with the law of trusts and estates, the humor is further enhanced by knowledge of the excruciating detail and formality of the legal rules governing will drafting, will validity, and will challenges.

One stock (and, for some, charmingly old-fashioned) context for cartoons is the "will-reading" trope. For most Americans, this is not a particularly compelling event because we know that our parents are going to bequeath us the little that they had. But, as Cartoons 3-5 and 3-6 show, the

"Now read me the part again where I disinherit everybody."

Cartoon 3-5 (cartoon 6—39953) Peter Arno/The New Yorker Collection/The Cartoon Bank

" *'And last but not least...'* "

Cartoon 3-6 (cartoon 5—TCB-67280) Whitney Darrow, Jr./The New Yorker Collection/The Cartoon Bank

drama that may accompany will reading for more affluent folks continues to provide entertainment for all.

Many relate to the notion of parents and grandparents wanting to control what offspring do. For some it is annoying, for others terrifying, and for yet others—it is simply cause for amusement. A lawsuit that for many caused at least a smirk, and perhaps a chuckle, concerned a will that provided that the five grandchildren (descendants) of a Jewish dentist (Max Feinberg) and his wife would each inherit $250,000 so long as they satisfied one condition. The operative language for the condition in Max Feinberg's will provided that "any such descendant who married outside the Jewish faith or whose non-Jewish spouse did not convert to Judaism within one year of marriage would be 'deemed deceasad for all purposes of this instrument as of the date of such marriage.' " Translation: you are cut out of the inheritance if you marry a gentile.[92] The will was challenged as an example of invalid dead hand control over "lives in being." (The law doesn't like it when dead people try to control the distant future—this is deemed not good for the most efficient allocation of resources during a future time that cannot be predicted accurately in a testamentary instrument.) But the court rejected the challenge to this will, reasoning in a courtly way that the money would be distributed according to the marital status of individuals as of the date of Max's death. Accordingly, the will would not control future behavior beyond that point and was a legitimate expression of preference as to those who would not inherit part of an estate.[93]

Max Feinberg's will is not an anomaly. The instinct for parents to express their disapproval of certain group affiliations for their offspring has a long history. Consider the will of one of the leading figures in Revolutionary America, Lewis Morris, a colonist from New York. Lewis Morris died in 1740—indisputably holding a dim view of the Puritans of New England, reflected in the following will provision:

> It is my wish that my son may have the best education that is to be had in England or America. But my express will and directions are, that he never be sent for that purpose, to the Connecticut colonies, lest he should imbibe in his youth, that low craft and cunning, so incidental to the people of that country, which is so interwoven in their constitutions, that all their acts cannot disguise it from the world; though many of them, under the sanctified garb of religion, have endeavored to impose themselves on the world as honest men.[94]

In today's jargon, this provision may be "precatory language," expressing only the will-writer's preference, rather than a legally enforceable condition. What is clear, however, is that Lewis Morris did not want his offspring to go to Yale!

Aside from providing a vehicle for release of anxiety about death, familial love, and the parental instinct to control children, do wills have other qualities that inspire humor? A look at actual wills that have made their way onto the Internet showcase them as a mirror of humanity's vengefully comic emotions. As one example, consider the following "let me use my wealth to make fools of others" will. A Toronto-based attorney fond of practical jokes died in 1926. His last will and testament bequeathed an impressive portion of his estate to any Toronto woman who produced the greatest number of offspring in the period of 1921–1936. This created a phenomenon known as the "Great Stork Derby." There were four winners, each producing nine children and receiving approximately $125,000. (Apparently two runners-up were given a small amount for their efforts.)[95]

Another funny genre is the "last laughs" will. Consider the will of Anthony Scott, who in his last will and testament reputedly wrote: "To my

first wife Sue, whom I always promised to mention in my will. Hello Sue!"[96]
Here are other examples of this impulse to tweak others from the grave:

- "I wish peace and affluence to all my friends and a piece of effluence to all my enemies."
- "To my daughter, I leave £1—for the kindness and love she has never shown me."[97]

And then there's the following: the German poet, Heinrich Heine, was not the type who begrudged his wife for a decision to marry after his death. In fact, he left his assets to his wife with the stipulation that she must re-marry. Why was that? Reports say that his will further provided: "Because, then there will be at least one man to regret my death."[98]

A glimpse at the instinct for revenge, an outlet for anxiety about death, a desire to subvert ill-advised impulses of our children, the world of last will and testament humor turns out to have considerable comic potential.

D. FUNNY LAWS

Here are some key qualities of law. First, it covers all of human society. When humans are ridiculous, law can be ridiculous too. Next, law tries—really hard—to be fair. In so doing, legal rules can make some ridiculous-looking distinctions. Finally, lawyers have the difficult position of having to act with slavish devotion to clients. They hold a fiduciary duty to their clients, meaning they stand in a special relationship and are obliged to do more than simply "a kinda good job." They need to act with unqualified loyalty to their clients. Over a period of time, this can require lawyers to make contradictory arguments and can stretch credulity in trying to do the best for those whom they represent. They are not necessarily clowns, buffoons, or liars. They are trying to fulfill their ethical duty. Morality's effect on legal doctrine can be funny. One can also see the impulse to do right by different segments of society at play in strange-sounding statutes, ordinances, and other legislative creations.

Some of what results defies usual rules of discourse and common sense. So, for example, one could say that the following sentence is semantically irregular under rules of English language usage: "My wife is not my wife." But state laws vary about who qualifies as a spouse. Even now that the Supreme Court has eliminated the effect of differences in same-sex mar-riage prohibitions, laws have different preliminary requirements about the procedures to be followed to obtain a marriage license (blood tests and the like), different prohibitions of degrees of "consanguinity" (blood relation-ship between relatives) that might nullify a union, and the like. It is still quite possible that—according to governing statutes—someone might be one's spouse in one state but not in another. In the world of the law, "my wife is not my wife" is quite possible.

The variety in spouse definitions is not an isolated example of law's apparently contradictory characterizations. Consider another example from the Supreme Court's 2012 decision upholding most of the Affordable Care Act (Obamacare). On the one hand, a majority of the Court held that the act did not include a "tax" because if it did have a tax, the litigation would violate a federal statute prohibiting federal court litigation preventing the imposition of a tax. On the other hand, a majority of the Court ruled that the statute fell squarely within a constitutional power of Congress.[99] What constitutional power would that be? Congress's power to tax, of course! Even at oral argument, the solicitor general admitted that he was currently arguing that the Affordable Care Act penalty was *not* a tax for the purpose of a statutory procedural obstacle to the lawsuit, but that he would return in the following days to argue that it was indeed a tax under the Congress's constitutionally granted taxing power.[100] A tax is not a tax. My wife is not my wife.

These facile mental gymnastics are common in the substance of the law. Cross burning is sometimes protected by the Constitution, sometimes not. A Ten Commandments monument sometimes violates the separation of church and state, sometimes not. A negotiable instrument can be a security for some purposes, but not for other purposes. It is also true that a woman has the right to sue herself under certain circumstances.[101]

Even the notoriously dense Internal Revenue Code has funny stuff. Case in point: the 2018 amendments to the Code. Let's start with the struggle over the name of the amendments. Using a procedural maneuver, Democratic legislators blocked Republicans from officially calling the amendments, "The Tax Cuts and Jobs Act." (Apparently, President Trump's preferred name, "the Cut Cut Cut Act," wasn't seriously considered.) Those who actually drafted the amendments ultimately got their way: the amendments are called "An Act to provide for reconciliation pursuant to titles II and V of the concurrent resolution on the budget resolution on the budget for fiscal year 2018."[102] Catchy, no?

Not to worry, though: those who actually drafted the text of the tax amendments showed a bit of the devil in framing the acronyms. (Acronyms are ubiquitous in all of law, and the Internal Revenue Code is no exception.) For a provision intended to provide an obstacle for companies seeking to shift profits offshore, the drafters choose the name "Base Erosion and Anti-Abuse Tax" ("BEAT," for short). Perhaps even better is the provision imposing a minimum tax on U.S. companies' foreign income, aptly named "GILTI," and pronounced "GUILTY."[103] The long form for this acronym is the "Global Intangible Low-Taxed Income" provision. No obvious logic mandates the choice of words in that phrase. In other words, drafters were cogitating about a memorable nickname. Witty or not, these folks were clearly trying to amuse themselves. The nation's tax bar is also tickled.

As a general matter, the law is nuanced in order to serve complex and conflicting policy purposes. From the outside, this can look silly: a farcical state of affairs meriting a giggle and a headshake. Reasonably, one may ask whether it is really high-level reasoning that makes possible the law's capacity for filigreed distinctions and multiple meanings. Or is it a sleight of hand at play to ensure that law serves selfish purposes at the hands of talented "hired guns" serving the interests of rich clients? Those trained in law's subtleties argue in favor of its good intentions—even if the result appears laughable for those who are not enmeshed in law's details and purposes.

In many instances, however, funny bits embedded in the law are not the product of anything analytically complex or even arguably nefarious. Some are just anachronisms; others are the product of life's oddities, artifacts of a strange occurrence that presented itself to a community, or a lascivious turn of mind. Here are some examples:

- According to the U.S. Code, it is generally illegal to make, distribute, sell, or possess a switchblade. Two exceptions exist, one of which can inspire a chuckle if one thinks about it: people with only one arm are allowed to carry switchblades.[104] (The other exception allows soldiers to carry switchblades—that's not as remarkable.)
- The U.S. Code prescribes detailed specifications for mailing live scorpions. Thankfully, the statute prohibits any "transmission . . . by means of aircraft engaged in the carriage of passengers for compensation or hire."[105]
- The Alabama Code prohibits billiard rooms from connecting with secret passages.[106]
- Apparently good culinary technique requires soaking a rabbit carcass in salty cold water immediately following slaughter. But California regulates how long it is lawful to do this: "It is unlawful for any person to immerse or soak the carcass of any slaughtered rabbit in water for a period longer than necessary to eliminate the natural animal heat in the carcass and in no event for a period longer than 2½ hours."[107]
- Sexual innuendo in legal jargon: horizontal merger (an anti-trust term), simultaneous attachment (dealing with security interests in an asset), and prophylactic effect (preventative impact).

Why are these amusing? Mostly incongruity—sprinkled with spicy topics—explains their comical character. But sometimes it is best not to dig too deeply. They are all a little weird, and maybe that's enough explanation. As E. B. White's classic admonition goes:

> Humor can be dissected, as a frog can, but the thing dies in the process and the innards are discouraging to any but the pure scientific mind.[108]

Conclusion

When touching law (and other aspects of life), jokes and other forms of humor work on multiple levels. Humor helps to process our internal tensions, resolve the wildly confusing contradictions that life throws at us, and give us a way to connect to others. Those functions bring together most of the ways that law intersects with humor—whether it be the ways that law regulates humor, the ways that humor pushes back on law, or the ways that humor manifests in the proceedings, substance, and text of laws.

But law also has important qualities that raise the stakes on meaningful analysis of humor's form and function. Because a legal system organizes

"A grand jury sitting in Terre Haute, Indiana, today handed up an indictment of society."

Cartoon C-1 (cartoon 11 TCB-42588) Dana Frandon/The New Yorker Collection/The Cartoon Bank

"The courts ruled that we had to open it up to all stuffed animals."

Cartoon C-2 (cartoon 67—TCB 25296) Mike Twohy/The New Yorker Collection/The Cartoon Bank

power and relations in human society, we can easily find much to condemn when we think about law.

Aside from quips about individual disputes and individual legal texts, a larger question on the intersection of law and humor hangs in the balance. Can humor improve governance? Does democracy work better when comedians are around to highlight how humor and law come together? In some ways the answer is easy: certainly humor empowers the population by connecting citizens to a common culture, binding together dramatically different ideas, and ultimately creating new ones.

The question, however, is whether humor can undermine oppressive power—whether it can mitigate or eliminate tyranny's force. The reason that this may occur arises from one of humor's wonderful qualities. Comedy is such fun that it can assuage pain, calm anxiety, and take the sting out of damage flowing from irresponsible uses of authority. Perhaps citizens might be better able to harness law for human benefit and fight against its misuse if they weren't entertained with the jests, wit, and hoopla of modern comedy—including comedy that is pointed at the most oppressive power.

Thus the following riddle remains: Does humor fight tyranny or support it? The answer may never emerge, but two things are certain. First, to make democracy work, we need to have an understanding of difference and allow group identities to flourish. Leveling all human culture to a common denominator is not the way to promote a rich society and culture. Cartoon C-2 does a good job ridiculing this impulse.

Second, and equally important, we need to protect free expression to ensure robust exchange of positive ideas as well as critique. While humor may not always be an equal match for true tyranny—and indeed can serve as a bromide that suppresses necessary dissent—stifling humor is surely not the way toward better government and society. Humor is too expressive in conveying ideas, too versatile in reaching diverse audiences, and too effective in creating bonds with others for a society to censor it vigorously. As Cartoon C-3 shows us, life would be barren with too much censorship.

Life would be also be considerably lacking without side-splitting laughs, chuckles, and giggles. Those joys alone are enough to tell the law to get out of the business of regulating taste, to keep lawyerly precision away from funny stuff, and to urge humor to continue its mission of unveiling the defects in law. As for the humor in law—the weird statutes, the weird case facts, and weird opinions—these may be an unavoidable symptom of the human condition. But we certainly can and certainly should laugh and enjoy them.

Cartoon C-3 (cartoon 68—TCB 121932) Michael Shaw/The New Yorker Collection/The Cartoon Bank

NOTES

INTRODUCTION

1. Kevin Underhill, *Lawsuit Against Food Critic Alleges that Steak Sandwich Misclassified,* Lowering the Bar (March 7, 2007), https://loweringthebar.net/2007/03/libel_suit_ agai.html [hereinafter Underhill, *Food Critic*].

2. *Hilarious Yelp Review: "It Ripped Its Way Out of Me in a Raging Fiery Whirlwind of Poopy Terror,"* IYCATT (Nov. 20, 2013), http://ifyoucanaffordtotip.com/hilarious-yelp-review/.

3. Underhill, *Food Critic, supra* note 1.

4. Underhill, *Food Critic, supra* note 1.

5. *Lawyer Joke Collection*, ICICLE SOFTWARE.COM, http://www.iciclesoftware.com/LawJokes/IcicleLawJokes.html (last updated Oct. 31, 2010) [hereafter Joke Collection].

6. Joke Collection, *supra* note 5.

7. Joke Collection, *supra* note 5.

8. Joke Collection, *supra* note 5.

9. John Leonard, *Fifty Years Old and All Grown-Up,* N.Y. TIMES BOOK REVIEW 1, FEB. 16, 1975 (reviewing Brendan Gill's HERE AT THE NEW YORKER).

10. Evidence of the magazine's dedication to quality is well illustrated by Brendan Gill's description of founding editor Harold Ross: "Ross . . . doted on immaculate writing and on stylish writing," wrote Gill. "He recognized beauty when it appeared," and was not diverted by fame and status, only "high quality." BRENDAN GILL, HERE AT THE NEW YORKER 390–91 (1975).

11. IAIN TOPLISS, THE COMIC WORLDS OF PETER ARNO, WILLIAM STEIG, CHARLES ADDAMS AND SAUL STEINBERG 4 (2005).

12. John Leonard, *Fifty Years Old and All Grown-Up,* N.Y. TIMES BOOK REVIEW 1, FEB. 16, 1975 (reviewing Brendan Gill's HERE AT THE NEW YORKER). For a look at the *New Yorker* television series through Amazon, *see* Internet Movie Database, *The New Yorker Presents,* http://www.imdb.com/title/tt4115864 (last visited June 4, 2016).

13. Lawyer joke studies have predominated, thanks to the enormously thoughtful work of Marc Galanter: MARC GALANTER, LOWERING THE BAR: LAWYER JOKES & LEGAL CULTURE (2005); Marc Galanter, *Changing Legal Consciousness in America: The View From the Joke Corpus,* 23 CARDOZO L. REV. 2223 (2002); Marc Galanter, *Anyone Can Fall Down a Manhole: The Contingency Fee and Its Discontents,* 47 DEPAUL L. REV. 457 (1998); Marc Galanter, *Lawyers in the Laboratory or, Can They Run Through Those Little Mazes,* 4 GREEN BAG 2D 251 (2001); Marc Galanter, *The Faces of Mistrust: The Image of Lawyers in Public Opinion, Jokes, and Political Discourse,* 66 U. CIN. L. REV. 805 (1998). For a jury joke study, *see* Valerie P. Hans, *Jury Jokes and Legal Culture,* 62 DEPAUL L. REV. 391 (2013).

14. Examples of studies of humor used in court proceedings include Ryan A. Malphurs, *"People Did Sometime Stick Things in My Underwear": The Function of Laughter at the U.S. Supreme Court,* 10 Comm. L. Rev. 48 (2013); Ryan A. Malphurs et al., *Too Much Frivolity, Not Enough Femininity: A Study of Gender and Humor at the U.S. Supreme Court,* (Oct. 3, 2013) (unpublished), *available at* http://papers.ssrn.com/sol3/papers.cfm?abstract_id=2335613; Jay D. Wexler, *Laugh Track,* 9 Green Bag 2d 59 (2005); Jay D. Wexler, *Laugh Track II—Still Laughin'!,* 117 Yale L.J. Pocket Part 130 (2007), *available at* http://www.yalelawjournal.org/forum/laugh-track-ii-still-laughin.

15. Subject-matter-specific studies tend to focus on intellectual property. *See, e.g.,* Dotan Oliar & Christopher Sprigman, *There's No Free Laugh (Anymore): The Emergence of Intellectual Property Norms and the Transformation of Stand-Up Comedy,* 94 Va. L. Rev. 1787 (2008); Jeremy A. Schachter, *That's My Joke . . . Art . . . Trick!: How the Internal Norms of IP Communities Are Ineffective Against Extra-Community Misappropriation,* 12 Va. Sports & Ent. L.J. 63 (2011); Conal Condren, Jessica Milner Davis, Sally McCausland & Robert Phiddian, *Defining Parody and Satire: Australian Copyright Law and Its New Exception,* 13 Media & Arts L. Rev. 273, 279 (2008).

  For a study focusing on humor's intersection with defamation, *see* Laura E. Little, *Just a Joke: Defamatory Humor and Incongruity's Promise,* 21 S. Cal. Interdisc. L.J. 95 (2011).

16. In this way, this book continues the global analysis of how legal doctrine intersects with humor reflected in two of my earlier works, Laura E. Little, *Laughing at Censorship,* 28 Yale Journal of Law and Humanities 161 (2016) (analyzing different forms of humor ridiculing, celebrating, and co-opting government censorship); Laura E. Little, *Regulating Funny: Humor and the Law,* 94 Cornell L. Rev. 1235, 1224–81 (2009) (identifying trends in humor regulation across legal subject matters).

17. Laura E. Little, *Regulating Funny: Humor and the Law,* 94 Cornell L. Rev. 1235, 1224–81 (2009) (surveying interdisciplinary humor scholarship).

18. Jon E. Roeckelein, The Psychology of Humor 13 (2002) (citing Rod A. Martin, *Humor and Laughter, in* 4 Encyclopedia of Psychology 202, 204 (Alan E. Kazdin ed., 2000)).

19. Rod A. Martin, The Psychology of Humor: An Integrative Approach 23, 126 (2007).

20. Joke Collection, *supra* note 5.

21. *Id.*

22. Charles M. Sevilla, Disorder in the Court 130 (1992).

23. Laughing Matters: A Serious Look at Humour 76 (John Durant & Jonathan Miller eds., 1988).

24. Conal Condren, Jessica Milner Davis, Sally McCausland & Robert Phiddian, *Defining Parody and Satire: Australian Copyright Law and Its New Exception,* 13 Media & Arts L. Rev. 273, 279 (2008).

25. Salvatore Attardo, Humorous Texts: A Semantic and Pragmatic Analysis 71, 87 (2001) (describing parody's connection to intertextualism and defining the term); Peggy Zeglin Brand, *Parody, in* 3 Encyclopedia of Aesthetics 441, 442 (Michael Kelly ed., 1998) (describing intertextualism); Jerry Palmer, *Parody and Decorum: Permission to Mock, in* Beyond a Joke 79 (Sharon Lockyer & Michael Pickering eds., 2005) (referring to parody's quality of intertextuality).

26. Jerry Palmer, *Parody and Decorum: Permission to Mock, in* Beyond a Joke 79 (Sharon Lockyer & Michael Pickering eds., 2005).

27. Arthur Asa Berger, Blind Men and Elephants: Perspectives on Humor 74 (1995) (discussing style of "authorship," style of "genre," and "specific text").

28. Hustler Magazine v. Falwell, 485 U.S. 46 (1988).

29. Conal Condren et al., *supra* note 24, at 280.

30. Richard Lederer, *A Primer of Puns,* 70 THE ENGLISH JOURNAL 32, 32 (1981).

31. Joke Collection, *supra* note 5.

32. Joke Collection, *supra* note 5.

33. *"The Comedy Rules-of-Three,"* HOLLYWOOD & LEVINE (July 25, 2013) http://kenlevine.blogspot.com/2013/07/the-comedy-rules-of-threes.html.

34. MATTHEW M. HURLEY, DANIEL C. DENNETT & REGINALD B. ADAMS, JR., INSIDE JOKES 61 (2011) (observing that puns, dirty jokes, and slapstick have little in common aside from the fact that they can all be fun).

35. *See, e.g.,* Rod A. Martin, *Humor and Laughter, in* 4 ENCYCLOPEDIA OF PSYCHOLOGY 202, 203 (Alan E. Kazdin ed., 2000); *see also* Anthony J. Chapman & Hugh C. Foot, *Introduction* to HUMOR AND LAUGHTER 1, 1 (Anthony J. Chapman & Hugh C. Foot eds., Transaction Pub. 1996) (observing that Cicero and Aristotle saw laughter as coming from "shabbiness or deformity," and degrades others in a way inappropriately in a civilized society). Similarly, Socrates advocated that society should restrict laughter that "mocks authority" and "notions of truth and beauty." MICHAEL BILLIG, LAUGHTER AND RIDICULE: TOWARDS A SOCIAL CRITIQUE OF HUMOUR 41–42 (2005). Finally, Plato believed that weak people use humor when they believe they are unlikely to face counterattack. Dolf Zillman & Joanne R. Cantor, *A Disposition Theory of Humour and Mirth, in* HUMOR AND LAUGHTER 94 (Anthony J. Chapman & Hugh C. Foot eds., Transaction Pub. 1996) (1976) (describing Plato's observation that "the weak and helpless" are handy ridicule targets as well as "a risk-free source of social gaiety").

36. THOMAS HOBBES, LEVIATHAN 48 (G.A.J. Rogers & Karl Schuhmann eds., Thoemmes Continuum 2003) (1651). Hobbes observed that humans tend toward insecurity. As a result, humans also tend to undervalue their own abilities, and look to satisfy their need for self-respect "by observing the imperfections of other men." *Id.*

37. This joke is derived from an example provided in MATTHEW M. HURLEY, DANIEL C. DENNETT & REGINALD B. ADAMS, JR., INSIDE JOKES 41(2011).

38. Giedrė, Bored Panda, *10+ of the Most Hilarious Things that Court Reporters Have Ever Recorded to Be Said in Court,* https://www.boredpanda.com/funny-court-reports-disorder-in-court/, citing CHARLES M. SEVILLA, DISORDER IN THE COURT 130 (1992).

39. As Max Eastman said: "Few certainly have never felt a pleasure in the debasement of others. It takes but a moment of honest recollection to establish the difference between these feelings and the feeling that something which has happened is funny." EASTMAN, *supra* note 32, at 33.

40. MICHAEL BILLIG, LAUGHTER AND RIDICULE: TOWARDS A SOCIAL CRITIQUE OF HUMOUR 86 (2005) (referring to humor's role in releasing pressure); JOHN LIMON, STAND-UP COMEDY IN THEORY, OR, ABJECTION IN AMERICA 39 (2000) (observing that jokes can release anxiety and fear about topics such as miscegenation and homoeroticism); SIGMUND FREUD, THE JOKE AND ITS RELATION TO THE UNCONSCIOUS (Joyce Crick trans., Penguin 2003) (1905) (discussing anxiety release through humor).

41. MICHAEL BILLIG, LAUGHTER AND RIDICULE: TOWARDS A SOCIAL CRITIQUE OF HUMOUR 86 (2005) (referring to humor's role in releasing pressure and tracing release theory to a dispute between Spencer and Bain); MURRAY S. DAVIS, WHAT'S SO FUNNY? THE COMIC CONCEPTION OF CULTURE AND SOCIETY 7 (1993) (naming Spencer and Freud as those who developed the theory).

42. MICHAEL BILLIG, LAUGHTER AND RIDICULE: TOWARDS A SOCIAL CRITIQUE OF HUMOUR 93–97 (2005).

43. SIGMUND FREUD, THE JOKE AND ITS RELATION TO THE UNCONSCIOUS 154 (Joyce Crick trans., Penguin 2003) (1905) (observing that joke technique is similar to "dreamwork:" "the processes of condensation . . . displacement, representation by absurdity

or...indirect representation"). MATTHEW M. HURLEY, DANIEL C. DENNETT & REGINALD B. ADAMS, JR., INSIDE JOKES 44– 45 (2011) (explaining release theory).

44. SIGMUND FREUD, THE JOKE AND ITS RELATION TO THE UNCONSCIOUS 92 (Joyce Crick trans., Penguin 2003) (1905).

45. *See, e.g.,* Vassilis Saroglou & Lydwine Anciaux, *Liking Sick Humor: Coping Styles and Religion as Predictors,* 17 HUMOR: INT'L J. HUMOR RES. 257, 257–66 (2004) (demonstrating correlation between coping styles and appreciation of jokes about disability, deformity, disease, and death); *see also Introduction* to MARK TWAIN: THE FATE OF HUMOR vii, xv (James Cox, Univ. of Mo. Press 2002) (1966) (arguing that humorists make possible release of "repressed tension" by exposing "the absence of meaning in existence").

46. This joke is derived from an example used in MARC GALANTER, LOWERING THE BAR: LAWYER JOKES & LEGAL CULTURE 88 (2005).

47. Giedrė, *Court Reporters, supra* note 38, citing CHARLES M. SEVILLA, DISORDER IN THE COURT 130 (1992).

48. *Id.*

49. *In re* Henderson, 343 P.3d 518, 520–23 (Kan. 2015).

50. SCOTT WEEMS, HA! THE SCIENCE OF WHEN WE LAUGH AND WHY 16 (2014).

51. Laura E. Little, *Regulating Funny: Humor and the Law,* 94 CORNELL L. REV. 1235, 1245 (2009) (describing Kant's and Schopenhauer's connection with incongruity theory).

52. PAUL E. MCGHEE, HUMOR, ITS ORIGIN AND DEVELOPMENT 10 (1979); *see also* Henry W. Cetola, *Toward a Cognitive-Appraisal Model of Humor Appreciation,* 1 HUMOR: INT'L J. HUMOR RES. 245, 245–46 (maintaining that "things that we find funny have to be somewhat unexpected, ambiguous, illogical, or inappropriate").

53. John Morreall, *Funny Ha-Ha, Funny Strange, and Other Reactions to Incongruity, in* THE PHILOSOPHY OF LAUGHTER AND HUMOR 188–89 (John Morreall ed., 1983); *see also* JOHN ALLEN PAULOS, MATHEMATICS AND HUMOR 9 (1980) (using the idea of opposites to define humorous incongruity).

54. HENRI BERGSON, LAUGHTER: AN ESSAY ON THE MEANING OF THE COMIC 112 (Cloudsley Brereton & Fred Rothwell trans., Macmillan 1914) (1900).

55. For Isaac Asimov, humor emerges when a point of view is altered and this creates an "anticlimax." ISAAC ASIMOV, TREASURY OF HUMOR 1 (1971).

56. Thanks go to my colleague Professor Finbarr McCarthy for this one.

57. BERGSON, *supra* note 54, at 94.

58. Mathematician John Paulos created a taxonomy of "opposites" that are contained in various humorous incongruities: expectation/surprise; mechanical/spiritual; superiority/ incompetence; balance/exaggeration; propriety/vulgarity. JOHN PAULOS, MATHEMATICS AND HUMOR (1980). Patricia Ewick & Susan S. Silbey, *No Laughing Matter: Humor and Contradictions in Stories of Law,* 50 DEPAUL L. REV. 559, 561 (2000) (reasoning that humor's "quality of suspense" results from placing "disparate elements in competition"); Victor Raskin & Salvatore Attardo, *Non-Literalness and Non-Bona Fide in Language: An Approach to Formal and Computational Treatments of Humor,* 2.1 PRAGMATICS AND COGNITION 31, 35–37 (1994) (discussing "recoil effect" and describing how listeners participate in joke-telling by looking for joke ingredients in the speaker's words).

59. *See, e.g.,* Salvatore Attardo & Victor Raskin, *Script Theory Revis(it)ed: Joke Similarity and Joke Representation Model,* 4 HUMOR: INT'L J. HUMOR RES. 293, 331 (1991); Tony Veale, *Figure-Ground Duality in Humour: A Multi-Modal Perspective,* 4 LODZ PAPERS PRAGMATICS 63, 74 (2008), *available at* http://versita.metapress.com/content/jp0413k02350. Theorist Marta Dynel describes two ways of tying incongruity humor with priming theory. One approach, Dynel argues, starts with priming that leads in one direction, but ends with a surprise, such as in the following: "War does not determine who is right but who is left." MARTA DYNEL, HUMOROUS GARDEN-PATHS: A PRAGMATIC-COGNITIVE

STUDY 25, 27 (2009). She observes that priming can also occur through an "ambiguous lead up," such as in the following: "She has her looks from her father. He's a plastic surgeon." *Id.* at 51.

60. Veale, *supra* note 59, at 75.

61. *See, e.g.,* Giovannantonio Forabosco, *Cognitive Aspects of the Humor Process: The Concept of Incongruity*, 5 HUMOR: INT'L J. HUMOR RES. 45, 60 (1992) (explaining that the humor process requires an "attention-shift . . . in which the project passes from the perception of congruence to the perception of incongruity and, sometimes, vice versa, with several shifts").

62. Veale, *supra* note 59, at 73.

63. *Id.*

64. *Id.*

65. ROD A. MARTIN, THE PSYCHOLOGY OF HUMOR: AN INTEGRATIVE APPROACH 63 (2007) (quoting Jerry M. Suls, *A Two-Stage Model for the Appreciation of Jokes and Cartoons: An Information-Processing Analysis, in* THE PSYCHOLOGY OF HUMOR: THEORETICAL PERSPECTIVES AND EMPIRICAL ISSUES 81, 90 (Jeffrey H. Goldstein & Paul E. McGhee eds., 1972)).

66. FREUD, *supra* note 44.

67. N.R.F. Maier, *A Gestalt Theory of Humor*, 23 BRIT. J. PSYCHOL. 69, 69–74 (1932).

68. AVNER ZIV, PERSONALITY AND SENSE OF HUMOR 90 (1984). For a description of the mental discomfort inspired by incongruity, *see* Benedict Carey, *How Nonsense Sharpens the Intellect*, N.Y. TIMES (Oct. 5, 2009), *available at* http://www.nytimes.com/2009/10/06/health/06mind.html.

69. Forabosco, *supra* note 60, at 57 (arguing that without resolution, "incongruity cannot be . . . used in the humor context" and the listener "would remain perplexed, confused, disoriented, and perhaps in extreme cases even frightened").

70. *See, e.g.,* ROD A. MARTIN, *supra* note 65, at 68–73 (describing various studies regarding the effect of incongruity resolution). Willibald Ruch & Franz-Josef Hehl, *A Two-Mode Model of Humor Appreciation: Its Relation to Aesthetic Appreciation and Simplicity-Complexity of Personality, in* THE SENSE OF HUMOR: EXPLORATIONS OF A PERSONALITY CHARACTERISTIC 109, 127 (Willibald Ruch ed., 1998) (finding that tolerance for ambiguity correlates positively with appreciation for humor with unresolved incongruity, bizarreness, and absurdity, while conservative and authoritarian personality traits correlate positively only with appreciating jokes that resolve incongruity); Willibald Ruch, *Assessment of Appreciation of Humor: Studies with the 3 WD Humor Test*, 9 ADVANCES PERSONALITY ASSESSMENT 27, 67 (1992) (finding that tolerance for ambiguity correlates positively with appreciation for humor with unresolved incongruity, bizarreness, and absurdity, while conservative and authoritarian personality traits correlate positively only with appreciating jokes that resolve incongruity).

71. Kevin Underhill, *Pants Judge Roy Pearson Is Back in Court* (January 29, 2010), https://loweringthebar.net/2010/01/still-unable-to-shut-up-pants-judge-roy-pearson-is-back-in-court.html.

72. *See, e.g.,* MARTIN, *supra* note 65, at 72 (summarizing current research and concluding that "some sort of incongruity (however defined) seems to be necessary for all types of humor").

73. The most prominent challenge to incongruity's essential role in the humor process comes from Gabriella Eichinger Ferro-Luzzi. Although asserting that incongruity occurs frequently in humor, she maintains that it is not essential to producing humor. Gabriella Eichinger Ferro-Luzzi, *On Necessary Incongruities*, 10 HUMOR: INT'L J. HUMOR RES. 117 (1997); Gabriella Eichinger Ferro-Luzzi, *Tamil Jokes and the Polythetic-Prototype Approach to Humor*, 3 HUMOR: INT'L J. HUMOR RES. 147, 152 (1990). Other humor scholars take

her work very seriously but believe it insufficiently theorized and insufficiently supported by examples. *See, e.g.,* ELLIOTT ORING, ENGAGING HUMOR 8–10 (2003) (arguing that Eichinger Ferro-Luzzi's analyses of jokes seem "incomplete or off the mark" and that her examples are "questionable"); Giovannantonio Forabosco, *Is the Concept of Incongruity Still a Useful Construct for the Advancement of Humor Research?,* 4 LODZ PAPERS PRAGMATICS 45, 55 (2008), *available at* http://versita.metapress.com/content/jp0413k02350/ (criticizing Eichinger Ferro-Luzzi's use of a standard "dictionary-based . . . definition" of incongruity rather than a theory-dependent use of the term).

Robert Latta also launched a broad-ranging attack on incongruity theory. ROBERT L. LATTA, THE BASIC HUMOR PROCESS: A COGNITIVE SHIFT THEORY AND THE CASE AGAINST INCONGRUITY 99–234 (1999). Other humor theorists have vigorously criticized his work as well. Forabosco, *supra,* at 55 (stating that Latta's "case against incongruity" has "been radically criticized in a close and tough analysis"); Elliott Oring, *Review of THE BASIC HUMOR PROCESS: A COGNITIVE SHIFT THEORY AND THE CASE AGAINST INCONGRUITY,* 12 HUMOR: INT'L J. HUMOR RES. 457, 457–59 (1999) (arguing that Latta's alternative theory is not firmly grounded in psychological literature and that Latta's attempt to impose "a strict logical standard" on incongruity is at odds with the nature of humor).

For an intermediate position on the incongruity debate, see Michael K. Cundall, Jr., *Humor and the Limits of Incongruity,* 19 CREATIVITY RES. J. 203, 211 (2007) (acknowledging that humor perception does require "recognition of an incongruity," but also arguing that incongruity theory "leaves too much of the act of perceiving humor unexplained").

74. Tony Veale, *Incongruity in Humor: Root Cause or Epiphenomenon?,* 17 HUMOR: INT'L J. HUMOR RES. 419, 424 (2004).

75. Veale, *supra* note 59, at 73 (explaining how "incongruity alone does not automatically produce either creativity or humour"); *cf.* MICHAEL BILLIG, LAUGHTER AND RIDICULE: TOWARDS A SOCIAL CRITIQUE OF HUMOR 76 (2005) (observing that one might conclude that incongruity often accompanies comedy, but this alone does not "explain why the perception of incongruity should be followed by a sense of pleasure and laughter").

76. MARTIN, *supra* note 65, at 68–73 (using the example of being hit by a car while walking on a sidewalk).

77. Veale, *supra* note 59, at 73 (citing ELLIOTT ORING, ENGAGING HUMOR (2003)).

78. MARTIN, *supra* note 65, 64–65 (2007) (summarizing literature on what "something extra" enables incongruity to be humor).

79. MATTHEW M. HURLEY, DANIEL C. DENNETT & REGINALD B. ADAMS, JR., INSIDE JOKES 53 (2011) (describing various surprise theories that posit that surprise is a necessary and perhaps sufficient condition for humor).

80. Victor Raskin & Salvatore Attardo, *Non-Literalness and Non-Bona Fide in Language: An Approach to Formal and Computational Treatments of Humor,* 2.1 PRAGMATICS AND COGNITION 31, 35–37 (1994) (analyzing how listeners participate in joke-telling by anticipating and searching for joke ingredients in the joke teller's words); *see also* TED COHEN, JOKES: PHILOSOPHICAL THOUGHTS ON JOKING MATTERS 28 (1999) (explaining that shared knowledge or experience between joke teller and listener can provide a "foundation of the intimacy" that develops if a joke "succeeds").

81. Hargus v. Ferocious and Impetuous, LLC, 840 F.3d 133 (2016).

82. *Id.*

83. CHARLES M. SEVILLA, DISORDER IN THE COURT 130 (1992).

84. The enterprise of this book is by its nature interdisciplinary. As explained earlier in this introduction, the existing humor scholarship spans a large mix of disciplines already.

By injecting law into the mix, I am expanding the mix. After structuring the study, I was pleased to discover that my structure for the book is similar to a classic interdisciplinary work, Richard Posner's study of the intersection of law and literature. Posner divides his study into "Literature on Legal Themes" (analogous to humor about law), "Law as a Form of Literature" (analogous to humor in law), and "The Regulation of Literature by Law" (analogous to law's effect on humor).

CHAPTER 1

1. St. John Barned-Smith & Michael Hinkelman, *Jury Clears White Electrician in "Noose" Trial*, PHILA. INQUIRER (Aug. 6, 2009), http://www.philly.com/philly/news/ pennsylvania/ 20090806_Jury_clears_white_electrician_in__noose__trial.html.
2. I thank Professor Robert Phiddian of Flinders University in Adelaide, Australia, for sharing this analogy with me.
3. Notice of Motion and Motion to Dismiss, Naruto v. Slater, No. 15-CV-04324-WHO, 2016 WL 362231 (N.D. Cal. Jan. 28, 2016), 2015 WL 9843651.
4. *Naruto*, 2016 WL 362231.
5. *See* ROGER E. SCHECHTER & JOHN R. THOMAS, INTELLECTUAL PROPERTY: THE LAW OF COPYRIGHTS, PATENTS AND TRADEMARKS § 29.1, at 637 (2003). Trademark protection derives from federal law (primarily the Lanham Act) and state antidilution statutes. *Id.* § 29, at 636, § 30.5, at 718.
6. Nike, Inc. v. "Just Did It" Enters., 6 F.3d 1225, 1228 (7th Cir. 1993).
7. Also subject to copyright protection, Mickey Mouse is a registered trademark.
8. Tommy Hilfiger Licensing, Inc. v. Nature Labs, LLC, 221 F. Supp. 2d 410 (S.D.N.Y. 2002).
9. Girl Scouts v. Personality Posters Mfg. Co., 304 F. Supp. 1228, 1230 (S.D.N.Y. 1969).
10. Jordache Enters., Inc. v. Hogg Wyld, Ltd., 828 F.2d 1482 (10th Cir. 1987).
11. *See* Pratheepan Gulasekaram, *Policing the Border Between Trademarks and Free Speech: Protecting Unauthorized Trademark Use in Expressive Works*, 80 WASH. L. REV. 887, 913–15 (2005) (noting problems with "line-drawing" and inconsistent results in trademark cases "related to drug use, sexuality, obscenity, and noxious behavior"). *See generally* Rochelle Cooper Dreyfuss, *Reconciling Trademark Rights and Expressive Values: How to Stop Worrying and Learn to Love Ambiguity*, in TRADEMARK LAW AND THEORY: A HANDBOOK OF CONTEMPORARY RESEARCH 261 (Graeme B. Dinwoodie & Mark D. Janis eds., 2009) (noting unpredictable results of First Amendment defense in trademark infringement suits against parodies of trademarked material, resulting in risk "for anyone who is contemplating an investment in expressive use").
12. Gen. Elec. Co. v. Alumpa Coal Co., 205 U.S.P.Q. (BNA) 1036, 1036–37 (D. Mass. 1979).
13. 15 U.S.C. §1052(a) (2012). The Federal Circuit Court of Appeals read this provision restrictively in *In re Tam*, 808 F.3d 1321 (Fed. Cir. 2015), *as corrected* (Feb. 11, 2016), *cert. granted sub nom.* Lee v. Tam, 137 S. Ct. 30 (2016) (mem.), a case I discuss further in connection with hate speech.
14. A similar example is *Dallas Cowboys Cheerleaders, Inc. v. Pussycat Cinema, Ltd.*, 604 F.2d 200, 202–03 (2d Cir. 1979), where the defendant had produced a pornographic film with women wearing Dallas Cowboys Cheerleaders uniforms engaged in sex acts. Although one could interpret this as a parody of provocative half-time performances during actual football games, the court of appeals, noting the "sexually depraved" nature of the film, found an infringement. *Id.* at 204–05.
15. RESTATEMENT (SECOND) OF TORTS § 559 (AM. LAW INST. 1977). The Second Restatement sets forth the actual elements of defamation.

  To create liability for defamation there must be:
  (a). a false and defamatory statement concerning another;
  (b). an unprivileged publication to a third party;

(c). fault amounting at least to negligence on the part of the publisher; and

(d). either actionability of the statement irrespective of special harm or the existence of special harm caused by the publication.

RESTATEMENT (SECOND) OF TORTS § 558 (AM. LAW INST. 1977).

16. Here is the full statement of this position:

> By definition, defamation requires a false statement of fact; parody, to the degree it is perceived as parody by its intended audience, conveys the message that it is not the original and, therefore, cannot constitute a false statement of fact. . . . If a parody could be actionable because, while recognizable as a joke, it conveyed an unfavorable impression, very few journalistic parodies could survive. It is not for the court to evaluate a parody as to whether it went too far, for the purposes of a libel claim; as long as it is recognizable to the average reader as a joke, it must be protected or parody must cease to exist.

50 AM. JUR. 2D *Libel and Slander* § 256 (2016). The Indiana Court of Appeals specifically adopted this approach in *Hamilton v. Prewett*, 860 N.E.2d 1234, 1244–45 (Ind. Ct. App. 2007). Although the court acknowledged that a humorous statement could be defamatory, the court nonetheless identified parody as "another beast that goes beyond mere humor." *See also* Garvelink v. Detroit News, 522 N.W.2d 883, 887 (Mich. Ct. App. 1994) (stating that "even if the writer is motivated by hatred or ill" a parody is still not to be actionable because it is "in the area of public debate concerning public officials").

17. Salomone v. Macmillan Publ'g Co., 411 N.Y.S.2d 105, 109 (Sup. Ct. 1978).

18. RESTATEMENT (SECOND) OF TORTS § 566.

19. *Id.* § 566 cmt. c.

20. There are many cases that exhibit the variety of approaches. *See, e.g.,* Knievel v. ESPN, 393 F.3d 1068, 1071, 1077–78 (9th Cir. 2005) (finding that a photograph with the caption "Evel Knievel proves that you're never too old to be a pimp" could not reasonably be interpreted as actual fact); Dworkin v. Hustler Magazine Inc., 867 F.2d 1188, 1193–94 (9th Cir. 1989) (dismissing a defamation claim by an antipornography advocate depicted in a *Hustler* cartoon because a reasonable reader could not interpret the cartoon as conveying a statement of fact); Keller v. Miami Herald Publ'g Co., 778 F.2d 711, 716 (11th Cir. 1985) (evaluating an editorial cartoon that referred to a nursing home as a haunted house by reference to the fact-opinion dichotomy as well as by reference to "hyperbole, exaggeration, and caricature"); Pring v. Penthouse Int'l, Ltd., 695 F.2d 438, 441 (10th Cir. 1982) (evaluating a beauty contest spoof by reference to rhetorical hyperbole case law and deciding that the spoof could not be interpreted as providing actual facts since the spoof presented "impossibility and fantasy within a fanciful story"); Filippo v. Lee Publ'ns, Inc., 485 F. Supp. 2d 969, 980 (N.D. Ind. 2007) (stating that under Indiana law a cartoon can be defamatory only if a reasonable fact finder could conclude that it implies "*objectively verifiable or testable* facts"); Sagan v. Apple Comput., Inc., 874 F. Supp. 1072, 1075–76 (C.D. Cal. 1994) (explaining in a defamation action based on changing a computer code name from "Carl Sagan" to "Butt-Head Astronomer" that using "the figurative term 'Butt-Head'" undermines the possibility that "a reasonable fact finder could conclude that the published statements imply a provably false factual assertion"); Freedlander v. Edens Broad., Inc., 734 F. Supp. 221, 228 n.13 (E.D. Va. 1990), *aff'd*, 923 F.2d 848 (4th Cir. 1991) ("Having found that the song is a comedic expression based on fact, the Court deems it unnecessary to pursue defendant's argument that the song constitutes protected opinion"); Couch v. San Juan Unified Sch. Dist., 39 Cal. Rptr. 2d 848 (Cal. Ct. App. 1995) (deciding that a mock examination in a student newspaper could not be interpreted as suggesting actual fact or anything other than parody); Hamilton v. Prewett, 860 N.E.2d 1234, 1245–47 (Ind. Ct. App. 2007) (deciding whether parody is protected as hyperbole and asserting that parody "is speech that one cannot reasonably believe to be fact because

of its exaggerated nature"); Newman v. Delahunty, 681 A.2d 671, 683–84 (N.J. Super. Ct. Law Div. 1994), *aff'd*, 681 A.2d 659 (N.J. Super. Ct. App. Div. 1996) (evaluating campaign literature for defamation liability by reference to whether it expressed facts or was "rhetorical hyperbole" or a "vigorous epithet"); McKimm v. Ohio Elections Comm'n, 729 N.E.2d 364, 371–72 (Ohio 2000) (evaluating whether election literature cartoons could be interpreted by a reasonable reader as asserting facts); Ferreri v. Plain Dealer Publ'g Co., 756 N.E.2d 712, 721–22 (Ohio Ct. App. 2001) (explaining that a cartoon may be defamatory only if a reasonable person would conclude that it contained a factual assertion rather than "exaggeration and hyperbole").

21. *See generally* Kathryn Dix Sowle, *A Matter of Opinion:* Milkovich *Four Years Later,* 3 WM. & MARY BILL RTS. J. 467, 474 (1994).

22. Pete Wells, *As Not Seen on TV,* N.Y. TIMES (Nov. 13, 2012), http://www.nytimes.com/2012/11/14/dining/reviews/restaurant-review-guys-american-kitchen-bar-in-times-square.html.

23. *Hilarious Yelp Review: "It Ripped Its Way of Me in Raging Fiery Whirlwind of Poopy Terror,"* IYOCAT (Nov. 20, 2013), http://ifyoucantaffordtotip.com/hilarious-yelp-review/.

24. Ron Culberson, *Is It Fact or Just Your Opinion?*, https://ronculberson.com/

25. Cockle Legal Brief, *"Who Says Judges Can't Be Funny,"* https://www.cocklelegalbriefs.com/blog/opinions/who-says-judges-cant-be-funny/.

26. Immanuel Kant explained: "Jest must contain something that is capable of deceiving for a moment." IMMANUEL KANT, THE CRITIQUE OF JUDGMENT 225 (J.H. Bernard trans., Prometheus Books 2000) (1892).

27. Salomone v. MacMillan Publ'g, 411 N.Y.S.2d 105, 108 (Sup. Ct. 1978).

28. Polygram Records, Inc. v. Superior Court, 216 Cal. Rptr. 252 (Cal. Ct. App. 1985).

29. *Id.* at 260–61.

30. New Times, Inc. v. Isaacks, 146. S.W.3d 144 (Tex. 2004).

31. *Id.* at 158.

32. Philosopher Max Eastman put the matter this way:

> The first law of humor is that things can be funny only when we are in fun. There may be a serious thought or motive lurking underneath our humor. We may be only "half in fun" and still funny. But when we are not in fun at all, when we are "in dead earnest," humor is the thing that is dead.

MAX EASTMAN, ENJOYMENT OF LAUGHTER 3 (1936) [hereinafter EASTMAN].

33. Hustler Magazine Inc. v. Falwell, 485 U.S. 46, 56 (1988).

34. *Id.* at 55.

35. *Id.* at 56.

36. *Id.* at 52, 57.

37. Martin v. Living Essentials, LLC, 160 F. Supp. 3d 1042 (N.D. Ill. 2016).

38. *Id.* at 1044–45.

39. *Id.* at 1044.

40. *Id.*

41. *Id.* at 1047.

42. *Id.*

43. Lucy v. Zehmer, 84 S.E.2d 516 (Va. 1954).

44. Conner v. Magic City Trucking Serv., Inc., 592 So. 2d 1048 (Ala. 1992).

45. 164 P.3d 454 (Wash. 2007).

46. The case was filed as *Berry v. Gulf Coast Wings, Inc.* Initial Complaint, Berry v. Gulf Coast Wings, Inc., No. 01-2642 (Fla. Cir. Ct. filed Jul. 24, 2001), 2001 WL 34131735; *see* Keith A. Rowley, *You Asked for It, You Got It . . . Toy Yoda: Practical Jokes, Prizes, and Contract Law,* 3 NEV. L.J. 526, 527 (2003) (summarizing *Berry*).

47. Augstein v. Leslie, No. 11-CIV-7512(HB), 2012 WL 4928914 (S.D.N.Y. Oct. 17, 2012).

48. Kolodziej v. Mason, 774 F.3d 736, 743–45 (11th Cir. 2014).

49. 88 F. Supp. 2d 116 (S.D.N.Y. 1999), aff'd mem., 210 F.3d 88 (2d Cir. 2000).

50. Id. at 128.

51. Id. at 128–29.

52. Oliva v. Heath, 41 Cal. Rptr. 2d 613 (Cal. Ct. App. 1995).

53. Caudle v. Betts, 512 So. 2d 389 (La. 1987).

54. Mason v. Wyeth, Inc., 183 F. App'x. 353 (4th Cir. 2006).

55. Swinton v. Potomac Corp., 270 F.3d 794 (9th Cir. 2001); Melissa K. Hughes, Note, *Through the Looking Glass: Racial Jokes, Social Context, and the Reasonable Person in Hostile Work Environment Analysis*, 76 S. CAL. L. REV. 1437 (2003).

56. Carter v. Ball, 33 F.3d 450 (4th Cir. 1994) (using a pun to associate the plaintiff with a gorilla); Parra v. Hous. & Cmty. Serv. Agency of Lane Cty., No. 05-6385-HO, 2007 WL 2401743 (D. Or. Aug. 16, 2007); Howard v. Burlington Air Express Inc., No. 93-C-7815, 1994 WL 722061, at *4 (N.D. Ill. Dec. 29, 1994) ("Let's call a spade a spade").

57. Hernandez v. Valley View Hosp. Ass'n, 684 F.3d 950 (10th Cir. 2012) (declining to find liability on the basis of a series of Latino jokes that the court found "boorish but not illegal"); Kelly v. Senior Ctrs., Inc., 169 F. App'x 423, 430 (6th Cir. 2006) (rejecting liability on the basis of racist jokes on the theory that the plaintiff had failed to establish how the hostile work environment interfered with his ability to do his job); Robinson v. Colquitt EMC, No. 7:13-CV-92 HL, 2015 WL 1471930, at *12 (M.D. Ga. Mar. 31, 2015) (concluding that the evidence around a series of jokes using the n-word and disparaging President Obama's black identity did "not warrant a finding that the off-color commentary and inappropriate jokes of Plaintiff's co-workers were so severe and pervasive to alter the conditions of Plaintiff's employment"). *But see* Streater v. City of Camden Fire Dep't, 567 F. Supp. 2d 667, 678 (D.N.J. 2008) (denying defendant's summary judgment motion and allowing the case to proceed to trial where the racist jokes and comments to an African American co-worker were threatening).

58. Oncale v. Sundowner Offshore Servs. Inc., 523 U.S. 75 (1998).

59. Faragher v. City of Boca Raton, 524 U.S. 775, 788 (1998).

60. 510 U.S. 17 (1993).

61. Id. at 19.

62. 760 F. Supp. 1486 (M.D. Fla. 1991).

63. Id. at 1498, 1500, 1504–05.

64. McIntyre v. Manhattan Ford, Lincoln-Mercury, Inc., 669 N.Y.S.2d 122, 125 (Sup. Ct. 1997).

65. Id. at 129.

66. Id. at 131 & n.5 (the challenged statements "[t]'aint funny").

67. Stanley v. Nw. Ohio Psychiatric Hosp., 7 F. Supp. 3d 731 (N.D. Ohio 2014).

68. 397 F.3d 1256 (10th Cir. 2005).

69. *Charges Alleging Sexual Harassment FY 2010–FY 2015*, U.S. EQUAL EMP. OPPORTUNITY COMMISSION, www.eeoc.gov/eeoc/statistics/enforcement/sexual_harassment_new.cfm (last visited Mar. 25, 2017); *Charges Alleging Race and Harassment FY 1997–FY 2015*, U.S. EQUAL EMP. OPPORTUNITY COMMISSION, www.eeoc.gov/eeoc/statistics/enforcement/race_harassment.cfm (last visited Mar. 25, 2017).

70. Nitsche v. CEO of Osage Valley Elec. Coop., 446 F.3d 841, 843 (8th Cir. 2006).

71. Lyle v. Warner Brothers Television Prods., 132 P.3d 211, 218 (Cal. 2006).

72. Id. at 217.

73. Hoffman v. Lincoln Life & Annuity Distribs., Inc., 174 F. Supp. 2d 367, 376 (D. Md. 2001).

74. Augustin v. Yale Club of N.Y.C., No. 03-CV-1924 (KMK), 2006 WL 2690289, at *6 (S.D.N.Y. Sept. 15, 2006), aff'd, 274 F. App'x 76 (2d Cir. 2008).

75. Martinez v. Rapidigm, Inc., No. CV-02-1106, 2007 WL 965899, at *2 (W.D. Pa. Mar. 29, 2007).

76. Goede v. Mare Rest., No. 95 C 5238, 1995 WL 769766, at *1 (N.D. Ill. Dec. 29, 1995).

77. Ryan v. Tau Labs., Inc., No. 87 CIV 8426 (MCG), 1989 WL 135901, at *3 (S.D.N.Y. Nov. 8, 1989).

78. Czemske v. Eastman Kodak Co., No. 01 C 6075, 2003 WL 21418319, at *6 (N.D. Ill. June 17, 2003).

79. Mel Watkins, On the Real Side: A History of African American Comedy 16 (Lawrence Hill Books 1999).

80. United States v. Kosma, 951 F.2d 549, 549 (3d Cir. 1991).

81. Watts v. United States, 394 U.S. 705 (1969).

82. *See, e.g.,* Roy v. United States, 416 F.2d 874, 877 (9th Cir. 1969) (stating that a "later statement that the threat was a joke would . . . not necessarily eliminate the mischief created").

83. Mustafa v. City of Chicago, 442 F.3d 544, 544 (2006).

84. Elonis v. United States, 135 S. Ct. 2001, 2005 (2015).

85. *Id.* at 2008.

86. 18 U.S.C. § 248 (2012).

87. United States v. McMillan, 53 F. Supp. 2d 895 (S.D. Miss. 1999).

88. Ruth Walden, Insult Laws: An Insult to Press Freedom (2000).

89. *All Things Considered, German Comedian's Crude Poem About Turkish President Sparks Controversy,* NPR (Apr. 13, 2016, 4:28 p.m.), http://www.npr.org/2016/04/13/474120891/german-comedians-crude-poem-about-turkish-president-sparks-controversy; Lizzie Dearden, *Prosecutors Drop Case Against German Comedian Jan Bohmermann over "Insulting" Erdogan Poem,* Independent (Oct. 4, 2016, 3:17 p.m.), http://www.independent.co.uk/news/world/europe/recep-tayyip-erdogan-poem-insulting-jan-boehmermann-affair-court-prosecutors-criminal-case-dropped-a7344791.html; Merritt Kennedy, *At Turkey's Request, Germany Allows Criminal Investigation of Comedian,* NPR (Apr. 15, 2016, 1:50 p.m.), http://www.npr.org/sections/thetwo-way/2016/04/15/474360749/at-turkeys-request-germany-allows-criminal-investigation-of-comedian.

90. FCC, *"Filthy Words" by George Carlin,* UMKC Sch. L., http://law2.umkc.edu/faculty/PROJECTS/FTRIALS/CONLAW/filthywords.html (last visited Mar. 25, 2017) (transcript of "Filthy Words").

91. FCC v. Pacifica Found., 438 U.S. 726, 740 (1978).

92. *Id.* at 749.

93. *Id.*

94. Timothy Bella, *The "7 Dirty Words" Turn 40, But They're Still Dirty,* Atlantic (May 24, 2012).

95. Ronald K .L. Collins & David M. Skover, The Trials of Lenny Bruce: The Fall and Rise of an American Icon 9 (2002).

96. Joe Randazzo, Funny on Purpose: The Definitive Guide to an Unpredictable Career in Comedy: Standup + Improv + Sketch + TV + Writing + Directing + YouTube.

97. Ed Payne, *Award-Winning Comedian George Carlin Dies,* https://www.radiowest.ca/forum/viewtopic.php?f=8&t=3698 (June 23, 2008, 1:19 a.m.) (last visited July 31, 2018).

98. The classic work on this subject is Dotan Oliar & Christopher Sprigman, *There's No Free Laugh (Anymore): The Emergence of Intellectual Property Norms and the Transformation of Stand-Up Comedy,* 94 Va. L. Rev. 1787 (2008).

99. Melvin Helitzer, Comedy Writing Secrets: The Best-Selling Guide to Writing Funny and Getting Paid for It 4 (1987).

100. Two particularly colorful examples include Joe Rogan's takedown of Carlos Mencia, Joe Rogan, *Carlos Mencia Is a Weak-Minded Joke Thief,* https://joerogan05.wordpress.com/

2005/09/27/carlos-mencia-is-a-weak-minded-joke-thief/ (last visited June 11, 2018), and Stewart Lee's particularly clever parable about another apparent joke-stealer, Stewart Lee, *Stewart Lee—Joe Pasquale Joke,* YouTube (Dec. 2, 2006), https://www.youtube .com/watch?v=0YE9Kthyaco (recording of Stewart Lee as broadcast on Paramount Comedy Edinburgh and Beyond in 2006). See text accompanying note 103 for the transcript for the Stewart Lee joke.

101. Stewart Lee, *Stewart Lee—Joe Pasquale Joke,* YouTube (Dec. 2, 2006), https://www.youtube .com/watch?v=0YE9Kthyaco (recording of Stewart Lee as broadcast on Paramount Comedy Edinburgh and Beyond in 2006).

102. Jason Newman, *"The Fat Jew" Joke Theft Victims Speak Out,* Rolling Stone (Aug. 20, 2015), http://www.rollingstone.com/culture/news/ the-fat-jew-joke-theft-victims-speak-out-20150820.

103. For discussion of related ideas, see Kimberlianne Podlas, *Respect My Authority! South Park's Expression of Legal Ideology and Contribution to Legal Culture,* 11 Vand. J. Ent. & Tech. L. 491 (2009).

104. Catherine Bates, *The Point of Puns,* 96 Mod. Philology 421, 422 (1999).

105. Joseph Tartakovsky, Op-Ed, *Pun for the Ages,* N.Y. Times, Mar. 28, 2009, at A21.

106. Eastman, *supra* note 32, at 119.

107. *See, e.g.,* Pac. Telesis Grp. v. Int'l Telesis Commc'ns, 994 F.2d 1364 (9th Cir. 1993) (holding that the designation "pun" would more likely trigger trademark protection); Marketquest Grp., Inc. v. BIC Corp., No. 11-CV-618 BAS JLB, 2015 WL 4064775 (S.D. Cal. July 2, 2015) (holding that the more obvious a pun, the less deserving of trademark protection); Schieffelin & Co. v. Jack Co. of Boca, 850 F. Supp. 232 (S.D.N.Y. 1994) (holding that an obvious pun does not establish a successful parody so as to avoid trademark liability).

108. *See, e.g.,* Alexandra Petri, *Chinese Media Banning Puns? End Pun Control!,* Wash. Post: ComPost (Dec. 5, 2014), https://www.washingtonpost.com/blogs/compost/ wp/2014/12/05/chinese-media-banning-puns-end-pun-control/.

109. Various political puns are collected in "The Grass-Mud Horse Lexicon," which compiles "resistance discourse of Chinese netizens" and posts them to Chinadigitaltimes.net.

110. For analysis of the role of political humor in contemporary Egyptian society, see Asmaa al-Ghoul, *Gazans Use Satire to Bypass Political Censorship,* Al-Monitor (Aug. 7, 2013), http://www.al-monitor.com/pulse/originals/2013/08/gaza-political-satire-palestinians-hamas.html#.

111. For a study of humor among Turkish protestors, see Ozan O. Varol, *Revolutionary Humor,* 23 S. Cal. Interdisc. L.J. 555, 564 (2014) (analyzing Turkish examples where protesters deployed humor in order to criticize the government's censorship efforts).

112. For analysis of the role of censorship and political humor in the Soviet Union and Russia, see William Henry Chamberlin, *The "Anecdote": Unrationed Soviet Humor,* 16 Russ. Rev. 27 (1957); Vadim V. Dementyev, *Russian Anekdots of 1970s: On the Material of the Soviet Humorous Journal "Krokodil,"* 2 Russ. J. Comm. 185 (2009); Martin Dewhirst, *Censorship in Russia, 1991 and 2001,* 18 J. Communist Stud. & Transition Pol. 21 (2010); Amei Wallach, *Censorship in the Soviet Bloc,* 50 Art J. 75 (1991); Victor Davidoff, *Russian Censors Are Dim-Witted and Dull,* Moscow Times (Nov. 26, 2012), http:// www.themoscowtimes.com/opinion/article/russian-censors-are-dim-witted-and-dull/ 471903.html; David M. Herszenhorn, *Bill to Give Russia's Government Broad Power to Restrict Web Content Is Criticized,* N.Y Times (July 11, 2012), http://www.nytimes.com/ 2012/07/11/world/europe/wikipedia-shuts-site-to-protest-bill-for-firewall-in-russia .html?_r=0; and *On the Media: Covering Nigeria, Russian Censorship, and More,* WNYC (May 28, 2014), http://www.onthemedia.org/story/on-the-media-2014-05-16/ [hereinafter *Covering Nigeria, Russian Censorship, and More*].

113. Rudolph Herzog, Dead Funny: Telling Jokes in Hitler's Germany (2012) (providing a detailed overview of humor during the Third Reich) [hereinafter Herzog]; John Morreall, Comic Relief: A Comprehensive Philosophy of Humor 119–20 (2009) (describing how jokes served a "coping function" during the Holocaust) [hereinafter Morreall]; Adam Phillips, *The Joy of Sex and Laughter*, 6 Index on Censorship 14, 19 (2000) (discussing humor in Nazi concentration camps) [hereinafter Phillips]. For contrasting discussions of censorship and humor during other periods of German history, see, for example, Kathy Heady, Literature & Censorship in Restoration Germany: Repression & Rhetoric (2009) (discussing censorship and opposition in nineteenth-century Germany); Gregory H. Williams, Permission to Laugh: Humor and Politics in Contemporary German Art (2012) (discussing trends in humor reflected in German art from the 1970s to the current time); Jefferson S. Chase, *Inciting Laughter: The Development of "Jewish Humor" in 19th-Century German Culture, in* 12 European Cultures: Studies in Literature and the Arts (2000) (providing history of Jewish humor (Judenwitz) in nineteenth-century Germany).

114. Victor Erofeyev, *The Unique Power of Russia's Underground Language*, Kenai Peninsula (Oct. 12, 2003), http://www.russki-mat.net/e/mat_VEvrofeyev.htm.

115. *See, e.g.,* David Remnick, *Putin's Four Dirty Words*, New Yorker: News Desk (May 5, 2014), http://www.newyorker.com/online/blogs/newsdesk/2014/05/vladimir-putins-four-dirty-words.html (discussing prohibition and fines).

116. *See Covering Nigeria, Russian Censorship, and More, supra* note 112 (discussing popularity of mat in social conversation in light of prohibitions).

117. *See Russian Jokes*, Wikipedia, http://en.wikipedia.org/wiki/Russian_jokes#Taboo_vocabulary (last visited July 17, 2014) (reporting egg-testicle joke under the "Taboo Vocabulary" section).

118. Victor Erofeyev, *Letter from Moscow: Dirty Words, The Unique Power of Russia's Underground Language*, New Yorker, Sept. 15, 2003, at 42 (describing how intonation can be used to make small changes in meaning using mat).

119. *See, e.g,* Herzog, *supra* note 113 (providing a detailed overview of humor during the Third Reich); Morreall, *supra* note 113, at 119–20 (describing how jokes served a "coping function" during the Holocaust); Phillips, *supra* note 113, at 19 (discussing humor in Nazi concentration camps).

120. Herzog, *supra* note 113, at 99.

121. *Id.* at 60.

122. *Id.*

123. *See, e.g.,* Satenik Harutyunyan, *Humor: Egypt's Revolutionary Ally*, Prospect J. (July 30, 2012), https://prospectjournal.org/2012/07/30/humor-egypts-revolutionary-ally-2/ (observing that Egyptian political humor thrives as "social humor"—often in the form of a "nukta" or "verbal cartoon" that is "often told during informal setting through word of mouth," thus eluding government attention).

124. The bridge between these two contexts is made more remarkable by how joke forms work differently in different languages. Puns are particularly apt illustrations of this difference, since some languages lend themselves more readily to punning than others. Interestingly, grammatical structure differences are quite significant to humor. German comedian Jan Böhmermann maintains that the structure of the German language inhibits effective joke telling: "In English you can make a joke and you don't . . . give away the punchline during the setup. But [German] is so complicated that you always give away the punchline during the setup, because we . . . put the verbs . . . at the end." Carol Giacomo, *Censored in Germany*, N.Y. Times: Taking Note (May 4, 2016, 4:57 p.m.), https://takingnote.blogs .nytimes.com/2016/05/04/censored-in-germany/?_r=0.

125. Brandenberg v. Ohio, 395 U.S. 444 (1969).

126. *See, e.g.,* Christopher Hooton, *Ricky Gervais on Outrage Culture: "Offence Is the Collateral Damage of Freedom of Speech,"* INDEPENDENT (Apr. 13, 2016), http://www.independent .co.uk/arts-entertainment/tv/news/ricky-gervais-on-outrage-culture-offence-is-the-collateral-damage-of-freedom-of-speech-a6982411.html.

127. GERARD GARDNER, THE MOCKING OF THE PRESIDENT 12 (1988).

128. PAUL LEWIS, CRACKING UP: AMERICAN HUMOR IN A TIME OF CONFLICT 117 (2006) (quoting anthropologist Mahadev L. Apte).

129. *CIA Realizes It's Been Using Black Highlighters All These Years,* ONION (Nov. 30, 2005), http://www.theonion.com/articles/cia-realizes-its-been-using-black-highlighters-all,1848/.

130. ROBERT R. PROVINE, LAUGHTER: A SCIENTIFIC INVESTIGATION (2000); T. C. Veach, *A Theory of Humor,* 11 HUMOR 161, 173 (1998).

131. A. Peter McGraw & Caleb Warren, *Benign Violations: Making Immoral Behavior Funny,* 21 PSYCHOL. SCI. 1141, 1142 (2010) (discussing the confluence of these two apparently contradictory conditions to create humor—the presence of a violation that is safe, playful, or, at least, non-serious). *See generally* PETER McGRAW & JOEL WARNER, THE HUMOR CODE: A GLOBAL SEARCH FOR WHAT MAKES THINGS FUNNY 9–14 (2014) (describing the development of the benign violation theory and critiques of the theory).

132. The pleasure for the audience here resembles the "joy of problem solving." *See* MATTHEW M. HURLEY, DANIEL C. DENNETT & REGINALD B. ADAMS, JR., INSIDE JOKES: USING HUMOR TO REVERSE-ENGINEER THE MIND 27 (2013) (observing that "[w]hen we 'get' a joke we feel a sense of discovery rather like the sense of triumph when we solve a problem").

133. The tendency to assume that the "negative" involves some kind of swearing may be well founded when the context suggests catharsis, pain, anger, or frustration—emotions that often inspire swearing. Marta Dynel, *Swearing Methodologically: The (Im)Politeness of Expletives in Anonymous Commentaries on YouTube,* 10 J. ENG. STUD. 29, 36 (2012) (explaining that swearing performs the function of venting anger, processing pain, and releasing tension).

134. *See, e.g.,* Texas v. Johnson, 491 U.S. 397 (1989) (criminalizing flag burning).

135. *See, e.g.,* Bethel Sch. Dist. No. 403 v. Fraser, 478 U.S. 675 (1986) (regulating speech of school students).

CHAPTER 2

1. MARC GALANTER, LOWERING THE BAR: LAWYER JOKES & LEGAL CULTURE 3 (2005) [hereinafter GALANTER].

2. Jacquelyn Smith, *These Are the Jobs Parents Want Their Kids to Have,* BUS. INSIDER (Nov. 14, 2014, 9:30 A.M.), http://www.businessinsider.com/the-job-parents-most-want-their-kids-to-have-2014-11 (citing 69 percent of parents); *see also* DAVID RAY PAPKE ET AL., LAW AND POPULAR CULTURE: TEXT, NOTES, AND QUESTIONS 73 (2d ed. 2012) (citing "a majority" of parents according to a 1999 Harris poll); Josh Crank, *Nearly Two-Thirds of Parents Want Their Kids to Become Lawyers,* LAWYERS.COM (May 30, 2013), http://blogs .lawyers.com/2013/05/two-thirds-of-parents-want-kids-to-be-lawyers/ (citing "nearly two-thirds of parents").

3. WILLIAM SHAKESPEARE, THE SECOND PART OF KING HENRY THE SIXTH, act 4, sc. 2.

4. William P. Skladony, *I'm Proud to Be a Lawyer Because Dick the Butcher Wants Me Dead,* 23 OHIO N.U. L. REV. 363, 376 (1996).

5. Maurice Kelman, *Is the Constitution Worth Legal Writing Credit,* 44 JOURNAL OF LEGAL ED. 267 (1994).

6. Lawyer and Court Jokes, http://groups.csail.mit.edu/mac/users/bentz/humor/lawyer .html.

7. Anthony D'Amato, *Minutes of the Faculty Meeting*, 1992 Brigham Young L. Rev. 359.

8. William H. Simon, *Moral Pluck: Legal Ethics in Popular Culture*, 101 Colum. L. Rev. 421 (2001).

9. Galanter *supra* note 1, at 16.

10. Christie Davies, Jokes and Targets 41, 82–93, 198–201 (2011).

11. Galanter, *supra* note 1, at 147.

12. Davies, *supra* note 10, at 41, 82–93, 198–201.

13. Richard Abel, Book Review, 57 J. Legal Educ. 130, 135 (2007) (reviewing Galanter, *supra* note 1).

14. Gerald F. Uelmen, *Id.*, 1992 Brigham Young L. Rev. 359.

15. Matthew M. Hurley et al., Inside Jokes: Using Humor to Reverse-Engineer the Mind 43 (2011).

16. Galanter, *supra* note 1, at 118.

17. Galanter, *supra* note 1, at 114.

18. *Lawyer Joke Collection*, IcicleSoftware.com, http://www.iciclesoftware.com/LawJokes/IcicleLawJokes.html (last updated Oct. 31, 2010).

19. Robert Hetzron, *On the Structure of Punchlines*, 4 Humor 61, 65–66 (1991).

20. Joke Collection, *supra* note 18.

21. *The Devil's Offer*, Aha Jokes, www.ahajokes.com/law013 (last visited Mar. 11, 2017).

22. *Funniest Lawyer Jokes*, Beer100.com, http://www.beer100.com/lawyerjokes.htm (last visited Mar. 11, 2017).

23. Galanter, *supra* note 1, at 165.

24. John Morreall, Laughing All the Way 130 (2016).

25. Nika Kabiri, *Lawyers Just Can't Get No Respect (Part 1 of 5)*, Lawyernomics (Nov. 16, 2015), http://lawyernomics.avvo.com/legal-marketing/lawyers-just-cant-get-no-respect-part-1-of-5.html.

26. Abel, *supra* note 13, at 135.

27. Kabiri, *supra* note 25.

28. Joke Collection, *supra* note 18.

29. Abel, *supra* note 13, at 158.

30. Galanter, *supra* note 1, at 39.

31. *Id.*

32. Rajani Gupta, Comment, *Trial and Errors: Comedy's Quest for the Truth*, 9 UCLA Ent. L. Rev. 113, 133–34 (2001) (quoting Christopher Morley: "Humor is perhaps a sense of intellectual perspective: an awareness that some things are really important, others not; and that the two kinds are most oddly jumbled in everyday affairs").

33. Robert J. Morriz, *The New (Legal) Devil's Dictionary*, 6 Journal of Contemporary Law 231 (1997).

34. Lisa G. Lerman & Philip G. Schrag, Ethical Problems in the Practice of Law 496–508 (4th ed. 2016).

35. Deborah L. Rhode, In the Interests of Justice: Reforming the Legal Profession 168–69 (2000).

36. Thomas W. Overton, Comment, *Lawyers, Light Bulbs, and Dead Snakes: The Lawyer Joke as Societal Text*, 42 UCLA L. Rev. 1069, 1082 (1995).

37. Abel, *supra* note 13, at 141.

38. Kabiri, *supra* note 25.

39. *Lawyer Q & A Jokes*, wbenton.tripod.com, http://wbenton.tripod.com/humor/Jokeindex228.html (last visited Mar. 11, 2017).

40. Hurley et al., *supra* note 15, at 215.

41. *Id.*

42. Paul Lewis, Cracking Up: American Humor in a Time of Conflict 7–9 (2006).

43. James A. Lynch & H. H. Friedman, *Approaching Ethics Through Humor—Using Lawyer Jokes to Teach Business Ethics*, 3 Soc. Sci. Int'l J. Econ. & Mgmt. 6 (2013).

44. *Funny Judge Jokes*, Funny Jokes, http://www.free-funny-jokes.com/funny-judge-jokes.html (last visited Mar. 11, 2017).

45. Lance S. Davidson, Ludicrous Laws & Mindless Misdemeanors 105 (2006).

46. *Id.*

47. *See, e.g.,* Richard Posner, *Emotion Versus Emotionalism in Law, in* The Passions of Law (Susan Bandes ed., 1999); Susan Bandes, *Introduction* to The Passions of Law, *supra.*

48. *Funny Judge Jokes, supra* note 44.

49. Jeffrey Abramson, *The Jury and Popular Culture*, 50 DePaul L. Rev. 497, 498 (2000).

50. Valerie P. Hans, *Jury Jokes and Legal Culture*, 62 DePaul L. Rev. 391, 412 (2013).

51. In using this four-part taxonomy, I owe homage to a similar organization developed by Valerie P. Hans in her work *Jury Jokes and Legal Culture. Id.*

52. Jeffrey Rosen, *One Angry Woman*, New Yorker, Feb. 24, 1997, at 54, 56.

53. Hans, *supra* note 30, at 406 (quoting Marshall Brown, Wit and Humor of Bench and Bar 511 (Chicago, T. H. Flood & Co. 1899)).

54. *Jury Quotes*, Dumb.com, http://www.dumb.com/quotes/jury-quotes/ (last visited Mar. 12, 2017) [hereinafter *Jury Quotes*, Dumb.com].

55. Gerd Herm, *A "Noisy Carnival": Parodies and Burlesques of Fourth of July Rhetoric, in* The Fourth of July: Political Oratory and Literary Reactions 1776–1876, at 239, 249 (Paul Goetsch & Gerd Hurm eds., 1992) (quoting Mark Twain, After-Dinner Speech: Meeting of Americans (July 4, 1873), *in* Mark Twain Speaking 74, 75 (Paul Fatout ed., 1976)).

56. Hans, *supra* note 50, at 410.

57. Abramson, *supra* note 49, at 499.

58. Hans, *supra* note 50, at 400.

59. *Common Nonsense Jury*, TV Tropes, http://tvtropes.org/pmwiki/pmwiki.php/Main/CommonNonsenseJury (last visited Mar. 12, 2017).

60. Hans, *supra* note 50, at 412.

61. *Juror's Excuse*, Jokes Journal, http://www.jokesjournal.com/jurors-excuse/ (last visited Mar. 12, 2017).

62. Katherine Boniello, *The Wackiest Excuses People Use to Get Out of Jury Duty*, N.Y. Post (Jan. 4, 2015, 8:58 a.m.), http://nypost.com/2015/01/04/the-wackiest-excuses-people-use-to-get-out-of-jury-duty/.

63. *Steve Martin Keeps the Jokes Rolling While Live-Tweeting During Jury Duty*, N.Y. Daily News (Dec. 22, 2010, 2:36 p.m.), http://www.nydailynews.com/entertainment/gossip/steve-martin-jokes-rolling-live-tweeting-jury-duty-article-1.471800.

64. *Jury Foreman Joke*, Funniest Clean Jokes, http://www.funniestcleanjokes.com/joke/jury-foreman-joke (last visited Mar. 12, 2017).

65. Hans, *supra* note 50, at 404.

66. *Id.* at 405.

67. *Id.* (citing Michael Wolfe, Comment to *Jurors Need to Know that They Can Say No*, N.Y. Times (Dec. 21, 2011), http://www.nytimes.com/2011/12/21/opinion/jurors-can-say-no.html).

68. Andrew D. Leipold, *Rethinking Jury Nullification*, 82 Va. L. Rev. 253 (1996).

69. Rosen, *supra* note 52, at 54, 56.

70. Alexis de Tocqueville, Democracy in America 127–28 (Richard D. Heffner ed., Mentor 1956) (1835).

71. Phoebe A. Haddon, *Rethinking the Jury*, 3 Wm. & Mary Bill Rts J. 29, 49 (1994).

72. *Jury Quotes*, BRAINYQUOTE, https://www.brainyquote.com/quotes/keywords/jury. html (last visited Mar. 12, 2017) [hereinafter *Jury Quotes*, BRAINYQUOTE].

73. Duncan v. Louisiana, 391 U.S. 145, 156 (1968).

74. *Id.*

75. Hans, *supra* note 50, at 408.

76. *Id.* at 407.

77. DENNIS J. DEVINE, JURY DECISION MAKING 21–39 (2012).

78. *Id.* at 198–200 (2012).

79. AM. BAR ASS'N, PERCEPTION OF THE U.S. JUSTICE SYSTEM (1999).

80. For an overview of possible explanations for "unflattering portrayals of the jury" in popular culture, see Nancy S. Marder, *Introduction to the Jury at a Crossroad: The American Experience*, 78 CHI.-KENT L. REV. 909 (2003).

81. Bradwell v. Illinois, 83 U.S. 130, 141–42 (1873).

82. GALANTER, *supra* note 1, at 147.

83. Joke Collection, *supra* note 18.

84. GALANTER, *supra* note 1, at 147.

85. *Id.* at 148.

86. COMM'N ON WOMEN IN THE PROFESSION, AM. BAR ASS'N, A CURRENT GLANCE AT WOMEN IN THE LAW (2012), http://www.americanbar.org/content/dam/aba/ marketing/women/current_glance_statistics_2012.authcheckdam.pdf.

87. LAUREN STILLER RIKLEEN, AM. BAR ASS'N GENDER EQUITY TASK FORCE, CLOSING THE GAP: A ROAD MAP FOR ACHIEVING GENDER PAY EQUITY IN LAW FIRM PARTNER COMPENSATION 20 (2013), http://www.americanbar.org/content/dam/aba/ administrative/women/closing_the_gap.authcheckdam.pdf.

88. *Id.*

89. Marlisse Silver Sweeney, *The Female Lawyer Exodus*, THE DAILY BEAST (July 31, 2013, 4:45 A.M.), http://www.thedailybeast.com/witw/articles/2013/07/31/the-exodus-of-female-lawyers.html.

90. William Bender, *A Supreme Court Justice's Indecent Inbox*, PHILA. DAILY NEWS, Oct. 8, 2015, at 3.

91. NICHOLA D. GUTGOLD, THE RHETORIC OF SUPREME COURT WOMEN: FROM OBSTACLES TO OPTIONS 11 (2012); Taunya Lovell Banks, *Judging the Judges—Daytime Television's Integrated Reality Court Bench*, *in* LAWYERS IN YOUR LIVING ROOM! LAW ON TELEVISION 309 (Michael Asimow ed., 2009).

92. Hans, *supra* note 50, at 401 (quoting GUS C. EDWARDS, LEGAL LAUGHS: A JOKE FOR EVERY JURY (2d prtg 1915)).

93. *Id.* (quoting *Jury Duty*, JOKES-FUNNIES.COM, http://www.unwind.com/jokes-funnies/ profession/juryduty.shtml).

94. The journal *Proceedings of the Natural Institute of Science* performed studies of the race and gender of those depicted in *New Yorker* cartoons in 2014. Sometimes written in a tongue-in-cheek tone, *see* Matt J. Michel, *Introducing the Proceedings of the Natural Institute of Science (PNIS): Come with us!*, PROC. NAT. INST. SCI. (Sept. 12, 2014), http://pnis.co/ editorial1.html, the journal has been described as "semi-satirical." The journal's statistical studies of the cartoons were nevertheless thorough and collaborated with earlier studies of political cartoons and cartoonists generally. For the full studies in the *Proceedings of the Natural Institute of Science*, see Matt J. Michel, *Racial and Gender Diversity of the Characters in* The New Yorker *Cartoons*, PROC. NAT. INST. SCI. (May 7, 2015), http://pnis.co/vol2/ h6.html, and Editorial, *Dispatch from the Obvious Department: The New Yorker Cartoons Drawn by Females Contain More Female Characters*, PROC. NAT. INST. SCI. (May 14, 2015), http://pnis.co/vol2/h7.html.

95. Quote Catalog, *TV Quotes/Seinfeld/Jackie Chiles,* https://quotecatalog.com/communicator/ jackie-chiles/ (last visited April 7, 2018).

96. *Chappelle's Show: Tron Carter's "Law and Order"* (Comedy Central television broadcast Feb. 18, 2004), http://www.cc.com/video-clips/3vk26x/chappelle-s-show-tron-carter-s--law---order----uncensored.

97. *Chappelle's Show: Celebrity Trial Jury Selection* (Comedy Central television broadcast Mar. 17, 2004), http://www.cc.com/video-clips/5uemlz/chappelle-s-show-celebrity-trial-jury-selection---uncensored.

98. Esther Zuckerman, *Watch Key & Peele Skewer Police Racism in This New Sketch,* Time (May 6, 2015), http://time.com/3849007/key-peele-police-racism-negrotown/.

99. Sharan Shetty, *Richard Pryor's Darkly Perfect Bit on Police Chokeholds,* Slate: Browbeat (Dec. 6, 2014, 4:10 PM), http://www.slate.com/blogs/browbeat/2014/12/06/richard_pryor_on_police_chokeholds_a_1977_bit_that_anticipates_eric_garner.html.

100. Dexter Thomas, Commentary, *Every Time a Black Person is Killed by Police, Americans Search for Chris Rock,* L.A. Times, July 8, 2016, 7:55 p.m., http://www.latimes.com/entertainment/tv/la-et-st-chris-rock-video-sterling-20160707-snap-htmlstory.html.

101. *The Nightly Show with Larry Wilmore: Racism in the Baltimore Police Department* (Comedy Central television broadcast), http://www.cc.com/video-clips/j8lad9/the-nightly-show-with-larry-wilmore-racism-in-the-baltimore-police-department; *The Nightly Show with Larry Wilmore: Ferguson Police Bias* (Comedy Central television broadcast Mar. 5, 2015), http://www.cc.com/video-clips/sytmii/the-nightly-show-with-larry-wilmore-ferguson-police-bias.

102. *Last Week Tonight with John Oliver: Mandatory Minimums* (HBO television broadcast July 26, 2015), https://www.youtube.com/watch?v=pDVmldTurqk.

103. *Boondocks: To Protect and Serve* (Cartoon Network Adult Swim television broadcast Mar. 12, 2006), http://www.adultswim.com/videos/the-boondocks/to-protect-and-serve/.

104. Caleb E. Mason, *Jay-Z's 99 Problems, Verse 2: A Close Reading with Fourth Amendment Guidance for Cops and Perps,* 56 St. Louis U. L. J. 567 (2012).

105. Bender, *supra* note 90.

106. Editorial, *Judge Cebull's Racist "Joke,"* N.Y. Times, Mar. 5, 2012, http://www.nytimes.com/2012/03/06/opinion/judge-richard-cebulls-racist-joke.html.

107. Kelman, *supra* note 5.

108. *Trial Jokes,* Jokes4all.net, http://jokes4all.net/trial-jokes (last visited Mar. 12, 2017).

109. *Funny Judge Jokes, supra* note 44.

110. *Id.*

111. *Justice Has Prevailed,* Expert Law—Law Laughs, http://www.lawlaughs.com/trials/justice.html (last visited Mar. 13, 2017).

112. Hans, *supra* note 50, at 410.

113. *Jury Quotes,* BrainyQuote, *supra* note 76.

114. *Justice Has Prevailed, supra* note 119.

115. *Jury Quotes: H.L. Mencken,* BrainyQuote, https://www.brainyquote.com/quotes/quotes/h/hlmencke101554.html?src=t_jury (last visited Mar. 13, 2017).

116. *Funny Judge Jokes, supra* note 44.

117. The Onion, *Bloomberg Defends NYPD's Controversial Stop and Kiss Program,* YouTube (Dec. 3, 2013), https://www.youtube.com/watch?v=GXXaj--a6-4.

118. *Courtroom Humor,* Gavel2Gavel.com, http://www.re-quest.net/g2g/humor/courtroom/index.htm (last visited Mar. 13, 2017).

119. *Lawyer Pick-Up Lines,* Pick Up Lines Galore!, http://www.pickuplinesgalore.com/law.html (last visited Mar. 13, 2017).

120. Kinsey Law Office, Lawyer Jokes, http://www.kinseylaw.com/JOKES/jokes.html (last visited April 7, 2018).

121. *Legal Humor & Lawyer Jokes*, GAVEL2GAVEL.COM, http://www.re-quest.net/g2g/humor/lawyer-jokes (last visited Mar. 13, 2017).

122. *Fibber McGee and Molly: Fibber Does His Income Taxes* (NBC radio broadcast Jan. 11, 1944), *quoted in* Lawrence Zelenak, *Six Decades of the Federal Income Tax in Sitcoms*, 117 TAX NOTES 1265 (2007).

123. *Roseanne: April Fool's Day* (ABC television broadcast Apr. 10, 1990), *quoted in* Lawrence Zelenak, LEARNING TO LOVE FORM 1040: TWO CHEERS FOR THE RETURN-BASED MASS INCOME TAX 94 (2013) [hereinafter Zelenak, LEARNING TO LOVE FORM 1040].

124. somduttprasad, *Welcome to /r/ Jokes: Lawyers and Loopholes*, REDDIT, https://www.reddit.com/r/Jokes/comments/34hrcq/lawyers_and_loopholes/ (last visited Mar. 13, 2017).

125. *Loopholes*, ANYJOKES.NET, http://www.anyjokes.net/lawyer-jokes/loopholes/ (last visited Mar. 13, 2017).

126. Douglas L. Parker, *Standing to Litigate "Abstract Social Interests" in the United States and Italy: Reexamining "Injury in Fact,"* 33 COLUM. J. TRANSNAT'L L. 259, 274 (1995).

127. Harlan F. Stone, *Some Aspects of the Problem of Law Simplification*, 23 COLUM. L. REV. 319, 321 (1923).

128. M. H. ABRAMS, A GLOSSARY OF LITERARY TERMS 166 (5th ed. 1988).

129. NANCY GOLDMAN, COMEDY AND DEMOCRACY: THE ROLE OF HUMOR IN SOCIAL JUSTICE 3 (2013), http://animatingdemocracy.org/sites/default/files/Humor%20Trend%20Paper.pdf.

130. *Id.*

131. Jonathan Coe, *Sinking Giggling into the Sea*, 35 LONDON REV. BOOKS 14 (2013), http://www.lrb.co.uk/v35/n14/jonathan-coe/sinking-giggling-into-the-sea.

132. Lewis *supra* note 42, at 205.

133. *Id.* at 7.

134. Justin E. H. Smith, *Why Satire Matters*, 61 CHRON. HIGHER EDUC. 9 (2015).

135. Christopher Hitchens, *Cheap Laughs*, THE ATLANTIC, Oct. 2009, at 101, 104.

136. Lewis *supra* note 42, at 159 (quoting 2 WILLIAM COWPER, *The Task, in* THE POEMS OF WILLIAM COWPER (John D. Baird & Charles Ryskamp eds. 1995)).

CHAPTER 3

1. CHARLES M. SEVILLA, DISORDER IN THE COURT: GREAT FRACTURED MOMENTS IN COURTROOM HISTORY 158 (NORTON 1193) [hereinafter SEVILLA].

2. Robert Cover, *Violence and the Word*, 95 YALE L.J. 1601, 1601 (1986).

3. SEVILLA, *supra* note 1, at 40.

4. *Pointer of the Month: Just Kidding, Really; Humor in Litigation*, PA. DISCIPLINARY BOARD: ATT'Y E-NEWSL. (Sept. 2016), http://www.padisciplinaryboard.org/attorneys/newsletter/2016/september.php.

5. JONATHAN SWIFT, A MODEST PROPOSAL (1729), http://art-bin.com/art/omodest.html.

6. John Forester, *Responding to Critical Moments with Humor, Recognition, and Hope*, 20 NEGOT. J. 221, 223 (2004); Richard Shore, *Three Tricks That Make Negotiations Work*, FORBES: LEADERSHIP F. (Jan. 1, 2014, 10:22 A.M.), https://www.forbes.com/sites/forbesleadershipforum/2014/01/31/three-tricks-that-make-negotiations-work/#389f573435d8.

7. T. Bradford Bitterly, Alison Wood Brooks & Maurice E. Schweitzer, *Risky Business: When Humor Increases and Decreases Status*, 112 J. PERSONALITY & SOC. PSYCHOL. 431–55 (2017).

8. Richard Carelli, *Fight Sexism with Humor, Women Told: Lawyers Panelists at Bar Association Meeting Recommend Immediate Response to Chauvinist Remarks, Preferably with Sharp Wit,*

L.A. Times, Feb. 20, 1994, http://articles.latimes.com/1994-02-20/news/mn-25162_
1_sharp-humor.

9. *Id.*

10. Forester, *supra* note 6, at 223.

11. *See, e.g.,* Whitney Meers, Note, *The Funny Thing About Mediation: A Rationale for the Use of Humor in Mediation,* 10 Cardozo J. Conflict Resol. 657, 682 (2009).

12. Notice of Motion and Motion to Dismiss, Naruto v. Slater, No. 15-cv-4324-WHO (N.D. Cal. Jan. 28, 2016), 2015 WL 9843651.

13. Martha Neil, *5th Circuit Mimics Filing's "Strange Hypothetical Conversation" in Their Ruling Denying Motion,* ABA J. (Mar. 1, 2016, 3:10 p.m.), http://www.abajournal.com/news/article/strange_hypothetical_conversation_in_filing_inspires_5th_circuit_ruling_tha?utm_source=feedburner&utm_medium=feed&utm_campaign=ABA+Journal+Daily+News#When:21:10:00Z; Petition for Panel Rehearing, Forum Subsea Rentals v. Elsharhaway, 631 Fed. App'x 236 (5th Cir. 2016) (mem.) (No. 14-20717) (citation omitted), https://www.scribd.com/doc/301465269/Motion-for-Rehearing [hereinafter Neil].

14. Neil, *supra* note 13.

15. Richard S. Arnold, *Why Judges Don't Like Petitions for Rehearing,* 3 J. App. Prac. & Process 29 (2001).

16. Pamela Hobbs, *Lawyers' Use of Humor as Persuasion,* 20 Humor 123, 139 (2007) [hereinafter Hobbs].

17. Erin Coe, *Courtroom Humor Has Risks but Also Benefits for Attys,* Law360, https://www.law360.com/articles/497835/courtroom-humor-has-risks-but-also-benefits-for-attys (last visited Mar. 23, 2016).

18. *See* Adam Goldberg, *George Zimmerman's Lawyer Tells "Knock-Knock" Joke at Trial,* Huffington Post (June 24, 2013, 1:45 p.m.), http://www.huffingtonpost.com/2013/06/24/george-zimmerman-knock-knock_n_3491367.html

19. 410 U.S. 113 (1973).

20. Geoffrey Sant, *8 Horrible Courtroom Jokes and Their Ensuing Legal Calamities,* Salon (July 26, 2013, 2:42 p.m.), http://www.salon.com/2013/07/26/8_horrible_courtroom_jokes_and_their_ensuing_legal_calamity/ [hereinafter Sant].

21. *Id.*

22. *Id.*

23. 501 U.S. 560 (1991).

24. Hobbs, *supra* note 16, at 139.

25. *Id.* at 142–45.

26. *Id.* at 146.

27. Matt Kaiser, *When Humor in the Courtroom Isn't Funny,* Above the Law (Aug. 13, 2015, 10:05 a.m.), http://abovethelaw.com/2015/08/when-humor-in-the-courtroom-isnt-funny/.

28. *Id.*

29. Neil J. Dilloff, *Humor in the Courtroom: Is There a Place?,* 20 MD. B. J. 20 (1987).

30. Lance S. Davidson, Ludicrous Laws & Mindless Misdemeanors 192 (1998).

31. Sant, *supra* note 20.

32. Hudson Hongo, *"Fuckman-Ass" Judge and "Donkey-Dicked" Murder Suspect Are America's Greatest Comic Duo,* Gawker (June 22, 2016, 8:45 p.m.), http://gawker.com/fuckman-ass-judge-and-donkey-dicked-murder-suspect-1782465086.

33. *Id.*

34. Steven Pinker, The Stuff of Thought 357 (2007); *see also* Steven Pinker, *What the F***?,* New Republic (Oct. 8, 2007), https://newrepublic.com/article/63921/what-the-f (observing that swearing "recruits our expressive faculties to the fullest: the

combinatorial power of syntax; the evocativeness of metaphor; the pleasure of alliteration, meter, and rhyme; and the emotional charge of our attitudes").

35. SEVILLA, *supra* note 1, at 42.

36. Jay D. Wexler, *The Laugh Track*, 9 GREEN BAG 59 (2005); *see also* Jay D. Wexler, *The Laugh Track II—Still Laughin'!*, 117 YALE L.J. POCKET PART 130 (2007).

37. Russell Goldman, *Who Is the Funniest Supreme Court Justice?*, ABC NEWS (Oct. 9, 2013), http://abcnews.go.com/blogs/headlines/2013/10/who-is-the-funniest-supreme-court-justice/.

38. ROBERT R. PROVINE, LAUGHTER: A SCIENTIFIC STUDY 3 (2000).

39. James Zinoman, *Why Do Comics Laugh at Their Own Jokes? It's No Accident*, N.Y. TIMES, Mar. 3, 2017, https://www.nytimes.com/2017/03/03/arts/when-comedians-laugh .html?emc=edit_tnt_20170303&nlid=59401804&tntemail0=y.

40. *Id.*

41. *Laughter with Dr. Sophie Scott*, ON HUM. CONDITION (July 15, 2015), https://www .onhumancondition.com/single-post/2015/07/15/LAUGHTER-with-Dr-Sophie-Scott.

42. *See, e.g.,* Ryan A. Malphurs, *"People Did Sometimes Stick Things in My Underwear": The Function of Laughter at the U.S. Supreme Court*, 10 COMM. L. REV. 48 (2012).

43. Anna Christopher, *Supreme Court Justice Stephen Breyer, Rock Star?*, NPR (Mar. 23, 2007), http://www.npr.org/about/press/2007/032307.breyer.html (including part of the transcript from the episode of *Wait Wait . . . Don't Tell Me!* that aired on March 24–25, 2007).

44. *See, e.g.,* Hugo Mercier & Dan Sperber, THE ENIGMA OF REASON (2017); Steven Sloman & Philip Fernback, THE KNOWLEDGE ILLUSION: WHY WE NEVER THINK ALONE (2017).

45. United States v. Tuttle, 627 Fed. App'x. 842 n.10 (11th Cir. 2015).

46. United States v. Grey, 648 F.3d 562, 568–69 (7th Cir. 2011).

47. Mello v. DiPaulo, 295 F.3d 137, 150 (1st Cir. 2002).

48. *Id.*

49. Lisa Ryan, *This Story About an Offspring Drummer Turned Ob-Gyn Has Everything,* The Cut (March 29, 2018), available at https://www.thecut.com/2018/03/offspring-ob-gyn-james-lilja-saves-juror.html.

50. Sharyn Roach Anleu, Kathy Mack & Jordan Tutton, *Judicial Humour in the Australian Courtroom*, 38 MELBOURNE U. L. REV. 62, 641 (2014).

51. *Id.*

52. *Id.* at 648–49.

53. Drayton v. Hayes, 589 F.2d 117, 119–20 (2d Cir. 1979).

54. *Id.*

55. *See generally* Marina Angel, *Sexual Harassment by Judges*, 45 U. MIAMI L. REV. 817 (1991).

56. *In re* Henderson, 343 P.3d 518, 520–23 (Kan. 2015).

57. Pamela Hobbs, *Judges' Use of Humor as a Social Corrective*, 39 J. PRAGMATICS 50, 50 (2006) [hereinafter Hobbs].

58. Laurence Baum, JUDGES AND THEIR AUDIENCE: A PERSPECTIVE ON JUDICIAL BEHAVIOR 40 (2006).

59. *Id.*

60. John C. Meyer, *Humor Functions in Communications, in* HUMOR COMMUNICATION: THEORY, IMPACT, AND OUTCOMES 24 (Rachel L. DiCioccio ed., 2012) [hereinafter Meyer].

61. Gonzalez-Servin v. Ford Motor Co., 662 F.3d 931, 934 (7th Cir. 2011).

62. *See, e.g.,* Diane Karpman, *"The Ostrich is a noble animal . . . ,"* CAL. B.J.: ETHICS BYTE (Jan. 2012), http://www.calbarjournal.com/January2012/EthicsByte.aspx.

63. Yxta Maya Murray, *Tragicomedy*, 48 HOW. L.J. 309, 335 (2004) [hereinafter Murray].

64. Mattel, Inc. v. MCA Records, 296 F.3d 894, 898 (9th Cir. 2002).

65. Mark Lane, *Courts' Attempts at Humor Aren't Funny*, COX NEWS SERV., JULY 29, 2002.

66. *Id.*

67. Gerald Lebovits, *Judicial Jesting: Judicious?*, 7 N.Y. St. B. Ass'n J. 64, 60 (2003).

68. *Most Self-Indulgent Legal Opinion?*, Volokh Conspiracy, http://www.volokh.com/posts/1179422540.comments.shtml (last visited Mar. 23, 2017).

69. Matt Zapotosky, *Federal Appeals Judge Announces Immediate Retirement amid Probe of Sexual Misconduct Allegations*, Washington Post (December 18, 2017), https://www.washingtonpost.com/world/national-security/federal-appeals-judge-announces-immediate-retirement-amid-investigation-prompted-by-accusations-of-sexual-misconduct/2017/12/18/6e38ada4-e3fd-11e7-a65d-1ac0fd7f097e_story.html?utm_term=.3aedbd269575.

70. For an overview, see Lauren Leatherby, *"Jiggery-Pokery": The Justices Have a Punny Way with Words*, NPR: It's All Pol. (June 30, 2015, 10:54 a.m.), http://www.npr.org/sections/itsallpolitics/2015/06/30/418645881/jiggery-pokery-the-justices-have-a-punny-way-with-words.

71. Benny Johnson, *People Are Leaving Broccoli, Fortune Cookies and Applesauce at Scalia's Memorial. Here's the Reason Why*, Indep. J. Rev. (Feb. 2016), http://ijr.com/2016/02/541908-people-are-leaving-broccoli-fortune-cookies-and-applesauce-at-scalias-memorial-heres-the-reason-why/.

72. Lawrence v. Texas, 478 U.S. 186, 597 (1986) (Scalia, J., dissenting).

73. Romer v. Evans, 517 U.S. 620, 636 (1996) (Scalia, J., dissenting).

74. Obergefell v. Hodges, 135 S. Ct. 2584, 2629 (2015) (Scalia, J., dissenting).

75. *Id.* at 2630 (alteration in original).

76. Stanley Mosk, *Courtesy on High*, 17 Nova L. Rev. 937 (1993) (quoting Lee v. Weisman, 505 U.S. 577 (1992)).

77. *Id.*

78. Aristotle, Poetics (Ingram Bywater, trans.), *reprinted in* The Pocket Aristotle 347 (Justin Kaplan ed., 1958).

79. Murray, *supra* note 63, at 335.

80. Pennsylvania v. Nathan Dunlap, 555 U.S. 964 (2008).

81. United States v. Prince, 938 F.2d 1092, 1093 (10th Cir. 1991).

82. *Id.* at 1092.

83. Nathan Koppel, *Court Jesting: These Sentences Don't Get Judged Too Harshly*, Wall St. J., June 29, 2011; Marshall Rudolph, *Judicial Humor: A Laughing Matter?*, 41 Hastings L.J. 175 (1989).

84. John B. McClay & Wendy L. Matthews, Corpus Juris Humorous (1991).

85. Meyer, *supra* note 60, at 25.

86. Mary B. Trevor, *From Ostriches to Sci-Fi: A Social Science Analysis of the Impact of Humor in Judicial Opinions*, 45 U. Tol. L. Rev. 291, 315 (2014) (citing Chem. Specialties Mfg. Ass'n v. Clark, 482 F.2d 325 (5th Cir. 2013)).

87. Ruth Carter, *Crazy Contract Clauses*, Carter L. Firm (Dec. 19, 2013), http://carterlawaz.com/2013/12/crazy-contract-clauses/.

88. *Id.*

89. Ken Adams, *"The Stormy Daniels Contract Is a Dumpster Fire," Adams on Contract Drafting* (April 13, 2018), http://www.adamsdrafting.com/the-stormy-daniels-contract-is-a-dumpster-fire/.

90. *Id.*

91. *Funny Lawyers Jokes*, WorkJoke, http://www.workjoke.com/lawyers-jokes.html (last visited Mar. 23, 2017).

92. *The Will with the Jew-Only Clause*, Patheos (Sept. 26, 2009), http://www.patheos.com/blogs/friendlyatheist/2009/09/26/the-will-with-the-jew-only-clause/.

93. *In re* Estate of Feinberg, 919 N.E.2d 888 (Ill. 2009).

94. John Stevens Cabot Abbott, Peter Stuyvesant: The Last Dutch Governor of New Amsterdam (1873), http://www.bookrags.com/ebooks/13811/140.html#gsc .tab=0.

95. Investopedia, *10 Strange Will and Testaments, Forbes* (Apr. 12, 2011, 3:07 p.m.), http://www.forbes.com/sites/investopedia/2011/04/12/10-strange-will-and-testaments/#72487f6d247b.

96. *Last Wills—Last Laughs*, Will Site, http://www.thewillsite.co.uk/wills-the-funny-side .php (last visited Mar. 23, 2017).

97. *Id.*

98. Yagana Shah, *7 of the Weirdest—But Very Real—Wills of All Time*, Huffington Post (Sept. 21, 2015, 4:23 p.m.), http://www.huffingtonpost.com/entry/7-of-the-most-unusual-wills-of-all-time_us_55fb0059e4b0fde8b0cd5bc5.

99. Nat'l Fed'n of Indep. Bus. v. Sebellius, 567 U.S. 519 (2012).

100. Margot Sanger-Katz, *Health Care Arguments Open with a Dry Tax Question, and a Few Laughs*, Nat'l J. Daily, Mar. 26, 2012.

101. *Utah Supreme Court Affirms a Woman's Right to Sue Herself*, Lowering the Bar (Feb. 3, 2017), http://loweringthebar.net/2017/02/utah-woman-right-to-sue-self.html.

102. Richard Rubin & Theo Francis, "Taxes Are Hard—So Is Pronouncing New Tax Law Acronyms Like FDII," Wall Street Journal 1, April 12, 2018.

103. *Id.*

104. 15 U.S.C. §1242-44, *cited in* Kevin Underhill, The Emergency Sasquatch Ordinance 59 (2013) [hereinafter Underhill].

105. 18 U.S.C. §1716(c); *see also* Underhill, *supra* note 104, at 59.

106. Ala. Code § 34-6-7, *cited in* Underhill, *supra* note 104, at 59.

107. Cal. Food & Agric. Code §26991, *cited in* Underhill, *supra* note 104, at 59.

108. E. B. White, *Some Remarks on Humor: Preface* to A Subtreasury of American Humor (E. B. White & K.S. White eds., 1941).

SELECTED BIBLIOGRAPHY

Abramson, Jeffrey, *The Jury and Popular Culture*, 50 DePaul L. Rev. 497 (2000).

Adams, Ken,*"The Stormy Daniels Contract Is a Dumpster Fire,"* Adams on Contract Drafting (April 13, 2018), http://www.adamsdrafting.com/the-stormy-daniels-contract-is-a-dumpster-fire/.

Attardo, Salvatore, Humorous Texts: A Semantic and Pragmatic Analysis (2001).

Attardo, Salvatore, & Victor Raskin, *Script Theory Revis(it)ed: Joke Similarity and Joke Representation Model,* 4 HUMOR: Int'l J. Humor Res. 293 (1991).

Bergson, Henri, Laughter: An Essay on the Meaning of the Comic (Cloudsley Brereton & Fred Rothwell trans., Macmillan 1914) (1900).

Billig, Michael, Laughter and Ridicule: Towards a Social Critique of Humour (2005).

Bitterly, T. Bradford, Alison Wood Brooks & Maurice E. Schweitzer, *Risky Business: When Humor Increases and Decreases Status,* 112 J. Personality & Soc. Psychol. 431 (2017).

Coe, Jonathan, *Sinking Giggling into the Sea,* 35 London Rev. Books 14 (2013).

Cohen, Ted, Jokes: Philosophical Thoughts on Joking Matters (1999).

Davidson, Lance S., Ludicrous Laws & Mindless Misdemeanors 105 (2006).

Davies, Christie, Jokes and Targets (2011).

Davis, Murray S., What's So Funny?: The Comic Conception of Culture and Society (1993).

Dynel, Marta, Humorous Garden-Paths: A Pragmatic-Cognitive Study (2009).

Eastman, Max, Enjoyment of Laughter (1936).

Ewick, Patricia, & Susan S. Silbey, *No Laughing Matter: Humor and Contradictions in Stories of Law,* 50 DePaul L. Rev. 559 (2000).

Freud, Sigmund, The Joke and Its Relation to the Unconscious (Joyce Crick trans., Penguin 2003) (1905).

Galanter, Marc, *Changing Legal Consciousness in America: The View from the Joke Corpus,* 23 Cardozo L. Rev. 2223 (2002).

Galanter, Marc, Lowering the Bar: Lawyer Jokes & Legal Culture (2005).

Giedrė, Bored Panda, *10+ of the Most Hilarious Things that Court Reporters Have Ever Recorded to Be Said in Court,* https://www.boredpanda.com/funny-court-reports-disorder-in-court/, citing Charles M. Sevilla, Disorder in the Court 130 (1992).

Grabosky, Peter, *Regulation by Ridicule: Humorous Denigration as a Regulatory Instrument,* Law, Culture and the Humanities (Jul. 22, 2013), http://lch.sagepub.com/content/early/2013/07/19/1743872113493079.

Hans, Valerie P., *Jury Jokes and Legal Culture,* 62 DePaul L. Rev. 391 (2013).

Herzog, Rudolph, Dead Funny: Telling Jokes in Hitler's Germany (2012).

Hilarious Yelp Review: "It Ripped Its Way Out of Me in a Raging Fiery Whirlwind of Poopy Terror," IVOCAT (Nov. 20, 2013), http://ifyoucanaffordtotip.com/hilarious-yelp-review/.

Hobbs, Pamela, *Judges' Use of Humor as a Social Corrective,* 39 J. Pragmatics 50 (2006).

Hobbs, Pamela, *Lawyers' Use of Humor as Persuasion*, 20 HUMOR 123 (2007).

HURLEY, MATTHEW M., DANIEL C. DENNETT & REGINALD B. ADAMS, JR., INSIDE JOKES (2011).

Kinsey Law Office, *Lawyer Jokes*, http://www.kinseylaw.com/JOKES/jokes.html.

Lee, Stewart, *Stewart Lee-Joe Pasquale Joke*, YOUTUBE (Dec. 2, 2006), https://www.youtube.com/watch?v=0YE9kthyaco.

LEWIS, PAUL, CRACKING UP: AMERICAN HUMOR IN A TIME OF CONFLICT (2006).

Little, Laura E., *Just a Joke: Defamatory Humor and Incongruity's Promise*, 21 S. CAL. INTERDISC. L.J. 95 (2011).

Little, Laura E., *Regulating Funny: Humor and the Law*, 94 CORNELL L. REV. 1235 (2009).

MANKOFF, BOB, HOW ABOUT NEVER—IS NEVER GOOD FOR YOU? (2014).

MARTIN, ROD A., THE PSYCHOLOGY OF HUMOR: AN INTEGRATIVE APPROACH (2007).

Mason, Caleb E., *Jay-Z's 99 Problems, Verse 2: A Close Reading with Fourth Amendment Guidance for Cops and Perps*, 56 ST. LOUIS U. L. J. 567 (2012).

MCGHEE, PAUL E., HUMOR, ITS ORIGIN AND DEVELOPMENT (1979).

MCGRAW, PETER, & JOEL WARNER, THE HUMOR CODE: A GLOBAL SEARCH FOR WHAT MAKES THINGS FUNNY (SIMON & SCHUSTER 2014).

McGraw, A. Peter, & Caleb Warren, *Benign Violations: Making Immoral Behavior Funny*, 21 PSYCHOL. SCI. 1141 (2010).

Meers, Whitney, Note, *The Funny Thing About Mediation: A Rationale for the Use of Humor in Mediation*, 10 CARDOZO J. CONFLICT RESOL. 657 (2009).

MORREALL, JOHN, COMIC RELIEF: A COMPREHENSIVE PHILOSOPHY OF HUMOR (2009).

OLIAR, DOTAN, & CHRISTOPHER SPRIGMAN, *There's No Free Laugh (Anymore): The Emergence of Intellectual Property Norms and the Transformation of Stand-Up Comedy*, 94 VA. L. REV. 1787 (2008).

PAPKE, DAVID RAY, ET AL., LAW AND POPULAR CULTURE: TEXT, NOTES, AND QUESTIONS (2d ed. 2012).

PROVINE, ROBERT R., LAUGHTER: A SCIENTIFIC INVESTIGATION (2000).

Raskin, Victor, & Salvatore Attardo, *Non-Literalness and Non-Bona Fide in Language: An Approach to Formal and Computational Treatments of Humor*, in 2.1 PRAGMATICS AND COGNITION (1994).

Richman, Barak D., & Dennis Schmelzer, *When Money Grew on Trees: The Untold Story of Lucy v. Zehmer*, 61 DUKE L.J. 1511 (2012).

Rubin, Richard, & Theo Francis, *Taxes Are Hard—So Is Pronouncing New Tax Law Acronyms Like FDII*, WALL ST. J. 1 (April 12, 2018).

Ryan, Lisa, *This Story About an Offspring Drummer Turned Ob-Gyn Has Everything*, The Cut (March 29, 2018), available at https://www.thecut.com/2018/03/offspring-ob-gyn-james-lilja-saves-juror.html.

SEVILLA, CHARLES M., DISORDER IN THE COURT 130 (1992).

Underhill, Kevin, *Lawsuit Against Food Critic Alleges that Steak Sandwich Misclassified*, Lowering the Bar (March 7, 2007), https://loweringthebar.net/2007/03/libel_suit_agai.html.

Underhill, Kevin, *Pants Judge Roy Pearson Is Back in Court*, Lowering the Bar (January 29, 2010), https://loweringthebar.net/2010/01/still-unable-to-shut-up-pants-judge-roy-pearson-is-back-in-court.html.

Varol, Ozan O., *Revolutionary Humor*, 23 S. CAL. INTERDISC. L.J. 555 (2014).

Veale, Tony, *Figure-Ground Duality in Humour: A Multi-Modal Perspective*, 4 LODZ PAPERS PRAGMATICS 63 (2008).

Veale, Tony, *Incongruity in Humor: Root Cause or Epiphenomenon?*, 17 HUMOR: INT'L J. HUMOR RES. 419 (2004).

WEEMS, SCOTT, HA! THE SCIENCE OF WHEN WE LAUGH AND WHY (2014).

Wexler, Jay D., *The Laugh Track*, 9 GREEN BAG 59 (2005).

Wexler, Jay D., *The Laugh Track II—Still Laughin'!*, 117 YALE L.J. POCKET PART 130 (2007).

INDEX

#MeToo Movement, 42
30 Rock, 104
99 Problems, but a Bitch Ain't One, 124

advertisements, potential liability for, 40
Affordable Care Act case, joking during oral argument, 156, 179
American Bar Association, 112, 117
Arguendo, 153
Aristotle, 10, 14, 78, 168
audience as co-author theory, 67–69
Australian legal humor, 163–164

Bain, Alexander, 12
Barbie, copyright claim, 166–167
Barnes v. Glen Theatre, Inc., oral argument, 153–154
Barsotti, Charles, 33, 67–68
Berle, Milton, 55
Bergson, Henri, 93, 159
Bierce, Ambrose, 57
benign violation theory, 67–69
billing practices, jokes about, 86–88
Bishop, Joey, 55
Boondocks, 124
bribing, jokes about, 101, 127–128
Bruce, Lenny, 52–53
Breyer, Justice, 156, 159, 161–162
Burke, Edmund, 57
Burton, Justice, 157
Bush, George W., 34

Caligula, 57
Candid Camera, 65, 67
Carlin, George, 21, 51–53, 64

Carrey, Jim, 84–85
Cartoon Bank of *New Yorker* cartoons, 4
Catch-22 (novel), 65
censorship by repressive regimes, 59–61
censorship humor
    humor mocking the censor, 65–67
    humor using censorship tools, 67–69
Charlie Hebdo attacks, 62–64
Chappel, Dave, 124, 160
Chiles, Jackie, 123
Cicero, 10
civil wrongs, defamation and other torts, 24, 28–36
Cochran, Johnny, 123
comedian self-regulation, 53–57
consumer protection laws, 73–74
contingency fee jokes, 86, 88
contracts
    contract law's regulation of humor, 36–40
    contracts with humorous content, 171–174
copyright law, 25–26, 54, 166
court proceedings, humor during, 148–155, 156–165
Cowper, William, 141
cross-examination, 130–132

Darrow, Clarence, 72
Defamation, 28–35, 37, 48, 192 n.16
Dick v. Phone Directories Co., Inc., 44–45
differentiation humor, 166, 170
due process of law, 136

Eakin, Justice, 165
Equal Employment Opportunity Commission, 45

Falwell, Jerry, 35
Federal Communications Commission
    (FCC), 51–53
Fibber McGee and Molly, 137
Finch, Atticus, 72
Feinberg, Max, 176–177
First Amendment
    exceptionalism, 23
    protection for defamation, 23, 30–33
    protection for parody, 27, 35
    protection for standup comedy, 52–53
Funt, Alan, 65, 67
Formal jokes, 5–6
Freedom of Access to Clinic
    Entrances, 50
French Press Law of 1881, 50
Freud, Sigmund, 12, 14, 17, 75
Fink, Werner, 61
Friends (television show), 45
Frost, Robert, 129

Galanter, Mark, 77, 83
Gervais, Ricky, 62
Ginsburg, Justice Ruth Bader, 100, 118
General Electric, trademark parody case, 27–28
Grass-mud horse, mythical Chinese
    creature, 59

Hansel and Gretel, 7
harassment, sexual, 6, 20, 24, 42–46
Halen, Van, 172
Harlan, Justice, 140
Harris v. Forklift Systems, Inc, 42–43
hate speech, 23, 61–63
Heine, Heinrich, 178
Hobbes, Thomas, 10
Hooters, 38
hostile work environment theory, sex
    discrimination, 41–46
Hughes, Langston, 46–47
humor categories, 5–9
Hustler Magazine, 7, 35
Hustler Magazine v. Falwell, 35

identification humor, 170–171
incongruity theory, defined, 14–18
incongruity humor
    preferred in contract law, 36–40
    preferred in defamation law, 34–35

preferred in intellectual property
    law, 26–28
    preferred in sexual harassment law, 45–46
insult laws, 50
intellectual property law, 2, 20, 24–26, 28,
    48, 56, 174
Italian legal system, 139–140

Jackson, Justice, 98
Jay Z, 124
Jimmy Kimmel Live! (television show), 67
Johnson, Samuel, 57
Jordache jeans parody, 27
Jordan, Michael, 172
judges, images in jokes, 94–100
judicial ethics, 150, 162, 164–165
judicial humor
    extrajudicial, 165
    in court, 154–165
    in opinions, 165–171
judicial misbehavior, 165
judicial self-importance, 94–95
juror images in jokes
    common-sense jurors, 101, 108–110
    lazy jurors, 101, 103–105
    misbehaving jurors, 101, 105–107
    stupid jurors, 101–103
    women jurors, 121
jury commissioners, 101–102
jury duty jokes, 103–105
Jury Duty (movie), 105
jury nullification, 107, 110

Kagan, Justice, 160
Kant, Immanuel, 14
Kennedy, Justice, 160
Key & Peele, 124
knock-knock jokes, 55, 131, 151
Kozinski, Judge, 166–167, 171
Krause, Jerry, 172

lack-of-exposure bias, 81
laughter, function of, 12, 33, 159–160
last-laughs wills, 177
lawyer images in jokes
    crafty and cunning, 79–85
    economic predators, 88
    lying, 84–85
    money-grubbing vultures, 79, 85–88

reproducing and proliferating, 79, 88, 90–91
women lawyers, 113–120
vain, 78
legal education, effect on lawyer
  jokes, 89–92
legal profession, source of negative views,
  71–73, 75–79
Lee, Stewart, 55
Lemon, Liz, 104
Leonard v. Pepsi Co, 39
Liar Liar, 84
libel, 28, 61
likelihood of confusion test, trademark
  infringement, 26–27
Little Red Riding Hood, 7
London Sunday Telegraph Magazine, 2

Mencken, H.L., 133
mandatory arbitration clauses, 74
Mao Zedong, 59
Mason, Perry, 72
Martin, Steve, 105–106
Martin, Trayvon, 151
Martin v. Living Essentials, 35–36
Marx, Groucho, 108
Mattel, 166
mediation, use of humor in, 146–148
metahumor, 9, 33
Miranda warnings, 134
Model Code of Judicial Conduct, 165
More, Sir Thomas, 72
Morris, Lewis, 177
Mosk, Justice, 168
Murphy, Eddie, 160
monkey selfie case (*Naruto v. Slater*), 25, 148

*National Federation of Independent Business
  v. Sebellius*, 156
National Public Radio, 161
negotiation, use of humor in, 146, 150
negativity bias, 81
The New (Legal) Devil's Dictionary (online
  article), 85
New Times v. Isaacks, 34
New York Times (newspaper), 4, 31, 107, 161
New Yorker (magazine)
  Cartoon Bank, 4
  cultural impact, 3–5
non-disparagement agreement (drafted for
  Donald Trump), 173

Obama, Barack, 125
O'Connor, Justice Sandra Day, 154
Oliver, John, 124
The Onion (Internet site), 65
Ostrovsky, Josh "The Fat Jew", 56
Oswalt, Roy, 172

Parody
  Defined, 7–8
  protected under intellectual property
    law, 24–28
  protected under First Amendment,
    27, 35–36
Pasquale, Joe, 55–56
personal jurisdiction, 135, 149–150
Pinker, Steven, 158
Planters Peanuts, 27
Plato, 10
political correctness, 64
Polygram Records v. Superior Court, 33
Posner, Judge, 166–168
practical jokes, 5–6, 21, 38, 160, 164, 177
pranks, defined, 164–165
priming laughter technique, 160
Preamble to the U.S. Constitution, 73
precatory language, 177
prior restraint on speech, 21–23
procedural rules, 134–138
Prophet Muhammad, 62
Provine, Richard, 159–160
Pryor, Richard, 124
psychology of dependency, effect on
  attitudes toward lawyers, 81–82
Putin, Vladimir, 60
public nudity prohibition, 153–154
puns
  definition of, 8–9
  preferences of U.S. judiciary, 42, 45–46
  regulation by Chinese, Russian and other
    oppressive authorities, 57–61

Race
  race and jokes about law, 123–125
  racist jokes, 10, 21, 41–42, 45
Rehnquist, Chief Justice, 160
release theory, defined, 12–14
release humor
  treatment in contract law, 40
  treatment in intellectual property law, 27–28
  treatment in sexual harassment law, 44–46

restaurant reviews, 2, 31–32
River Crab, Chinese pun humor, 59
Roberts, Chief Justice, 156, 160, 169
Rock, Chris, 124
Robinson v. Jacksonville Shipyards, Inc., 43
Roe v. Wade, oral argument joke, 152
Rolling Stone (magazine), 56
Rosanne (television show), 138

Safford United School District v. Redding,
    oral argument, 156
Sagal, Peter, 161–162
Saint Peter jokes, 86, 100, 135
satire
    about legal system, 72, 75
    as a social corrective, 63, 140–142, 166
    debate about effectiveness, 75, 125,
        140–142, 166
    defined, 7
Schopenhauer, Arthur, 14
Scott, Anthony, 177
Sophie Scott, 160
Scalia, Justice, 153, 156, 159–161,
    167–169
Seinfeld (television show), 123
Seinfeld, Jerry, 137
Seven Dirty Words, stand-up routine,
    21, 51–53
sexual harassment, 6, 20, 24, 42–46, 57, 165
Shakespeare, 23, 57, 73
Shore, Pauly, 105
Simpson, O.J., 123
The Simpsons (television show), 8
situational humor, 6
slander, 28
Stevens, Justice, 153–154
Socrates, 10
Soviet Union, humor in, 50, 60–61
Spencer, Herbert, 12, 102
speech codes, for schools, 64
stand-up comedy, 22–23, 48, 51, 53–55,
    57, 64, 160
statutes
    jokes about, 127
    with humorous content, 178–181
stop and frisk, practice of, 134
Stormy Daniels, 173
superiority theory, defined, 10–11

superiority humor
    censorship humor, 65–66
    directed at lawyers, 72, 75, 78
    treatment in defamation law, 26–35
    treatment in sexual harassment law,
        41–43, 46
Swift, Jonathan, 141, 146

tax law, jokes about, 137–138
Terry v. Ohio, 134
Third Reich, humor during, 60–61
Thomas, Justice, 159
Three Little Pigs, 7
Tina Fey, 104
Tommy Hilfinger, 27
Tony Veale, 15
tort litigation crisis, 74
trademark law, treatment of parody, 21,
    24, 26–27
TripAdvisor, 31
Trump, Donald, 72, 87, 173, 179
Twain, Mark, 51, 102

U.S. Copyright Act, 25

Venue law, 135

Wait, Wait . . . Don't Tell Me! (radio
    show), 161
Walt Disney Company, 27
E.B. White, 181
Williams, Robin, 33–34
will-reading trope, 13, 175
wills with humorous content, 175–178
Wizard of Oz, 8
Woo v. Fireman's Fund Insurance Co, 38
Workplace humor, jokes and pranks, 40–46

Yelp, 31
YouTube, 53, 56, 134
Youngman, Henny, 55

Zimmerman, George, 151–152